In Memoriam

ELLEN SWALLOW

ELLEN SWALLOW

The Woman Who Founded Ecology

Robert Clarke

𝒻 Follett Publishing Company / Chicago

First Printing

Library of Congress Catalog Card Number: 73–82198

ISBN 0–695–80388–3

To Chris, Monty, and Rachel

Contents

Preface

Environment is a popular word today. Only a few years ago it was a word used more often to describe the atmosphere of a favorite club or restaurant, rather than the vast and intricate life support system it is.

As our awareness has evolved since 1968, I'm not sure "environmental awareness" has taken on all that much more meaning. There seems to be a certain mindlessness accompanying that awareness; a mindlessness that seems to be building toward an inevitable showdown between the so-called environmentalists and establishmentarians. If we are to judge from the proposals and programs presented by either group so far, whichever one comes out ahead, it seems certain we'll have far less than what we will need in our environment in the years ahead.

It would not be the first time that an "environment movement" has dissipated and died. It has happened before. Then, "mindlessness" was more ignorance, built on a lack of information and a refusal to take seriously what evidence was available or the people who presented it.

This time, the movement seems threatened by an opposite force: an overload of evidence, argument, and arguers. It is in danger of being beaten to death on one side and rejected out of hand on the other because of the hard realities involved. If either should come to pass, it would be tragic. There may not be a next time.

As the doomsayers and soothsayers collide over today's environment crisis, one thing becomes increasingly clear. Of all the solutions and counter solutions proposed by either side, no one or no one group seems to be getting to the core of the problem, let alone its cure. None of what we hear or see today touches the truth of the matter or the depth of its solution proposed seventy years ago.

The environment movement of the late nineteenth century in- cluded more than air and water pollution, urban decay, transportation, architecture, and waste disposal. It was also the genesis of America's public health, consumer, and nutrition movements incorporated into reforms of the education, economics, and politics that permitted it all.

In today's fragmented and programmed world, it seems hard to believe that a single movement encompassed all those issues that today give fame, following, and even some degree of fortune to the likes of Rene Dubos, Barry Commoner, and Stuart Udall; to Jean Mayer, Robert Choate, and Adele Davis; to Ian McHarg, Buckminster Fuller, and Palo Solari; to Ralph Nader, Virginia Knauer, and more than fifty thousand others in the United States alone.

It may be even more difficult for some people to cope with the fact that the movement encompassing all these issues almost one hundred years ago was organized and mobilized under the leadership of a single individual. Perhaps in reliving that person's life and struggle, each of us can find something to help us live through the crises predicted by that person.

Robert Clarke

Acknowledgments

Telling a story a century old takes help. Albert Newman, Ph.D., and Sally Wagner Jones were original in their encouragement, and, with Sol Roy Rosenthal, M.D., Ph.D., were constant in their support. In the same sense, I would like to express my appreciation and gratitude to Lydia Kerr Lee, John A. Kennedy, Albert Sullivan, Ph.D., William Lundin, Ph.D., Robert Walker, Ph.D., Robert Malcomson, the Butlers, and the Furlongs for the support and advice they gave when it was needed.

In research, Marilu Glover in Boston was tireless; Jeannine Addams in Pittsburgh, Bonnie Binney in Washington, Charlotte Hennessey in Oakland, and Caroline O'Neal in Florida made it easier. The charming and hospitable Laura Richards Wiggins of Gardiner, Maine, was an invaluable source of personal recollections of the times and events we do not know personally. Likewise, all of us are indebted to the Anne Mineahs of the world who recognize genius and history in the making and collect its correspondence.

Even still, we would be without link to the past, and hence less able to understand the present or future, without libraries and librarians. Those of particular help in preparing this book were Professor E. N. Hartley, archivist, and his staff, Elizabeth Bartlett, Barbara Linden, and Bonnie Salt of the Massachusetts Institute of Technology; Frances Goudy, the cooperative and resourceful head of the Vassar College Library and Archives; Winifred Collins of the Massachusetts Historical Society; Dorothy Dwyer, Massachusetts Department of Public Health; Mary Litterest,

Massachusetts Department of Education; Virginia Jeffrey, Women's Industrial and Educational Union, Boston; and many managers and more staff at the great public libraries of Boston and Chicago—particularly Mr. Wagner at the Philadelphia Public Library and the marvelous facilities and the freedom to use the John Crerar and Newberry Libraries in Chicago.

The New England Genealogical Society is unsurpassed in tracing old Yankee bloodlines, a remarkable achievement considering it spans not just time but oceans, too. Charles Neiring and Stanley Auerback were helpful in recalling the early days of the Ecological Society of America. Patricia Devane of R. S. Weeks, Chicago, worked in a variety of ways to backstop day-to-day details, and Diane Dozer helped type early manuscript drafts.

There are other debts that can never be fully repaid and are all the more keenly felt: for Richard and Esther Whitsell; George and Karen, Cherry and Bill; the Goldins; the Roots; Tom, Ron, and Meredith; and more. Professionally, for whatever value this book may have, I thank Eugenia Fawcett and Friend for their original interest; Herb Luthin for his expert management; and most of all, Jean Adams, for her long hours and shortening editorial criticisms.

Finally, it is my family who helped me understand the deeper dimensions of Ellen Swallow's life work.

ELLEN SWALLOW

Prologue

At the Massachusetts Institute of Technology they move quickly through the halls to class and laboratory; architects of yesterday's, today's, and tomorrow's environments flow as constant as the Charles River just outside the door.

Three hundred years ago the Charles helped open America for settlement and commerce. It moves slowly now, polluted from the banks of Boston to Cambridge; from Hopkinton, down to Boston Harbor and out into the ocean beyond; thickened with the chemistries of human and industrial waste.

Barely a hundred yards from the river, inside MIT's old chemistry building, on a corner wall in a shadowed hallway, hangs a plaque. It is a plaque of a human face in relief, black with age.

Except for the nose.

The nose alone catches light in that dark place. It shines in bronze brilliance, polished by thousands of student rubbings over the years.

It's a common custom, rubbing the noses of old statues for good luck. Not even the rational oblates of this citadel of science and technology are immune to an old wives' superstition. But in this day of environmental crisis there is a curious irony to this particular shining nose. Not one in a hundred of the keepers of tomorrow's environment knows the name or the deeds of the person memorialized on the wall. Each, when asked, was unaware that the nose they rub for luck in life belonged to the person who first warned and worked against a polluted world.

At a time when the earth's population belatedly bleats its

rising concern for an environment that threatens to extinguish life in any form, a highly buffed nose is all that recalls the brilliant career of MIT's first woman student; its first woman graduate; and its first woman faculty member—the First Lady of Science and Technology 100 years ago.

Hidden under the tarnish of time is the face of the rebuffed founder of consumer and environmental sciences: Ellen Swallow.

This is her story.

ONE

The Beginnings

The person who would synthesize food and consumer and environmental sciences, Ellen Henrietta Swallow, was well named. The only child of Peter and Fanny Taylor Swallow was born on a bleak December day on a farm near Dunstable, Massachusetts. It was 1842.

Both Peter and Fanny Swallow, two of 550 citizens spread over Dunstable's sixteen and a half miles, were sixth generation Americans. Ambrose Swallow came over from England before 1666. Fanny's ancestors made the trip even earlier, 1640, settling in Concord before moving to New Ipswich, New Hampshire, in 1776. Life was hard and punishing in New England then. It hadn't changed much by 1842.

Both lines of the family were forged in the wilderness struggle. Ambrose Swallow's sons and neighbors worked years to remove the huge "bowlders" jutting out of the flat field where they built their home. Fanny, too, knew about those days. As a young girl, she listened to how Indians and wild beasts attacked the early families on their way to church; about the "dog-whipper" appointed by the village to keep the animals quiet while the preacher said his Sunday piece.

Ellen Swallow's parents met at the Academy at Ipswich. Such schools were a rarity then—teaching above the high school level —and Peter and Fanny were well educated for that time and place. Both were teachers before their daughter was born. Peter had gone back to the land, but he still took a turn at teaching school when the crop was poor.

Fanny taught, too, but she was ill more often than not. Her condition seemed to become worse after Ellen was born.

The daughter seemed to have inherited her mother's poor health. From her father, she learned will and determination. With two people sick in a family of three, a lesser man might have been driven away from the hard life-style of a northern farm. But Peter, a descendant of a Revolutionary War patriot buried in a grave near the house, refused to go. So constant illness became another member of that rural household, and the family doctor a frequent caller.

The physician's Rx of the early nineteenth century was basic: good food, fresh air, and plenty of sunshine. The Swallow farm filled that prescription in full supply. In this environment of nature and necessity, the girl slowly overcame inherited weakness. Here, too, the perseverance and perceptions that she would merge in her remarkable life were acquired.

Away from the three-story house, beyond an unpainted barn and across the field where the earth was too stoney to cut or plant—in a meadow dotted with wildflowers and rising suddenly to form a hill where tall, majestic trees pierced the changing colors of the New Hampshire sky—Ellen Swallow began her lifelong pact with nature.

The meadow and hill were seamed with a meandering rock-bottomed brook fed by a spring somewhere up in the craggy White Mountains. The water, still cold in its rush to the meadow, foamed white and filled the dark pools where the banks widened as the brook wound its way, slower, to the Merrimac River, nearby. There, over a century and a quarter ago, beside a clean, sparkling stream, a frail, spindly child breathed the pure fresh air of the country.

In that setting, grew the thoughts that Ellen Swallow would write down later: "Air and Water are Food." They were a very special food to the fertile mind housed in that frail body.

The child who would one day "ignite the United States Public Health movement" was small as well as weak. Her thin, small-boned frame was topped by a mass of long black hair that made her pale face seem even whiter. The hair, meticulously braided into an intricate knot by an often bedridden mother, was pulled taut along the little head. With little variation, it became the style of a lifetime.

Her pale face was plain, but it never struck others that way. It wasn't the smile, which seemed even then to slant slightly upward (or the slightly prominent nose that shines so well in posthumous bronze) that people remembered. They remembered the eyes in that face; large blue eyes with gray flecks the color of flint steel; intense eyes that seized and held on what they saw.

A "steadfast gaze" and "quickness of motion and speech" were the most marked characteristics of this girl, according to her friend, associate, and biographer, Caroline Hunt. The girl's quick mind turned out thoughts so fast she had to practice speaking more slowly for others to understand.

As the child took nature's tonics, she grew stronger. The frail frame stabilized. The steps grew quick and sure. The pale face took on color, tanned by the summer sun, blushed by the cold New Hampshire winters.

Fanny Swallow worried that the doctor's orders were making her girl a "tomboy." Ellen seemed to spend too much time out doors: with her father while he cut the stubborn soil, riding the horse, on the hay wagon, and driving the cows to pasture. Ellen even liked to pitch hay, and her father let her. But Fanny Swallow drew the line at milking the cows. That will make her hands "large and unsightly," she said. Maybe she had a point. These were the hands, "deft and dainty," that would pick the intricate lock on the doors of science, then closed to women, and open new knowledge to man.

Peter Swallow was a stern father. He "carefully reserved his approval" in that provincial household. His demands and the needs of an often incapacitated mother may have been the basis of the girl's "two great passions in life: . . . a longing for usefulness and a love of pioneering." By this measure of her sixty-eight years on earth, Ellen Swallow's was a full and satisfying life.

Educating a child was uncomplicated in those days before Horace Mann and George Ticknor forced Massachusetts to make public education compulsory. Many still thought it was unnecessary. Domestic skills were more important. Some "readin', writin', and numbers" were available in the one-room, all-grades country school. But the Swallows placed great importance on education, and they were extremely critical of Dunstable's schools. So for the first sixteen years of her life, Ellen was educated at home.

She learned her domestic skills early; early in life and early in the day. Other subjects were taught in the field, as well as in the house. Her father taught her history and logic. In the evening by the fire and lamp she learned numbers and letters from her mother. From both she learned mathematics and from both she learned literature.

The future scientist also learned to cook and bake, to sew and clean. These were creative skills then—human expressions incorporated in mental and physical enterprise. When she was thirteen, "Miss Swallow" won two grand prizes at the county fair: one for the best loaf of bread, another for the finest embroidery. She had learned those skills well. Now she began to explore beyond the farmhouse and the field into the world beyond Dunstable—into the past and future, with the increasing number of books she shared with her parents.

There was an extraordinary comprehension in this learning that wed theory to fact, concept to practice, dream to reality. It enabled an understanding of the world and her relationship to it, far superior to the rote of memorizations and repetitions of the public school.

In 1859, Ellen Swallow was an unusually "bright" seventeen-year-old. Realizing her needs had changed from body to mind, Peter and Fanny Swallow packed up and moved by wagon to the town of Westford, a few miles away. There, Peter Swallow bought a small general store and enrolled his daughter in Westford Academy for her first formal education.

The academy was located in the center of Westford, at the edge of the Common, a village green around which the New England town was settled. Directly across the Common was the Swallow store; a short walk down a street lined with fruit trees was the white, flower-bordered house where the family lived. Early in the morning, after the girl helped with the beds and breakfast, she walked to the store with her father, where she helped uncover the barrels, baskets, and sacks of goods. Then she took her books across the green in time for school.

The succession of headmasters of Westford Academy usually

was comprised of young graduates of Harvard College in Cambridge, Massachusetts. The curriculum followed the classic lines. Latin was a new challenge for Ellen. She did so well she was permitted to take French and a little German, a rare language north of New York (formerly New Amsterdam); rarer still in the cultural center of Boston that dominated nineteenth-century New England. At Westford, the girl also dug deeper into the splendors of the thoughts of classical Greece, the works of Rome. Now she began to show her genius for mathematics. She was also learning that she had bottomless energy and a superior talent for organizing it.

Working more and more in the store, she learned the fundamentals of business supply and demand. When she wasn't in school or tending the store, she practically ran the house—cooking, cleaning, sewing, papering walls, and caring for her mother. If it was much easier than the farm, she missed the animals. In the backyard she soon "worked up" a little garden of her own.

The girl had still other interests. Somehow she found time to pursue them. In the woods and fields around the village, she collected plants and fossils. She had an uncommon devotion to living things. At home, in class, and in her diary and letters, she classified what she found and presented her observations. She also read. "Too much," an uncle warned.

Not long after she entered Westford Academy, Ellen Swallow was asked to tutor other students, especially in Latin and mathematics. She enjoyed "making the little ideas shoot," she said. At the store, other ideas were taking seed.

Even as a teenager, Ellen Swallow took more than a casual interest in the lives of others. From behind the counter, she observed and tested their habits, their knowledge of foods and fabrics or the lack of it. She was amused by a debate between women over the merits of "saleratus" and "soda" as an ingredient for better biscuits. Both, she knew, came from the same sack in the store. She was amazed that people had such little knowledge of what they put into their bodies and what they "kept out of their heads." Personal experience had taught her the benefits and dangers of such commissions and omissions.

Even then, it was said, she related the conditions of mind and body to their "fuels"—the inputs of food and information to the outputs of energy and intelligence. If she knew no replacement for knowledge, she also knew no substitute for quality in the water she drank and the air she breathed. She hated tobacco.

A customer recalled the time Ellen objected when a group of men sat down next to the potbellied stove in the store to light their pipes and talk. They were indignant when the young girl asked them to smoke outside, please.

"You sell us the tobacco! Do you expect us not to smoke it after we buy it?" bellowed one man.

"We sell you molasses, too," Ellen snapped. "But we don't expect you to stay here and cook it up."

She softened that Yankee candor in later years, but she only took a harder line on health and environment. Without knowing it, she was charting a course for a life that would take her out of the home and store and into the public arena where she would organize the consumer and environment movements of the nineteenth and twentieth centuries.

The girl was already the peer of her elders in home skills. She knew better than her customers what should be bought, sold, and used. At school, too, she was often more familiar with her subjects than her teachers. Especially when it came to nature.

Walking through Westford, she noted its topography, the flow of its streams, and the growth of its plants, the habits of its animal life. She made her observations in ways that were always instructive—drawings, maps, descriptions—and often more thorough in detail than school manuals of that time.

She had a passion for flowers and plants. Very few of her early letters fail to mention some species that was "doing fine" in her care. She showed an appreciation for other elements of nature, too.

"I wish you could come and stay with us," she wrote a sick friend. "The bracing air would do you good."

In the time when her mind was not otherwise occupied, she read. There was always a book in her bag. At the store, shoppers remembered, there was "always an open book" on the counter beside her.

Peter Swallow was not an exceptional businessman. "His daughter's got the dollar sense," the townspeople said. But he was more than the average parent in that age. The most ardent supporter of her search for knowledge, he was quietly proud of his daughter. She kept the store's books and managed the inventory. She traveled, a young woman alone, to Boston to purchase "from the large wholesaler markets." There, too, merchants commented on "her quickness of perception."

In her last year at Westford, Ellen spent a vacation in Lynn, Massachusetts, visiting family friends who also operated a store. She rode up front on the wagon that delivered groceries to the big houses along Boston's swank suburban North Shore. "The other half," she noted. The country girl's suburban experience would contrast sharply with what she was about to see in an urban environment.

The Swallows moved again in the spring of 1863 when their daughter graduated from Westford Academy—this time to the larger town of Littleton, where Peter Swallow opened a bigger store. A post office was attached to the store, and Ellen managed the substation. Soon most of the incoming mail was magazines and books she ordered. She expanded her "input," and she developed her curiosity about the places she learned of from the postmarks of cities and towns far beyond Littleton.

If Peter Swallow was counting on his daughter's full-time services in the store, however, he was disappointed. The next year, 1864, he agreed to her taking a teaching job on the other side of town.

She was twenty-two; a small but fully developed black-haired young woman seen driving a buckboard back through Littleton Friday nights and out again on Monday mornings, commuting two miles back and forth to "teach over thirty class calls of forty-one pupils" a day. She enjoyed teaching. More, she enjoyed being on her own. But that freedom was cut short when her mother's illness forced her home to help once more. This time though, Ellen made it a point to "hire out" to other families—tutoring, cooking, cleaning, and nursing the sick. She put away the money she earned.

The mind's appetite was whet and growing. Ellen had plenty of outlets for her knowledge now, but she wanted more knowledge. As her mother got over one more illness, Ellen Swallow took the dreaded big step, one of prodigal sons and scandalous daughters of the nineteenth century. Leaving home and parents in Littleton, in late fall of 1865 she moved to the large city of Worcester, Massachusetts. She was alone for the first time in her life.

Worcester was too far to commute. But it wasn't too large to overcome the provincial stigma of a young woman living apart from her family. Other young women might have been intimidated. Ellen ignored it.

". . . I enjoy the privileges here very much . . ." she wrote her cousin Annie Swallow, "[and] . . . I have . . . the opportunity of doing good, too, for Deacon Haywood has taken me to his Mission school and given me a class of bright little boys to look after. And I go with him to the Jail . . ." to help his missionary work there. The Deacon and his aide also visited the frightful asylums for the insane of the 1860s.

To attend a school in Worcester—the name of which is lost—again she "hired out" to families in the city. Living "mainly on bread and milk," she managed to save some money.

During this period, young Ellen "saw" several young men. "But," she wrote, ". . . there is no possibility of your dreams proving true at the present, for the young or old gentleman has not yet made his appearance who can entice me away from my free and independent life."

Nor was she looking for him.

"I know of no lady with whom I would exchange places. The gentleman whom I think the most of and who comes the nearest to my ideal . . . does not treat his wife as I wish to be treated . . . I often tell him we could not live together . . . more than a week."

She had good reason for her point of view.

"Oh! Annie, the silent misery I am discovering . . . among my friends whom I thought happy . . . makes me shudder. Some things I learned yesterday . . . almost made me vow I would never bind myself with the chains of matrimony. . . . girls don't get behind the scenes as I have, or they could not get up such an enthusiasm for married life. . . ."

As for children, ". . . the world will be peopled without my help," she said.

Witness to unhappiness among her friends, miseries in jails, hospitals, and asylums brought out a social sensitivity in Ellen Swallow. The urge to help engulfed her.

"Pray to God for me, Annie," she asked her cousin, ". . . that I may be of some use in this sinful world."

The experience also hardened her resolve and gave her confidence.

"I have an almost Napoleonic faith in my star," she wrote. Then that star seemed to fall from the sky. Once again she was called home to Littleton. Beginning in the spring of 1866, for the first time in her life, Ellen succumbed to frustration. Frustration turned to depression. She had savored the satisfaction of service and touched the world beyond Littleton. Now in her mid-twenties, she was back at the beginning. Alone in her room with its plants and books, depressed, she suffered long meaningless days.

"Did not go to meeting . . ." "Tired . . ." "Tired . . ." "Indifferent . . ." "Tired . . ."

The next month was worse.

"Busy . . . tired . . ." ". . . wretched . . ." ". . . lay down sick . . ." "Oh, so tired . . ." "Tired . . ." "Tired . . ."

The next, worse yet.

"I lived for more than two years in purgatory," she later wrote a woman in similar confinement. During those years, she worked, skimped, and saved for something she could sense but not find. More than anything, she had the urge to learn. But what? Where? From whom? She was the town tutor. Who would teach *her*?

There were no colleges for women in New England then. There were precious few anywhere in the world. Woman's place was Home. Wellesley and Smith would not open for almost ten years or more. But in "Up New York State," she read, a beer baron had opened a "higher school" for young women. In 1865, Matthew Vassar, encouraged by his niece, had begun the experiment that shocked the good townspeople of Poughkeepsie. Ellen Swallow thought about Vassar College for Women.

A relative visiting Littleton about that time remembered the day Ellen told him, "You know, Mr. Tuttle . . . I have been to school a good deal, read quite a little, and so secured quite a little knowledge. Now I am going to Vassar College to get it straightened out and assimilated. What do you think of my little plan?"

Whatever Tuttle's reply, at 10 AM September 15, 1868—a century before the extension of man into the moon's environment —Ellen Swallow said good-bye to her family and boarded the "express train" from Littleton to faraway Vassar College. It was no small step for a woman of that day. It was to be a significant step for man's earthly environment.

The trip was tiring. Was it excitement or foul air and stale water on the train? Westward the train made its way, with its stream of cindered smoke streaking the clear sky. Going through towns and villages, she saw the growing concentrations of people and the filth and decay in the streets, the Civil War's harvest of wasted human lives.

At Albany, a five-hour layover, she walked outside the station for some fresh air. With soot and ash on her clothes, mud on her buttoned shoes, she came back to wait in the station with its dead, dank air. Then, reboarding the train, a full day after leaving Littleton, she arrived at Poughkeepsie.

An hour later, after a hot bath, Ellen Swallow crawled between the new sheets of her bed and wrote in her diary:

"September 16 . . . arrived at Vassar . . . pleasantly welcomed . . . very tired. . . ."

TWO

Discovery

Ellen Swallow was twenty-six years old when she enrolled as a third-year "special student" in Vassar. She had saved $300. Without her help at the family store, she could count on very little financial help from home. She was on her own.

Poughkeepsians were still whispering about Matthew Vassar's school and the young women "radicalizing" themselves there. "They are too frail and delicate." "They will ruin their health." "Their nervous systems will not adapt to higher learning." All this and more was said and written at the time. Since this was supported by medical opinion, it was believed. If nothing else, the girls would ruin their reputations or the town's. Beneath it all was the widespread opinion that women should not be educated "beyond their needs."

Vassar's administration was acutely aware of public opinion. School policy reflected the sensitivity. Always under scrutiny from the outside, pressures also developed within the school. Everything from deportment to dress was planned or unplanned in paranoia. More than one activity—like a proposed visit to the "cannon factory" at West Point—was cancelled for fear the scandal "would get into the papers." Lecturers were screened for their social acceptability as much as for their subject matter.

Students were advised not only how to behave off campus, but if, where, and when they might go. "It is not proper to be found off grounds in groups no less than three," the rule book stated. Rare trips into town were sudden and quick, the girls hardly alighting from their "common conveyance" until they were back on board and gone in a cloud of dust and gossip.

Such forays reinforced the mystery surrounding Matthew Vassar's experiment. If the girls were inhibited in town, in class they were fortified against opinion. They were encouraged by tales of educated women who had succeeded in spite of their sex: eighteenth-century musician Caroline Herschel, "who helped her brother's astronomical work"; of Mrs. Somerville, mathematician; and others. Much more often than not, woman's success was told in relation to man's. Such was the world for women at that time and for a long time to come.

Struggling against thousands of years of male suppression, nineteenth-century woman was doing more than any before her to rise above the status marked down for her. At Vassar, Ellen Swallow joined them. "They won't let us study enough," she wrote home. A male guest lecturer "spoke down to us," she complained. "He told us sand comes from stones rubbed together." She was very dissatisfied with the lecture. The next day, Vassar officials took the girls to task for their apparent boredom, but at least one was not cowed by the scolding. Ellen Swallow illustrated the fallibility of male knowledge.

"There were 208 bones in the human body when I was seven . . . now there are 238 . . ." A male-written text gave the precise date of the earth's origin as 4004 B.C., which prompted Ellen to comment "The world moves . . . but we move with it."

As she learned she grew eager for more. She wanted to pioneer, she said, ". . . in the expansion of women's boundaries." Yet she was objective about her sex. "I wish the women's rights people would be more sensible. I think a lot of them have a great deal to learn before they are fit to vote." She sympathized with the ideals and courage of the nineteenth-century woman's movement, but not with its fringe of sexual separatists. "The men are here to stay; we might just as well work with them," she said.

She admired many feminist leaders of the day, but she wished their followers would reflect ". . . a higher standard of knowledge and responsibility." "Women are able to reason—we must," she wrote. She felt if men would do the same, the world would be better off. The path to reason, she believed, is education. She spent her life and energy removing obstacles in that path for men and women alike.

Hard work in her first year at Vassar paid off in the second. The "special student" was accepted as a senior. Frustration and depression had disappeared completely. Her letters showed excitement and enthusiasm. Not for the rest of her days would those spirits lag again, not even when censored and criticized by her male scientific peers. At least one member of the class of 1870 had found herself.

Two people at Vassar had particular roles in her discovery: astronomy instructor Maria Mitchell, and Professor A. C. Farrar, head of the Natural Sciences and Mathematics Department. Mitchell showed Ellen the universe. From Farrar, she discovered the chemistry connecting its infinite elements.

Recognizing the power of this student's mind, both educators vied to win it to their respective disciplines. It looked like Maria Mitchell would win. She would have won ". . . had not Astronomy been so far removed from the Earth and its needs," as Caroline Hunt put it. Ellen herself said ". . . a leaning toward social service," curiously, turned her from the observatories and telescopes of astronomy to the microscopes and laboratories of chemistry.

It was no easy choice. She enjoyed and excelled in both sciences. The steel-blue eyes found star clusters and meteors even her instructor couldn't identify. And in the chemistry lab, she analyzed everything ". . . from shoe black to baking powder." Even "saleratus" and "soda." Chemistry slowly gained on the ethereal outer world because it allowed for Ellen Swallow's obsession for practical application of knowledge.

Her intelligence had never been questioned; at Vassar, her genius became obvious. Both Mitchell and Farrar pressed to hone the mind sharper.

"I think Father would be delighted to see Miss Mitchell lecturing me, as she did this morning," she wrote home. ". . . I ignored the one hundredth of a second in an astronomical calculation. 'While you are doing it you might as well do it to a nicety' she told me." It was a lesson never forgotten. She deliberately practiced greater attention to detail. "I find myself going up and down 250 steps a day," she noted in her diary. Her friends noticed, too.

"Her concentration was so great she would not be aware of a friend who sat down beside her for an hour if she was reading a book," classmate Anne Mineah remembered. She even organized her anxieties. "I hope you are feeling better," she wrote her mother. "I don't worry because I can do nothing . . . If you need me you must send for me and I will come. Then will be soon enough to worry."

She was developing powers that would expose new knowledge in science and win her a place in its world.

With vitality belying her small figure, she examined everything. Even the school menus were subjected to chemical analysis. She wrote her father ". . . of the dangers of Butyric Acid that forms in strong butter. Its slow workings are undetectable as it undermines the body's health."

She became known among her classmates for her desire to absorb all accessible knowledge: in required classes, in electives, at lectures, on class field trips or those she organized among her friends. She had the Farmer's Daughter's analogy for knowledge, comparing it with "spreading guano in the field" to fertilize those "shoots in the mind." Knowledge was a "flowing stream" to feed human development, Ellen wrote.

Students and faculty alike noticed this small but awesome dynamo. "Nellie" became a topic of conversation when she read, oblivious to all else, while walking to class; knitting as she took the five flights of stairs to her dormitory room. In class, she had more than just answers—she had more questions. After class, she had the time and patience to help others with their work and to volunteer for extra assignments.

But books and classrooms weren't enough. The outdoors still was her first love. Outdoors was her true home. She brought all of it she could carry into the laboratory to know it better. There, in her shapeless white smock, her braided hair pinned tight against her head, her sharp eyes made sharper by the microscope, she studied fossils, rocks, soil, animal and plant life. And water. Nothing was so revealing to Ellen Swallow as was the magnification of water. In water she learned to see how all things had a common heritage; that it was a vital source of all life under the sun. She thirsted to know it all.

With a rare ambition for the times, to say nothing of it as acceptable behavior, she took up surveying to know nature from another dimension. If this wasn't rash enough, her costume was —a modified bloomer-style athletic suit.

"I am getting a reputation for knowing all that goes on outdoors," she wrote to her proud father. But more and more she was learning the outdoors indoors: in the chemistry laboratory that would become her unparalleled realm.

When the Smithsonian Institution sought help from Vassar in taking early meterological recordings, student Swallow was selected for the careful work. When classmates fell behind in their studies, "Nellie" was asked to lend a hand. With her $300 long since gone, she supported herself—frugally and by denying herself frills and fashions—with $5 monthly from fees for tutoring in Latin, math, and German. In her last year, Vassar helped too, with a small "scholarship assistance."

To explore every avenue of thought, Ellen also learned some political craft. A controversial lecturer was denied permission to speak on a sensitive issue. Ellen organized a way around the objection. "By charging admission," she argued, "only those who want to hear his views will be exposed to them." Speaking for less outspoken classmates, she said, "we are tired of pokey lectures." He spoke.

The senior year drew to a close. Any sadness Ellen Swallow may have felt was submerged in the wake of her dreams for the future. As graduation neared, her lack of money denied her the traditional feminine celebration of a new wardrobe. She'd spent all she'd earned to stay in school. Peter Swallow was hard pressed and little help, but his daughter eased his conscience.

"I have enough in my head to balance what is wanting on my back," she wrote. Indeed, what she had in her head had become her most evident apparel. At graduation, surrounded by expensive fineness, Ellen wore her white Sunday dress, "the only one of its kind at commencement," she rationalized.

On her last day at Vassar, "Nellie" Swallow walked to class with her well-to-do Newport friend, "Lizzie" Coffin.

"You will make valuable discoveries in your life," Maria Mitchell told her.

"Professor Swallow," Farrar greeted her prophetically.

The graduate added her own prophesy in a happy note home.

"My life is to be one of active fighting."

It was an accurate vision.

THREE

Opening the Door

The year 1865 figured prominently in Ellen Swallow's life. That year Vassar, which she attended, had opened; the Civil War ended; and ". . . to advance instruction and make a connection with the industrial arts . . ." that had won the war for the North, the Massachusetts Institute of Technology opened in a brick building on Boylston Street in Boston's Back Bay.

The Civil War had been a turning point for America's two largest disenfranchised groups: blacks and women. Though history often overlooks the connection between these groups, the rank and file of the antislavery movement was mostly women. Thirty years before Fort Sumter was fired upon, there were " . . . at least a hundred feminist anti-slavery societies . . ." in the United States. More than half the thousands of signatures on The Great Abolition Petition were women's. Nearly all were obtained by the women who circulated that congressional document.

Even more important to Emancipation—if we are to believe Abraham Lincoln—was the role played by the book, *Uncle Tom's Cabin*. This best seller and the thousands of stage plays adapted from it awakened the American conscience and built the public opinion required to wage civil war. Even those who didn't read the book or see it played out were aware of its message.

A woman, Harriet Beecher Stowe, wrote this dramatic indictment of slavery. When Union troops marched south, they did so to the tune of "The Battle Hymn of the Republic," by Julia Ward Howe. The success of these and others in bringing about abolition established the women's movement in America. After the war,

20

women went on to become a major force in other reforms of the nineteenth century.

These were improvements of the social environment of the times. But physical environment, too, was becoming more victimized by man's increasing exploitation through the offices of science and technology. And the order of science and technology was absolute patriarchy.

Once the black man's cause was won, women returned to their own cause: suffrage. But for black men and white women alike there were very few opportunities other than those set aside for them by a white man's society. Five years after the war, in 1870, Ellen Swallow came face to face with this hard fact. She was in love with science, but there was no place to pursue the relationship, let alone consummate it.

Nursing already had its pioneers, and Ellen had had her fill of nursing. Teaching was very nearly the only other field open to women, and Horace Mann's niece, Mary Pennel Dean, had opened that trail in colleges. Science was a closed door, although a few women like Maria Mitchell had managed to work their way into the ethereal science of astronomy. The patriarchs could hardly keep a woman from reading about the stars or from sitting in a tower somewhere looking up through a telescope. The science laboratory, however, was another thing.

Stargazing was not suited to Ellen's personality. She wanted the mainstream, the "hard" science of chemistry Farrar had exposed to her. It simply wasn't available to women in 1870, she was told. At graduation, she decided to combine the best of the few opportunities available to educated women. Along with five others, she signed a contract to teach astronomy in Argentina, then rushed home to prepare for an adventure that never came.

The family had moved once again while their daughter was away at school—from Littleton to Worcester. With the money from the sale of his store, Peter Swallow set himself up in "artificial stone," a kind of forerunner to cement and cinder block building materials. Artificial stone was a spin-off of the new technology. In on the ground floor, he thought, he moved to the larger city of Worcester where there would be a larger demand, he hoped.

Ellen found time to help organize the business and examine the new materials. Then she made the rounds of her old Worcester friends to find work and money for the trip. The same old job offers convinced her she'd done the right thing in electing to go to Argentina. She was packed and ready with a small nest egg when word came that war had broken out there. President Sarmiento cancelled the teachers' contracts.

"Hired and fired before I started," Ellen wrote. With no plans for the future, she decided to explore the past. In the family buggy she made a three-week tour back through the towns she'd known as a child. Old friends and relatives gathered in Littleton, Westford, and Dunstable, eager to get a glimpse of a curiosity of the time: a college educated woman.

"I saw the great trees planted by my hand . . . boys nearly six feet high whom I had rocked in their cradles," she wrote. Time was passing.

In her diary and to friends, she outlined her options.

"Well, here I am, no nearer to my winter's work than when I left. I have tried several doors . . . but they won't open."

Back she went to the old subsistence: helping in the family business, hiring out, reading, and attending evening lectures around town.

"I'm not discouraged or blue at all. I've full faith that the right thing will come in time. I've only to work and wait. I've lived in the greatest calm all summer, not feeling the old unrest and fretting against the fetter, and I know the blessings of contentment," she told her diary.

It was a dramatic change from her earlier bout with limbo. Education had made the difference. She felt confident, and others shared that feeling.

"I often feel as if I must have something good in store for me, so many people give expressions of confidence in my future," she wrote.

"Never a croaking word do I get. I hope I shall not neglect the right thing when it comes, but I begin to feel anxious to see something done. I can't lie idle . . . I must stir in some direction."

But which? For women, any course other than home or school was frontier. Horace Greeley advised young men to "Go West." Should she? She wrote to some friends there. "I wonder if there would be any chance for me to take private pupils . . . in the

Western cities? I think I would do it, though I believe I would go into a chemist's shop in preference."

She wrote to a friend in Ohio. "Does Dayton boast any drug stores or the like? Would it be advisable for me to advertise, think you, for a situation in such a place? I rather want to dip into some science."

She sealed that letter, then wrote to Merrick & Gray, a Boston chemical company. She selected a commercial house, since the schools a woman could attend offered no more chemistry than she had already mastered at Vassar, and no science school admitted women. Merrick & Gray replied routinely. They did not hire women. They suggested she try the "new Institute of Technology" in Boston.

It was well known that women weren't accepted there, either. More than one had tried. Her friends advised it was folly for her to try. "There's no sense going further; you are at the edge of cultivation, now," they told her.

But she was drawn to that edge. In a letter, she innocently asked if the Institute would accept a female student. She gave Professors Mitchell and Farrar as references. When no answer came, she wasn't surprised. Instead, she wrote to another chemical firm, Booth & Garrett in Philadelphia.

The Quakers regretted, too. But they expressed their desire "to see proper means of livelihood thrown open to women." That sympathy encouraged her to write again, restating her plea. The Quakers were moved, but not much. They couldn't hire her, but she could hire them, they said. For $500 they would take her on as a student. But there was no $500. Only desire. And determination.

"I've quite made up my mind to try chemistry for a life's study," she told her diary, "and have been trying to find suitable opportunity to attempt it, but everything seems to stop short at a blank wall. I trust something will come to pass. . . . I feel I shall get impatient."

She was entitled to impatience. Soon she would be twenty-eight. In those days, much younger women, unmarried, won the unattractive title of "old maid." Worse words were used for those strange creatures "educated beyond their needs."

Then, the morning of December 3, her birthday, the post

brought her most memorable gift. The Massachusetts Institute of Technology's impressive letterhead confirmed they had "formally received" her application. After thinking about it for four weeks, they had decided, they said, to postpone a decision until the next meeting. Fortunately, that was only a week away.

On December 10, 1870 ". . . the question of the admission of Miss Swallow was resumed and after some discussion it was voted that the Faculty recommend to the Corporation the admission of Miss Swallow as a special student in chemistry. . . ." That was not all the faculty resolved that day. The admission of Miss Swallow was "only to be considered an experiment." The answer to her question, "Does the Institute admit women?" was, "We'll see." On December 14, she received an historic document.

> My Dear Miss Swallow:
> The Secretary of the Institute, Dr. Kneeland, will notify you of the action of the corporation in your case at a meeting held this day. I congratulate you and every earnest woman upon the result. Can you come to Boston before many days and see me? I will say now that you will have any and all advantages which the Institute has to offer *without charge of any kind.* (Author's italics.) I have the pleasure of knowing both Miss Mitchell and Mr. Farrar of Vassar. Hoping to have the pleasure of seeing you, I am,
> Faithfully yours,
> J. D. Runkle
> President of the Institute

"Without charge!" She could hardly believe it. But it wasn't philanthropy that motivated the Institute. They had couched their position. Admitting her without charge, they took on the "Swallow Experiment" without obligation. When she learned this later, Ellen said she wouldn't have gone if she'd known. Luckily, this once her perceptiveness had overlooked something. Regardless of the benevolence, she still needed money to live in Boston. The holidays were approaching, so she took a job as a department store Christmas clerk. December 25, 1870, Ellen Swallow could sing "God Rest Ye Merry, Gentlemen" with a special joy to the world and peace toward men. She wrote:

"I have the chance to do something no one else ever did . . . to be the first woman to enter the Institute of Technology, and so far as I know, any scientific school. . . ." She was deeply touched and honored, vowing ". . . to proceed with caution."

In Boston she lodged at a boardinghouse at 532 Columbus Avenue run by the mother of her friend from Westford Academy, Isa Blodgett. Half a century later when Vassar opened its unique center for interdisciplinary environmental science, it would be named Blodgett Hall for the woman who gave a sizeable part of her fortune to realize Ellen Swallow's long sought vision.

In January 1871, however, the future environmental scientist was all but broke. With only enough money for a room at Mrs. Blodgett's, she took her meals elsewhere. Then the proprietor, impressed by the energy and organization of the new boarder, offered her board and a job managing the house. Eagerly, she accepted. And soon she was also looking after the Boston offices of a family friend.

A few days later, Ellen Swallow arrived at the Massachusetts Institute of Technology, a five-story brick building on Boylston Street in Back Bay Boston. It was a heady moment for the young woman from a Dunstable farm. She went directly to the office of the president. Runkle spoke seriously of the challenges facing her. Then he took her to the segregated laboratory where she would study. He introduced her to the only other woman in the school, Mrs. E. A. Stinson, "Assistant in Charge" of the chemical supply room. After an hour or so, Ellen Swallow thanked Runkle and left. Watching her go, he went back to the chemical supply room. Drawing Mrs. Stinson aside, he asked her to ". . . look after" the new student. Mrs. Stinson was unsettled. "She looks rather frail to take on such a difficult course," she said. "Yes," the president nodded, "but did you see her eyes? She will not fail."

FOUR

A Woman in the Patriarchy

When Ellen Swallow entered MIT, science was in its fourth century of the explosion that began with the Renaissance. Founded by Hippocrates 2,000 years before, science slept in the shadow of the Church for 1,500 years until wakened by the printing press. The Reformation unpried the private grip on knowledge even more.

By the seventeenth-century Age of Reason, rapid acceleration and chaotic accumulation of knowledge had changed man's mind and his environment. Where was it going? What was the purpose? Sir Francis Bacon tried to answer those questions by "reorganizing the whole of knowledge upon a proper platform." To make sure mankind would benefit, rather than fall prey to exploitation of knowledge, Bacon joined science to philosophy.

This fruitful union mothered the eighteenth-century Enlightenment, which in turn sired the social sciences of economic and political theory used for the new world's democracy. Technology, the application of science and mechanics, was still new. The word itself was not yet in existence. But it was about to be born.

It is a sad commentary on today's education that the father of technology—Count Rumford—is practically unknown in his native land and the capital nation of technology. Perhaps that is because technology today is not the true technology he intended. Count Rumford, nevertheless, had a strong, if posthumous, influence on Ellen Swallow's career.

As one of the more curious figures of the Enlightenment, Rumford was the opposite of the Man Without a Country. Although named and titled by Bavaria's Elector, he was first knighted and then loaned to Bavaria by George III of England. Later, he became a clause in Napoleon's peace talks with Bavaria, which stipulated that Rumford would live at and advise the French court.

An organizational genius, Rumford had overhauled England's Home Army. In Bavaria, he saved the crown from a starving, hostile population by transforming the military from an ineffectual force of destruction into an efficient environmental improvement corps. Draining swamps to plant huge agricultural acreage, he nurtured the nation back to health. "Uniting the interest of the soldier with the interest of the civil society . . . subservient to the public good," he employed them in public works and introduced "military gardens." Each soldier was given "a plot of three hundred and sixty-five square feet . . . to keep in good condition . . ." and cultivate. He rid the nation of poverty, enlisting beggers and vagrants in agriculture and sanitation and providing them with clean food, comfortable shelter, and wages for their work. Rumford's achievement was hailed as "the greatest philanthropic experiment in history."

In doing it, he also founded the science of nutrition. Believing that most food value never reached plate or palate, he formulated scientific principles of food growing, storage, and preparation. He invented the closed oven and the double boiler, introduced coal for cooking, and saved "seven-eighths" of cooking fuel costs. He studied times, heats, pressures, and foods required to prepare the most healthful meals at the lowest cost. It was Rumford who believed "water must become nutritious in the process of cooking soups." His experiments with potatoes, which he introduced to Bavaria, gave them their German name.

For healing Bavaria, England's knight was made a Bavarian count. His service there and later in France gave those countries head starts in food science and public nutrition.

But Rumford was not English anymore than he was Bavarian or French. He was American, born Benjamin Thompson in Woburn, Massachusetts, just twelve miles down the road from his contemporary, Benjamin Franklin. American mythology credits Franklin as the founder of modern technology, perhaps because Thompson, accused of sympathy to England when revolutionary fires were being lighted, fled the country. Chauvinism aside, however, in the founding of technology, the role of the man who had founded the science of nutrition was much more precise than Franklin's.

After a term at the French court, Rumford returned to England to convince George III ". . . to form a Public Institution for Diffusing the Knowledge and Facilitating the General Introduction of Useful Mechanical Inventions and Improvements and for Teaching by Courses or Philosophical Lectures and Experiments, the *Application of Science to the Common Purposes of Life. . . .*" (Author's italics.) It was the founding of the Royal Institution.

But if Rumford was an innovator, he was also an American. He couldn't ignore either. He felt something was missing from the mechanics and manufacturing evolving during the Industrial Revolution. He saw it in England, and to lesser extents in Germany and France. But in a younger nation, it might be different.

Some people thought that "Tory" Benjamin Thompson had repented when he began to contribute to the American Academy of Arts and Sciences (he was its largest benefactor) and to Harvard College. The exile himself must have felt satisfaction when the United States asked him to become the first superintendent of the new Military Academy at West Point and Inspector General of Artillery for the United States Army. Now married to the widow of the French chemist Lavoisier, Thompson declined, from Europe. But at his death, the true nature of his interest in America's future showed—he left his estate to Harvard "for the purpose of founding a new institution and professorship in order to teach by regular courses of academic and public lectures, accompanied with proper experiments, the utility of the physical and mathematical sciences for the improvement of the useful arts and for the extension of the industry, prosperity, happiness and well being of society."

Rumford wanted Harvard and America to find a humane ethic for the Industrial Revolution.

From the first occupant of the Rumford chair came a new word for the world lexicon: *Technology.* Thus, Count Rumford of Bavaria, nee Benjamin Thompson, Woburn's advisor to king, elector, and emperor, tried to give democracy a professionally ethical application of science and mechanics that he saw as the runaway children of the breaking union of the Enlightenment's science and philosophy.

A family of English brothers who came to America in the early nineteenth century agreed with Rumford's concept. While the eldest, Patrick Rogers, gave the first free public chemistry lectures in America, two younger brothers, Henry and William, alternately taught, studied, and performed the earliest professional geological surveys that set up knowledge needed for the great engineering projects of the era: tunnels, bridges, dams, canals, railroads, modern mining, and metals refining to supply the conquerors of the continent.

Henry and William Rogers had a dream: to extend Rumford's concepts and incorporate them into American education. Since Harvard was the pinnacle of intellectual America, Henry applied to fill the Rumford chair when it became vacant. Turned down, in 1846 he and his brother proposed that the Massachusetts legislature charter a new school. Teaching applied science, arts, and agriculture would "diffuse the knowledge" needed to develop America's environment, they argued.

If Boston was the Athens of the New World, Harvard was its aristocracy. And Harvard was opposed to the Rogers's plan. The idea of a new school was one matter. To propose general dissemination of the secrets of science—especially to artisans, mechanics, and farmers—like so much fertilizer, was heresy. Science must be kept pure, chaste, within the elite priesthood where life sciences—medicine and biology—reigned supreme.

The Rogers's proposal languished in the legislature. How much pressure was put on that body by Boston's Brahmins, or how, is not known. "If" is hardly debatable. But the opening of the Scientific School of the University of Cambridge at that time was not just coincidence. It undermined the Rogers's argument for more science education. Yet there was only one university in Cambridge. If Harvard's Overseers declined to put their real name on it, at least they could control the who and what of science education.

The Rogers were turned down by the state. Henry went back to England to follow a distinguished career. William left Boston to take a chair at the University of Virginia. But a slit had been made in the holy garment of science worn by the classicists. The slit would widen. From it there would evolve a competition between "pure" and "applied" scientists. Sometimes silent, sometimes outspoken, it was often bitter. And it was always there. At one point near the turn of the century it would erupt briefly in a way that would dramatically affect the rise and fall of environmental science. Ellen Swallow would find herself in the middle of that conflict.

William Barton Rogers came back to Boston from Virginia, this time with a powerful sponsor, James Savage of Provident Savings Bank and father of Emma Savage, the woman whom William Rogers married. Appointed State Inspector of Gas Meters, Rogers built support for his idea in influential circles. He realized a school for science and engineering could not flourish at Harvard, where the "classical tradition" was too strong. Again he applied for a charter for a new school to merge science, agriculture, and arts into technology. This time he had the apparent support of the governor.

"Should not Massachusetts . . . provide for the initiation of a work which would enable her instructed people to trace the separate stages of evolution . . . from nothing to divinity?" asked Governor Banks in defense of the plan. Not quite, said the legislature. Leave evolution and divinity to Harvard. Yet time had shown the need for more technologists to speed up America's production. When economics entered the picture, science, no matter how pure, faltered. Bowing once more to the jealousies of Cambridge, the politicians approved the charter with the condition that MIT ". . . could not interfere with the interests of the established schools of general literary and scientific education."

In 1865, William Rogers took Rumford's "word" from Harvard to temporary rooms in Boston's Mercantile Building on Summer Street, where a Society of the Arts, a Museum of the Arts, and a School of Industrial Science were merged into the Massachusetts Institute for Technology. It was off to a slow start; of the first class of twenty-eight men, only half were around for graduation two years later. By then the state had deeded land on Boylston Street to the Institute, and in February 1866, a chemistry laboratory was opened there. By fall, the rest of the operation had moved in.

William Rogers smarted from the campaign against the Institute and the attempts to castrate MIT's curricula. But he found enough men who shared his views to make the school work. In hindsight, Harvard Overseers would realize their error. In years to come, alternating scowls and smiles across the Charles River accompanied intermittent efforts by Harvard to acquire MIT.

The stage was set. The shape and function of the world 100 years ago was drawn more and more under the powers of science and technology. It was controlled by a small, tight little circle of men. As the links to profits increased, science and technology became ever more a man's competitive game. Into this foreboding atmosphere came, in 1871, the diminutive figure and the perceptions of a woman—Ellen Swallow.

Ellen was not the only pioneer at MIT. She was merely the only female. Everyone from faculty to the lowest student was opening a controversial path in education. It was bad enough that the Rogers's heretical band had opened the temple of science to commoners. Now they had committed original sin, admitting a woman. Everyone connected with the school felt the pressures of their unpopular position. In a pecking order with sexual as well as scientific gravity, she was at the bottom of an inverted pyramid of pressure.

The faculty was small in number. But it comprised large, impressive figures to Ellen; courageous for allying themselves to a cause while fully aware of the enmity of their peers. She looked with admiration on the men she saw in the halls: men like Edward C. Pickering, Charles W. Eliot, Frank H. Storer, Silas W. Holman, and William Atkinson. She absorbed the words and motions of those assigned to teach: Professor Crafts, Ordway, and Nichols; she learned new and basic branches of chemistry and physics. Mining was a major field by which MIT hoped to connect with industry so she studied mineralogy under Professor Robert Richards.

Ellen paid particular attention to the young and brilliant William Ripley Nichols. ". . . stepping out from the ranks of the 'first and oldest college' to adopt MIT made him at once an object of attention." She had another interest in this serious young man. Rumor had it he was the least enthusiastic in the faculty meeting that voted to admit a woman.

MIT's most infamous feature, aside from its woman student, was the "Universal Laboratory." Up until then, the laboratory had been the exclusive habitat of "pure" scientists. By making it a part of every student's instruction, MIT ". . . led the world in the introduction of laboratory practice. So far as known . . . this was the first laboratory of such a character . . . in the world. Certainly . . . the first in the United States."

It was soon apparent to those supervising this unique facility that they had no more adept student than the woman in their midst. Ellen Swallow also knew that recognition could become a liability, as well as an asset, in an all-male environment.

"Roil no waters," were her bywords.

"I hope in a quiet way I am winning a way for others . . ." she wrote her Vassar classmate, Anne Mineah. She "picked her steps" along that unmarked road.

Starting with appearance, she emphasized her plainness. By making her own clothes, she not only saved money, but tailored a more austere wardrobe. She eliminated the full leg o'mutton sleeves and disdained the bustle, even after school. Nearly everything she wore to school was dark; cottons mostly; some wools in winter. High-collared, long-sleeved dresses touched the tops of her buttoned black or brown shoes. Four or five petticoats— fashionable then—were too cumbersome. She wore two or three petticoats and a corset, only because it was "morally proper" and only for a few years. With her black hair pulled straight back, gripping her books and papers tight against her, she walked quickly and quietly through the halls.

Classes were another problem. She had to draw a fine line between eagerness to learn and the appearance of being too bright or too competitive. What impressed one professor could offend another. Deliberate, cautious, plain and quiet, humble and soft spoken, instead of an intruder, she earned a tolerant, even curious, welcome.

She went out of her way to be "useful."

Prof. A accords me his sanction when I sew up his papers or tie up a sore finger, etc. Last night, Prof. B found me useful to *mend his suspenders* which had come to grief, much to the amusement of young Mr. C.

I try to keep all sorts of such things as needles, thread, pins, scissors, etc, around . . . they are getting to come to me for anything they want and they almost always find it. . . . As Prof. D said

the other day, "when we are in doubt we go to Miss Swallow."
You see, I am useful in a decidedly general way . . . they can't
say study spoils me for anything else.

I think I am making good progress in my study too. They say
I am going ahead because Prof. Ordway trusts me to do his work
for him, which he never did anyone else. The dear good man, I am
only too happy to do anything for him.

It was wise willingness on her part. John Ordway was one of
the earliest industrial chemists. As he found more and more work
for this talented student's skills, unique opportunities opened for
her.

By today's standards, it's easy to think of Ellen's eager help-
fulness as subservience. Perhaps it would have been, even then,
if she had allowed it. But her purpose was very clear to her. And
she was, as shown in her childhood and throughout her life, dedicated to human service. It made no difference if they were men or
women. Her desire to help was true altruism. Service was her
ambition.

Endurance was something else she was learning. It was part of
every day. She was up early in the morning to organize Mrs.
Blodgett's instructions to the help, menus for the day, budgets,
interviewing the poor and often ill Irish men and women and
children at the back door, looking for work—and then to school.
"A good walk to start the day," she recommended. But her day
had started much earlier. School was invigorating mentally, but
the close, stuffy rooms and halls left her tired, she noticed. She
did not complain; not yet.

Boston was the largest city she had seen so far. She was en-
raptured by its great museums and schools, the world port. It was
America's ultimate center of commerce and culture. The Hub,
Oliver Wendell Holmes named it. Everywhere she looked, she
could see liberty's heritage. And its horrors.

She was shocked by things she saw on the way to school and
around town. Filth. Disease. Suffering. She'd read about the ex-
cessively high rates of death and illness, the epidemics that ran
through the city. Now she saw why. Horse wagons carrying uncovered food over dirty, unpaved streets through pools of stag-

nant swill made of everything from animal waste, human spit, and garbage. Alleys were worse: open sewers. Indoors, many homes weren't much better.

Children were hit hardest by these conditions. She read that sometimes less than half a city's children lived to be adults. Many made it only with deformed bodies or with crippled minds.

Cities: the best and worst of civilization, she thought; people crowding together for greater human opportunity and suffering. And not just disease, either; she read about the terrible fire in Chicago that year; how the winds had fanned the flames to turn a whole city to ash. She saw young children and women employed in inhuman labor in equally inhumane conditions.

The strain of her busy schedule in that new environment weakened Ellen Swallow. In her first semester, she came down with an illness of some unrecorded kind. Excusing herself from classes, she pulled her affairs in order and took a train home to rest for a few days at Worcester. She had hardly arrived when tragedy struck.

"I was just able to lie around on the sofa . . . [when] word came Father was being brought home." Peter Swallow had been hit by a train in the Worcester station. The injuries were serious; a crushed right arm would have to come off.

In 1871, when anesthetics were not commonly used, his daughter had to help with the amputation. "Oh . . . the terrible agony he suffered 'in the arm that is gone'," she wrote. Fanny Swallow was helpless with grief. ". . . he looked to no one else, trusted all in my hands, night and day for four days, a few hours delirium, then sleep and a glorious awakening in heaven," Ellen recorded her father's death.

> I had strength to go through it all, calm, without a tear, but it almost took [my] reason. I sometimes fear I shall give up. . . . So many things I have to do which almost kill me, business which calls him up to me, seeing people who want to talk of him and yet I will not allow myself to shirk. I could not leave Mother alone tho it is torture for me to be here and so I shall go back and forth to Boston every day. . . . What special mission is God preparing me for? Cutting me off from all earthly ties. . . .

Then she answered that question by throwing herself into her work.

> Let the mind know there is a will power to control it. . . . This is possible. I could never have lived thru these sad months. . . . When you feel an indication of a certain morbid feeling, set your mind in another direction and don't give up easily. Now when the thought comes to my mind I shut the door tight and run to the other side [of my mind] and take a book or pencil or plan something for the future and so turn the attention. . . .

Until the summer hiatus at MIT, Ellen Swallow supported herself, executed her father's estate, took care of her mother by commuting daily from Boston to Worcester, and completed her first semester's studies at the Institute. If there was ever a doubt in her mind, she resolved it. When fall came around, she was back for the second semester of her "experiment."

FIVE

First Lady of Science

In 1869, while Ellen Swallow studied at Vassar, Massachusetts established America's first state board of health. The statement by which it was created made a permanent impression on Ellen.

"No Board of Health," its preamble said, *"if it rightly performs its duty, can separate the physical from the moral and intellectual natures of man. . . . These three qualities are . . . indissoluble, and mutually act and react upon one another. Any influence exerted to the injury of one, inevitably, though perhaps indirectly, injures the other and are acted upon [in turn] by the forces of nature that surround us."* (Author's italics.)

The intelligence of that statement more than 100 years ago carries a comprehension on which Ellen Swallow would build the foundations of environmental science. To her, *the physical, moral, and intellectual natures of man* were the three relative forces of environment by which man lived and developed his physical, social, and perceptual environments.

These elements of "man's nature" were relative, she knew. Through this perspective she saw that the definitive value of all knowledge was subordinate to the health of man and the quality of his environment. To this concept, she dedicated her life. In its course, she would organize and disseminate new bodies of knowledge to awaken the three institutions she held responsible for the condition of man and his environment: government, industry, and the public. That she was a woman before her time was only because of the rejection of her work by the mankind she worked for.

Even the resurrection of her work by later environmental scientists to solve the crisis she predicted lacks the depth and scope of the environmental sciences she began to form in April 1872.

The concern of Massachusetts with health stemmed from England's. Industrialization began there first, but on smaller, more densely populated land. As far back as the fourteenth century, England legislated a futile effort to clean up the Thames, an open sewer for London's growing population and industry. By the sixteenth and seventeenth centuries, air pollution compounded the problem. Laws were passed against open fires and certain fuels. But little abatement was brought to the ever accelerating exploitation known as industrialization.

By the mid-nineteenth century, England's environment was so bad that a Rivers Pollution Commission was formed. The oldest manufacturing area in the new world, England's former colony, Massachusetts, decided it should follow the lead. In the words of Dr. George E. Derby, head of the first Massachusetts Board of Health:

> The pollution of streams by industrial establishment and by the sewage of towns has been several times during the past year brought to [our] attention. Judging from the history of still more densely populated manufacturing areas in other parts of the world, the general subject will continue to claim the attention of the people of Massachusetts for many years to come. As the interests of life and health become more definite and more valued, and as manufactories and population grow and multiply, the apparent conflict in this respect between health and industry will yearly become more evident. *It is our duty, if possible, to show that these important interests are not irreconcilable, and to give a word of warning in season to prevent their relations from being forgotten until it is too late to remedy the omission except at an enormous cost.* (Author's italics.)

That foresight indicated America would not be caught napping. MIT's William Ripley Nichols was called in to test the water ". . . not because there was any serious menace, but as a basis for future comparison. . . ." In 1870, as Ellen Swallow finished her work at Vassar, Nichols took his crude equipment to little Mystic Pond on the outskirts of Boston.

Water analysis was a new branch of science. In England, differing methods and opinions had produced not much more than scientific squabbles. Nichols, alone in his work in the United States, had no such opposition. He was allowed to make a major contribution to the new discipline, which was just that: discipline. Only rigid, precise controls, the most thorough and uniform procedures in the laboratory could remove debate on water content, its source, and its future.

Nichols tested for "mineral constituents . . . no attempt being made to determine organic impurities. . . ." Nevertheless, his nineteen samples of water from Mystic Pond sounded the first warning of America's water pollution. It was not exactly Paul Revere's ride, however. The first scientific testing of America's water reached a small, isolated audience of politicians. Two years later they approved another study. Again Nichols was called in ". . . to collect information concerning sewage and the possibility of using it, the pollution of streams, and the water supply of towns and report at the next session" of the legislature. It was April 2, 1872. Ellen Swallow had entered the picture.

The classic water-sewage study was an enormous challenge to a new science in which laboratory analysis was paramount. Laboratory science itself was in its infancy. Although Nichols had been part of the contingent opposing the admission of women to the Institute, that was two years before. Now, from all the state resources at his command, all the personnel available to him, he picked the now obvious talent and discipline of the Institute's only woman, second-year student Ellen Swallow.

"A new work has been put in my hands . . . by a professor who does not believe in women's education," she wrote. "I have made about 100 analyses so far and that is only part of my daily duties. I . . . prepare my lessons . . . evenings."

While Nichols was in Europe to observe techniques there, Swallow made the actual tests of Massachusetts sewage, streams, and water supply. For two years, her flint-steel eyes saw Massachusetts through the matter under her microscope and in her test tubes. It made a special impact on the mind of a once sickly girl nature helped cure.

Nichol's 1873 report to the state legislature showed his rehabilitated faith in educated women—at least one of them.

"Most of the analytical work has been performed by Miss Ellen Swallow. . . . I take pleasure in acknowledging my indebtedness to her valuable assistance by expressing my confidence in the accuracy of the results obtained." Those two sentences were not small words for a man of science at the time. Coming from this man, they were even more significant.

The eyes that had gazed wonderingly into a bubbling brook so many years before had completed a scientific study that went far beyond its initial recognition. Today, no less than six scientific and professional specialties can be traced back to that 1872 study. In the years ahead, Swallow would help develop these fields.

Once again, the study was made more for future comparisons. Again the state accepted the findings. It would be fifteen years before the complete examination of the state's water and sewage would give the world its first Water Purity Tables and the United States would be given its first state water quality standards. When that time came, Ellen Swallow would play a much more central role.

To those who could admit it (the liberated Nichols was one), the study made her a preeminent international water scientist even before her graduation. Her interest equalled that often-ignored status, and she began a life-long collection of water from the world over, bringing it to analyze in the laboratory. While still a student, she managed to get ahold of samples from as far away as Turkey. It was dirty water she saw, but unlike that she was finding close, and then not close, to American manufacturing sites.

If the years immediately before incubated environmental science, 1873 marked its birth. Water was the appropriate medium for this event. But it was a medium for more than Swallow's work. While the chemist studied water in America, a biologist at the University of Jena, in Germany, was approaching environmental science from another direction.

Ernst Haeckel in his lifetime coined the names for nearly a dozen new sciences. As early as the late 1860s he is credited with suggesting a science be developed to study organisms in their environment. By 1873, Haeckel had come up with a name for that science. Then, leaving "Oekologie" for others to develop, he concentrated on other sciences he named, particularly

"Phylogeny," and conceived the Phylogenetic Scale of Life, a tree from the smallest life form up to man.

Fluent in German, Swallow traced the German word Oekologie to its origin—the Greek word for house. "Oik" for house; "Oek" for "every-man's house"—environment. The "Oe," she knew made it universal—"oecumenical." If Haeckel, a male biologist, saw that a science of everyone's house environment needed to be developed, the female chemist slowly began to take up residency in the structure. She was well aware that men wore the pants in science, and in science no one wore them quite as possessively as life scientists. But chemistry could provide a distaff side for environmental science, not just life but the environment that influences that life. It would take the organization of an irrefutable body of knowledge.

Haeckel and Ellen Swallow started at the same time and at the same place: with water, the source of all life and its first environment. In Oekologie—the "universal house"—biology was the science of life; chemistry, as Ellen Swallow saw it, was the science of environment.

MIT was a near perfect incubator for environmental science. In addition to Nichols's and Swallow's study of water, Professor Frank Storer had begun, in 1870, the study of air. She would study this element, too, and physics along with chemistry, at the Institute. In a vague but constant effort to put it all together, she also went to that part of the laboratory where another MIT professor studied the earth itself. From mineralogist Robert Richards she would add earth to air and water science, to build Oekologie.

Richards was an interesting figure. By his own account, he had been a "slow" young man while preparing in England for the usual Harvard education given sons of prominent families. When his mother wrote that her cousin's husband, William Barton Rogers, was opening a technical school, "I leaped at the chance," Richards said. At MIT, "the scales fell from my eyes and I could see for the first time in my life." The "slow" student was found to be a technical genius. Seventh student in the Institute's first graduating class, he was hired immediately as an instructor of mining and chemistry.

Richards was not opposed to the higher education of women.

There were many educated women in his family. But according to his diary, he was against *coeducation*. As his colleague Nichols was won over, however, Richards too changed his mind. Swallow's fluency in German was the first step in that conversion.

In the 1870's, the best professional journals in mineralogy and mining were German, an "almost unspoken tongue" in Boston at the time. Richards subscribed to the magazines anyway. He could understand the graphs and charts. Chemical equations were fairly universal. But when it came to the text of an article, the "scales" flew back to his eyes. When he discovered a student who could translate German spontaneously, his argument against coeducation began to evaporate.

In the mineralogy laboratory, where chemistry and mining met, Richards and Swallow became metallurgists and mineralogists together, a relationship that spun off unexpected benefits for science and technology, as well as for their own careers.

In 1872, Dr. T. T. Bouve, president of the prestigious Boston Society of Natural History with which the Institute had a relationship, stopped by to see Richards. He brought a piece of samarskite, a rare ore he thought the professor would like to examine. Richards introduced Bouve to this woman student, who was making a kind of natural history of her own. Benevolently, the professor and doctor turned over the samarskite sample to the student.

"Eminent men had examined samarskite" and identified various rare metals in it. Their analyses were considered the last word on the ore. Yet Ellen's very first examination did not match that of the experts. Repeating it, she got the same results. "What am I doing wrong?" she wondered. Again, she meticulously made her calculations: the same. In a paper published by the Natural History Society, she boldly stated, ". . . there is an insoluable residue that is not accounted for" in samarskite. While some doubted the woman's word, a Kentucky scientist devised a new method of analysis and discovered samarium and gadolinium. Richards was astounded.

"She came near to being one of those immortals who have identified new elements in the earth's crust," he wrote. She was still a student.

In the summer of 1872, Swallow and a friend, Bea Capen, a

teacher at Boston High School for Girls, made a mineralogical expedition. They studied ore deposits in upstate New York, and examined silver, lead, and copper mines in Maine and Canada. Surprisingly, they were allowed into the mines. Swallow's report impressed Richards that fall when school resumed. He decided to put her mineralogical skill to the ultimate test with the new and rare metal, vanadium.

Only a few scientists had yet worked with this metal, named for the Scandinavian deity Vanadis. Although it had been found in Europe, Mexico, Canada, and America—and even in sea water—it was always found in infinitely small quantities and was almost beyond detection, "given the present state of scientific knowledge." Vanadium was not only hard to find, it was more difficult to prove its presence because of its varied reactions to different methods.

Richards gave his student an ore "reported to contain Vanadium." Others had examined it unsuccessfully. The professor himself was uncertain of its content. After six months, in which she culled from and corresponded with international sources, Swallow succeeded in isolating .02 percent vanadium in the ore. It was said of vanadium, "There is no more difficult metal to obtain." She agreed, and Richards was now convinced he had a genius in his lab.

Two other seemingly unrelated events of her student years helped influence the course of Ellen Swallow's environmental science. The first was the Boston Milk War of the early 1870s. Unscrupulous milk and railroad interests customarily added half or more water to bulk milk on the way to the homes and bellies of Bostonians. In one year alone, of the $4 million the city spent for milk, $600,000 was calculated as the cost of the water added. A group of concerned citizens met at the Temple Flower Mart to organize the Consumer Protection Association and a new milk distribution system. On the cold March morning they started, their wagons were stolen or broken, the drivers beaten or bribed to foul the milk. There were horses crippled or killed. In spite of the criminal acts against them, the C.P.A. managed to get a pure milk supply through to the city. Ellen watched the drama unfold. She wanted to join with them, but her precarious position at MIT prevented her. Milk, she knew, is the first food. The event rekindled her old interest in another environmental element: the purity or pollution of the human diet.

The year 1872 was also the year of the Great Boston Fire.

It is a strange feeling to stand out in the still night and see so intense and angry a monster eating up stone walls. It was only property that was destroyed and mainly the merchandise we put on our bodies, so we can do with less and not suffer.

But it was a still night. A shift of wind and the flames would have taken a far worse toll, she knew. As the fire destroyed the city's structures, it convinced her that new building materials must be developed by science and technology. She thought about her father's "artificial stone" and mentally designed a "Home of the Future" of it or a modified fire-resistant material. She envisioned new products and processes inside the house that would improve the quality of the man-made environment.

Soon it was 1873. The full, busy undergraduate years had passed quickly. In June, a Thomas Wentworth Higgins came to Boston to address the American Social Scientists convention on "The Higher Education of Women." He was all for it. So was the American Association for the Advancement of Women meeting in the city that year. Both groups had their best example at the school on Boylston Street. There, Ellen Swallow, A.B. Vassar 1870, became Ellen Swallow, S.B. MIT 1873.

It was the school's first degree of any kind to a woman and probably the first science degree for any American woman. Immediately, the graduate applied for membership in the American Association for the Advancement of Science, which William Barton Rogers had helped reorganize.

At the same time, Vassar College awarded Ellen a master's degree, based on and praising her brilliant thesis on vanadium. Farrar and Mitchell were especially proud. But Vassar knew its place. Master of Arts was the only degree it could offer, even for a scientific thesis.

Ellen Swallow was thirty-one and America's First Lady of Science, a title she would earn internationally in the remaining thirty-eight years of her life. First, she wanted a doctor's degree. "But while there were many to make use of her skill, there were few to encourage and help her surmount the difficulties which at that time lay in the way of a woman securing such an honor."

In plainer words, Doctor of Chemistry was not a title MIT was willing in 1873 to concede to a woman. Already she'd got back papers marked "A.O.M."

"What does that mean?" she asked Ordway.

"Actium Omnium Magistra," he politely suggested.

She knew better. "An Old Maid, I see it." Three quarters of a century later, Professor Emeritus Robert Richards recalled the hopes of his prize student.

> She wanted a Doctor's Degree more than anything else, but she had to give up the idea, one of her greatest disappointments in life.

Then he touched the real reason for MIT denying genius its potential.

> She was treated for some time as a dangerous person. . . . It seems to me . . . that some of the difficulties may have arose from the fact that *the heads of the department did not wish a woman to receive [MIT's] first D.S. in Chemistry*. (Author's italics.)

Disheartened, Ellen thought about her future. There was so much she wanted to do. But where? Argentina came to mind again. Then, in a perverse sort of way, the Institute helped make up her mind. Whether from guilt, recognition, intercedence, or a combination of factors, they let her know she could stay on at the school. After all, there was still a water-sewage study to complete. She could assist with other things around the school. But they could give her no title. Worse, they would give her no pay. They didn't object to her presence, apparently; nor to her work, obviously. Just as long as she kept an anonymous place in the patriarchy's pecking order, she was welcome. She could even have the use of the laboratories. That did it.

In the five years since Littleton, Ellen Swallow had done more than others dared dream. Now, suddenly, the reality of her sex came back to the Bachelor of Science. By example she had opened the door for women in science. But here it was, ready to swing shut again.

The feisty Yankee made her decision. The Institute hadn't taken her money for the knowledge it had given her. Now she would repay that debt. She would finish the water study. She would learn what else she could at the Institute. Pay or not, title or anonymity, she would stay in the doorway and hold it open for others.

She could "hire out" again. This time, as a chemist, she would tend a much larger environment than the homes of Littleton and Worcester. This time, the home and hearth of the environment itself would be nurtured by the hand, the eye, and the mind of Ellen Swallow, scientist.

SIX

The Blowpipe Conspiracy

An officer of the MIT Corporation recalled, years later, "the tradition of a long controversy with Miss Swallow, President Runkle and a few faculty members on one side, and the rest and all the Corporation on the other. Why [they] asked, 'should a female take up scientific studies reserved for men? Woman's place is in the Home . . . and if one woman is admitted, others will follow; and think of the disastrous effect on the young men'."

Another observer recorded, "She was put on trial for all women."

Ellen Swallow was her own counsel in that trial. The verdict was less than a complete vindication of women in science. But she won probation for herself and a stay of execution for others of her sex. She was not the first woman to try to enter MIT—two others had tried and failed—but for five years it seemed she might be the last. At one point in her second semester, it seemed even she might not make it.

The Faculty Committee, meeting on October 21, 1871, voted:

> . . . the name of Miss Swallow who takes a special course in chemistry, be omitted from the list of students in the catalogue . . .

Tenuous from the start, her position fell to its low point. It was only a couple of weeks since she had been taken off "segregation" and allowed to study with the men. Apparently, something had happened. Perhaps someone complained. In any event, her expertise in the lab and her improving relations with Ordway,

Nichols, and Richards helped President Runkle ease faculty criticism. By mid-December, she had passed the crisis. The Faculty Committee met again.

> The vote not to introduce the name of Miss Swallow into the Catalogue was reconsidered, and it was voted that her name be inserted in full under the head of "special students."

From that point on, she consolidated her position. When other women were finally permitted to cross the line at MIT, Ellen Swallow's subtle strategies had made it possible.

To Ellen, science was like a language. It had a literacy all its own. In a world being changed by science and technology, she saw a need for ordinary people to have some basic grasp of that language—if not its command—if they were to have some say in their own destinies. She appointed herself responsible for translating the elite language of science into a vernacular for everyday use. Directly, she made possible the science education of thousands. Indirectly, she reached millions in generations yet unborn. It does not overstate her case to say Ellen Swallow was a dominant force in humanizing American science by opening its doors to greater human participation.

MIT recognized the need to increase awareness of science. The growth of anything is limited to its participation. In the economically recessed years of the early 1870s, that fact was brought home painfully to the specialty school. Enrollment was small, facilities limited, and the budget cut and pared again.

The Lowell Lectures, begun in 1865 with a gift of $250,000, were MIT's main means to channel science information to the public. The lectures were a popular intellectual attraction to which writers, educators, and other "opinion leaders" came to get abreast of the emerging scientific miracles before the age of mass media. As a mass medium though, the Lowell Lectures were grossly ineffective. A bigger and better channel was needed.

In 1872, the lectures were limited in yet another way. Financial austerity at the Institute led to cancellation of the all-important chemistry lectures. Charles W. Eliot, who with Frank Storer was an author of what was called the best chemistry textbook for schools, left MIT enroute to a career that would see him become president of Harvard. Loss of the chemistry lectures created a serious problem for teachers who had found them the only available supplement to the complex science textbook.

If science is a language, Ellen thought, chemistry is its alphabet. The real bottleneck for science education was the public school. Very little science, if any, was taught there then, even in the so-called upper "Normal Schools." There simply weren't enough qualified science instructors. And a textbook, no matter how good, was worthless if a teacher couldn't interpret it.

Obviously, if teachers shied from science, there was no science exposure for students. If students had no idea of its subject matter, they had practically no way to develop interest in the work or to know their aptitudes for it. Sooner or later, the lack of science knowledge in public schools would be felt by the school specializing in science. To MIT, in those lean years, it felt like sooner.

Ellen Swallow related the paucity of science education in the public schools to the main problem facing college women. In each she saw a potential solution for the other. The number of women able to go to college was increasing. But there were still few opportunities, other than teaching, after graduation. As more women graduated from college, the ratio of women teachers grew. Why not equip women to teach science in public schools?

Swallow had opened the gate to science for women. Rather than merely hold it open by example, she felt it should be unhinged altogether. Events in the early 1870s gave her the opportunity to try.

In the fall of 1872, an optimistic young woman came to Boston to prepare for a career in medicine. But she could not be admitted to a medical school. Before one would accept her, she had to find a school where she could study chemistry.

The official record of what happened that winter is vague. But somehow, we are told, the aspiring medical student was put in touch with Professor James Crafts at the Institute. Crafts, who just happened to be one of Ellen's teachers, took the young woman's case to another Eliot, Dr. Samuel P., head of Boston's Girls High School. Eliot just happened to be Bea Capen's employer. This man in turn put the problem to the newly formed Woman's Education Association in Boston. Both Ellen and Bea Capen just happened to be members of the W.E.A.

"If the Association will pay for materials and instruction,"

Eliot said, the young woman could study chemistry in the evenings at the new Girls High School. The w.e.a. was looking for just such projects, they said, having failed in their initial plan the year before to open a course for women at Harvard. In February 1873, sixteen young women began a class in advanced chemistry at Girls High School. Most were teachers looking to augment their meager science knowledge. Their instructors: Bea Capen of the Girls High School and Ellen Swallow, MIT student.

Ellen had more to do with this development than teaching. She had known Bea Capen for at least a year, her diary shows. Their friendship had expanded Bea Capen's education. She was teaching science at Boston Girls High. Now that friendship hatched a conspiracy. The Crafts-to-Eliot-to-w.e.a. parlay seems logical enough on the surface, but whose logic was it really? How did an aspiring female physician "happen" to meet Ellen's chemistry professor? It would seem natural for a girl hoping to study chemistry to look up the only girl at the only science specialty school in the city. What led Crafts, Ellen's professor, to Eliot, Bea Capen's employer? As for Eliot's decision to approach the w.e.a, nothing else would have occurred to him, since he'd helped organize the group the previous year. And at the w.e.a, Swallow and Capen had prepared the response.

If the space between coincidence and conspiracy is hidden by time, the outcome of the project is not. Also labeled "in the nature of an experiment," this time it was Ellen Swallow's experiment. She lost no time in merchandising its success. In casual conversation at MIT, with periodic progress reports to the w.e.a., she built her case.

"Fully half of [the women science students] are teachers," she explained, "hoping to expand their potential. Soon they will be sending you more young scientists to train." To the association, she praised their good use of funds to "improve the present methods of education for women." The seeds were planted. For the next three years, as the classes continued, she irrigated the idea. Attitudes began to change. "After all," she explained to Professor Richards, "I'm not the only one. There are a great many able young women coming through college. They will be very important to science education if we allow them to have one first."

Richards was not yet fully converted to coeducation. Ellen Swallow, to his mind, was an exception. Just how exceptional she was can be seen in the fact that Richards, unsuspecting, now became a major figure in the plot to open MIT to women: The Blowpipe Conspiracy.

Related to MIT's founder by marriage, Richards was a member of a very prominent family in his own right. He carried more weight than he knew or used in the daily affairs managed by the school's Faculty Committee and Acting President Runkle. His work in the "glamor" industry of the day, mining, added another dimension to his stature. Each summer he visited remote mining areas in the North, South, or Wild West. Young, handsome, and single, with a six-foot frame and a lean 179 pounds, he was a much sought figure in Boston's social circles, where his tall tales of the frontier added to his charm. The fact that no less than two Maine towns carried his family names; that his brother Henry, a Harvard architect, had just married the daughter of Samuel Gridley Howe and Julia Ward Howe; that another brother, George, was an internationally famous sportsman and a repeating winner of Newport's Americas Cup Race with England, all added up to a substantial advantage to a new school trying to hold its own in Brahmin Boston.

Robert Richards was not one to use his influence, if indeed he was conscious he had any. But "innocently vain," as his niece recalls, Richards's ethics did not prevent others from cultivating his approval. He was a serious, hardworking young man of twenty-nine, always ready to lend a hand to his colleagues, mostly his seniors. One helpful task Richards was called upon to perform from time to time became a fulcrum for Ellen Swallow's campaign to open MIT to women.

Of all Richards's hobbies—archery, photography, boating among them—he was proudest of his glass blowing. It was more than a hobby to the school, however. Built on laboratory science at a time when laboratories were few and far apart, MIT's scientists were always upgrading their processes. New processes required new equipment. But there were fewer science supply houses than laboratories. What there were followed, rather than led, in the development of new instruments.

When a colleague felt he'd worked out a new system, very

often he needed a new piece of laboratory glass. Even if the piece was available from commercial sources, it often took too long to get it. Richards was always there to help.

Glass blowing, a fascinating craft to watch, requires great patience and skill. Ellen Swallow delighted in watching her handsome professor heat up the sand, take the blowpipe in his strong hands, put it to his mustachioed lips, and slowly blow out the glistening form of a delicate glass instrument. If she was captivated by the show, Robert Richards was human enough to enjoy the audience. One day, he was particularly flattered when Miss Swallow asked if he would terribly mind demonstrating glass blowing to her science students at the Girls High School. Thus having met Miss Capen and the class of would-be science teachers, Robert Richards was pleased to see them stop by the Institute to visit Miss Swallow. In the winter of 1875, these casual visits had evolved considerably. Ellen confided to her friend Anne Mineah:

There has been a private class in chemistry in our little laboratory this winter. . . . 8 members of whom Miss Glover is one." A main bolt on the last hinge was removed from the door.

By this time, Richards appears to be aware of his role. In his diary, he argued the pros and cons of coeducation. A few pages after the insertion, "Classes in Blowpipe . . . Miss Capen . . . Ventilation . . . Swallow . . ." he outlined the case:

Men & Women Together: Statement and Answer (Swallow)
Statement: Introduces Feelings, interests foreign to lecture room.
Answer: But those feelings do less harm . . . than in cars & street corners.
Statement: Together in the Family, why not in class?
Answer: Mother warmly interested in each one; Teacher cannot be; numbers too great.

However convincing the argument may have been, Robert Richards was not about to make a formal plea for the women to the faculty. Swallow knew this. The most she hoped for, and she was fairly sure she'd made her point, was for Richards's silence at worst, or his support at best if the subject came up. Perhaps he might just mention it favorably to Dr. Rogers, his mother's cousin by marriage, if the occasion arose.

In November 1875, Swallow spoke to her fellow w.e.a. members—the Cabots, Lodges, Wolcotts, Lowells, Endicotts.

> I have reason to believe that if you will provide the funds, [they] will provide the space for a women's laboratory at the Institute.

Once again the ladies agreed. A committee was appointed to explore the idea with the Institute. Innocently, like a fox, Swallow brought the groups together and then left them alone, but only after she'd primed them both.

Logic overcame resistance. The profit motive was more modern than old fashioned ideas about women. Now, Swallow thought, if the w.e.a. can make good on its end. "Its" end came to be very much hers.

"Now all I need is $2,000 to have a special room fitted up for 10 or 12 women. . . . I am making a strong effort to interest people in it," she wrote in February 1876. She had become the project's fund raiser as well.

"Success is assured," she wrote in May. Then later that month: "I must tell you the good news. Yesterday, the government of the Institute passed a vote that hereafter special students in chemistry shall be admitted without regard to sex. . . . I can assure you I am very happy."

Again, the faculty hedged. ". . . without regard to sex" applied only to Swallow's ". . . special students in chemistry . . ." An old garage tabbed for renovation as a men's gymnasium was set aside to segregate the special students. The "cautious and reluctant authorities placed her and her small band of disciples in a sort of contagious ward located in what we students used to call the 'dump' . . .", remembered a male student who became an officer of the MIT Corporation.

Nevertheless, in November 1876, twenty-three women, most of them teachers, began training for careers in science through chemistry at MIT. In the centennial year of American independence, a determined Yankee farm girl made possible the celebration of a sexual independence of sorts on the Boston side of the historic Charles River.

The world's first women's science laboratory was put in John Ordway's charge. But its day-to-day operation was the responsibility of one Ellen Henrietta Richards, nee Swallow, A.B., S.B.,

A.M. During the Blowpipe Conspiracy, "cupid was found among the test tubes and retorts of the Laboratory." On June 5, 1875, Ellen Swallow married Robert Hallowell Richards, professor of mining engineering and head of the new metallurgical laboratory that was opened at the Institute. The conspiracy had benefited both. Many, many more would profit in the future.

Through 1878, when MIT abandoned its "special student" label for women, until 1884, when the old garage was torn down and the sexes integrated in the school, and ever after, women came from all parts of the United States to study and to take back the knowledge of science to instill in new generations. As MIT's men went on to careers in industry and government, its first women found their way into high schools, seminaries, academies, preparatory schools, colleges, and universities. There they founded, enlarged, and improved science departments that brought ever more students through the doors of science unhinged by Ellen Swallow; students who otherwise might never have had the chance or inclination for science.

She started the development that would play a major if unstated role in the nation's course: arming public education with the subject and substance by which America would grow to international scientific and technological supremacy in the next century. But for as long as Ellen Swallow lived, she worked to nurture a balance between exploiting and improving the environment with science.

Until the Women's Laboratory was fully established, however, it was her main interest. Soon after it opened, she began adding new disciplines, new projects, and new significance to its student portfolio. For all this, she was unpaid. Instead she paid out $1,000 a year of her own money to reduce the lab's operating cost. Her friend John Ordway joined her in this gesture, waiving his salary for the women's lab work.

In 1878, the Institute recognized Ellen Swallow as an "assistant instructor." If they added a token financial reward—Robert Richards said they didn't—she waived it, continuing her annual contributions to the school. She continued to solicit funds from others for scholarships to help bright but poorer students.

She recruited them, gave crash courses to prep them for exams, found lodging, part-time work, and full-time careers. With

Robert Richards she taught, chaperoned, counseled, and fed them. When they graduated she stayed in touch, recruiting their students and finding jobs for hers.

After she died, receipts were found to show she had paid the tuition of more than one young woman—or young man.

She was the "Dean of Women" at MIT, although like the doctorate she wanted so badly, MIT never quite got around to giving he either title, actually, honorarily, or posthumously. It remained for another major college to bestow an honorary Doctor of Science degree on Ellen Swallow. When that happened, one of her young protégées was present to receive the same honor.

For all MIT's myopia, the American Association for the Advancement of Science (she called it A₃S) saw Ellen Swallow in a clearer light, however. In 1878, they elevated her from "member" to "Fellow," a designation given the scientist who performs above the Ph.D. level. Her only recognition by the school she served so well and so long is a bronze plaque tarnished black on the wall of a hall in the chemistry department she helped bring to world leadership.

In 1883, when the women were integrated, she raised "eight or ten thousand dollars" for a lady's lounge and named it The Margaret Cheney Room for one of the women who had helped her open the lab. It was called the "Center of Life for Women at MIT." But she, Ellen Swallow, was the original and lasting center of life for American women in science, then and now.

Chemistry, threshold to all science, was an appropriate choice for this unusual woman's work. By securing its literacy for others, she brought the female's sensitivity to science's patriarchy. In a very real sense, she brought to science's elite language a vernacular that allowed more of the population to share the benefits of knowledge. Ellen Swallow was the mother from whom this tongue was learned.

The hinges were undone. The doors were down. The way was open for greater participation in science. It was enough for a lifetime's work. Focused on newer, larger horizons, hers was just beginning.

SEVEN

Ellen and Robert

Romance between a teacher and student wags tongues in any age. In nineteenth-century Boston, the love of a very proper professor for his puritanical protégée was a closely kept secret.

The romance seems to have started in the winter of 1872. Robert Richards's diaries during his wife's undergraduate years hint at the momentum of their relationship. References to "EHS" became "Miss Swallow" by spring. By the time the young man fancied "Nellie" in the confidence of his diary, the name of Mrs. Swallow also made its appearance. The courtship may have been concealed from MIT, but not at home.

"The inevitable happened," as Richards put it, "shortly after she received her B.S." On June 6, 1873, in the MIT laboratory, the professor whispered his proposal. But Ellen wanted time to think it over. Her future was confused at the time. As the Blowpipe Conspiracy unfolded, however, any doubts she may have had about her professor disappeared. Two years and a day later, June 7, 1875, Robert and Ellen were married in Boston's Union Chapel.

Their scientific acumen notwithstanding, on their wedding day the bridegroom forgot his necktie and the bride the keys to their new house. He'd hoped for a little cottage along a river somewhere outside the city, but she vetoed the idea. Malaria and other epidemic diseases struck first and hardest along the polluting rivers of the nineteenth century. The newlyweds spent the first week of their marriage organizing a house "on the corner of a shaded street" in Jamaica Plain, four miles from the Institute.

Then they were off on a Nova Scotia honeymoon with his entire class to see the mines in the region.

Ellen wore high boots and a short skirt—anything above the heel was short then—as the odd party toured the mines. So many ore samples were stuffed into their trunks, she arrived back in Boston still wearing her outdoor habit. On their way to drop off the rocks at the Institute, they met a friend "in the company of a party of fashionable women." The ladies were shocked. They refused to believe they'd just seen "a Vassar graduate," let alone a bride, returning with a couple of dozen males from a wedding trip.

The honeymoon was only the first of countless such excursions. Europe, Canada, Mexico, Alaska, the Caribbean, over the North Pole by ship, and across the North American continent to every major city and most of its states and provinces, Ellen became the most traveled woman of her time. Many of those trips Ellen and Robert made together as she helped him in his work. But as her sciences expanded, she traveled more and more alone. During the first years of the marriage, however, she concentrated on the needs of husband, home, and the Women's Laboratory.

Apart or together, the marriage was a true symbiosis—two lives never intruding but always an advantage to the other. She believed in the synergism of the sexes, that the sum of their relationship should be greater than its parts. This was a physical law. She saw no reason why it should not apply to social nature as well.

Symbiosis and synergism worked for Robert and Nellie. Marriage enabled each an output neither could have achieved alone. Partly because of her, he became an internationally recognized mineralogist, metallurgist, and educator who "revolutionized academic instruction," according to *The New York Times*. On the other hand, he provided opportunities for her that would otherwise have never advanced.

Uncomplicated by petty competition, their union was marked by mutual interests of opposite personalities. He was "slow, deliberate, and judicious"; she was "quick to see, move, and act."

"She was of great assistance in my work . . . took more than her share from the beginning," he wrote. "Some twenty papers a week come into our house," she noted. She read, translated, and excerpted them for him. Her speed at reading amazed him. He put two dots on a piece of paper an inch apart. "Are you aware if you move your eye when you look at them?" he asked. She studied the dots. "Yes, I do," she said. He concluded, "Her eyes report much more quickly to the brain than mine."

A niece of Robert, Laura Richards Wiggins, recalled in 1972 the aunt and uncle she knew as a teenager. The marriage was then more than thirty years old.

> They were the most opposite people you could imagine. He was a handsome man . . . vain about his good looks . . . we used to see him pat his curls and got quite a good chuckle out of that. She wasn't a strikingly pretty woman . . . not pretty in the physical sense that we evaluate beauty today. She was quite plain. But even though she was not pretty, she was striking. . . .
>
> She had the most intent, keen eyes. A pleasant sense of humor very much her own . . . not silly, but very feminine. She didn't waste words on humor for humor's sake. When she said something clever or comical, it had a point.

Robert on the other hand, had a bit of the ham in him; he liked to tell a funny story. With his deep, resonant bass voice, he enjoyed singing with Boston's Handel-Haydn Society.

Ellen had great self-confidence, Laura Wiggins recalls. "She was the boiled-down essence of New England . . . like the hard granite under every inch of New England soil, she was there . . . even when she wasn't in the room, you were aware of her presence. . . . She gave you the impression of permanence.

"It was obvious to all of us how much Aunt Ellen adored our Uncle Bob. She called him Robert. Always. Her career was quite important to her—but it was not so important to her as his was to her. That seems hard to imagine now, looking back at all she did. But it was true, nonetheless. There were quite a few rules in her household . . . but there was one rule to which all others were subordinate . . . that nothing whatsoever should interfere with her husband's work."

A year after her daughter's marriage, Fanny Swallow moved into the Richards's household. "A small-minded woman who had no conception of what her daughter was," Robert observed. "It is well that she was not with us in the beginning . . . she would have tried to force her personality on us. By spending the first year by ourselves and forming our own happiness, we were not influenced by her presence afterwards."

Fanny had her own parlor and a harmless run of the house, as long as she didn't interfere with Robert's routine.

In the second year of marriage, there was a population explosion in the house at 32 Eliot Street, Jamaica Plain. First came Ellen's friend Minnie Glover. She had full room and board there while studying at the Women's Lab. Her tuition she exchanged for secretarial help to "The Professor." Another student from the Lab, Sarah Wentworth, soon joined them. Then, Katy Carty, a fourteen-year-old niece "of one who calls himself Patsy Ashes, as he earned his living emptying ashes," was taken in, housed, trained, and educated until "she married well."

In what Robert called "my own incompetent way," he said when Katy married, "Here we have spent all this time and money on her and now we will have to start all over again." His wife's silence "spoke volumes." The next time one of the invested help "bettered herself," he would say, "God bless her! Isn't it splendid that we have been able to help her?" It was a story Robert Richards liked to tell on himself to illustrate his wife's personality. But neither husband nor wife ever mentioned the tubercular girl they brought into their home to nurse until she died.

There were other student helpers who came and went. "One . . . is doing quite well now at Smith College," Ellen wrote. A Swedish girl, Edna, and then Augusta were long-time and faithful live-in housekeepers. When Augusta's mother took sick, after Fanny Swallow died, she was given the empty bedroom. When Augusta fell ill, too, Nellie nursed them both back to health. It was a large but always efficient group. "We have plenty of ready hands and quick minds to help in any emergency," said Ellen. Robert enjoyed it.

"Last evening the professor and I were reading in the library when the sound of [the girl's] cheery voices reached us. 'Nellie, you have a happy home,' he said," she told a friend who wondered at the crowd.

The scientist retained the farm girl's love for animals. "My babies are my cats . . . one, the handsomest creature God ever made," she wrote a friend in Maine. "Dutchess," a chestnut horse, doubled as a personal pet and power for the family carriage. She also liked birds. "Carmen" was a silent parrot for whom Ellen bought a feathered friend, "Dayoko," to stimulate conversation. But in that busy house, both birds just sat in their cages, looking, listening to the inordinate comings and goings around them. With Louisa Hewins, an always present next-door neighbor, these were the core of the commune at 32 Eliot Street. But many others came to add to its life.

If Ellen Swallow helped her husband to greater heights, perhaps his most valuable complement to her was the exposure he made possible to the intellectuals and personalities of the time. Foremost among these was his family and its many distinguished connections.

Robert's brothers, George and Henry, were both Harvard men —lawyer and architect respectively. George, the eldest, rivaled his sister-in-law's altruism. "An Honest Man's the Noblest Work of God," said his obituary. A renowned gentleman, George was constantly on the go at sporting events in Europe and America. He never had time to settle in one place until his eyes failed him. Then "he would not presume his handicap on a woman," a relative said.

Every Tuesday afternoon Ellen stayed at home to prepare the week's activities. Her routine was built around the Tuesday evening adventures she organized for George and the Thursday nights she held for Robert's uncle, Richard Sullivan.

An even closer tie formed between Ellen and Henry Richards's wife, Laura Howe Richards. A mutual esteem drew these exceptional women together—the artist and the scientist—the one urbane and the other from a rural background. The daughter of Samuel Gridley and Julia Ward Howe would create some seventy literary works in the course of her life, the first "written on the back of my first born" of seven children. Children's stories and operas and a Pulitzer Prize winning biography were included in her productive lifetime.

"I can see Mother and Aunt Ellen," Laura Wiggins says. "Ellen with her hands on her hips, drawing herself up to my mother in mock determination: 'Now see here, sister Laura!' But her eyes gave her away. We all knew how close they felt to one another."

One of those "see-here-sister-Laura" incidents came about when Laura Howe Richards very considerately made a special

mince pie for her visiting sister-in-law. Knowing she was a tee-
totaler, Laura left the brandy out of the mince meat. At the table,
Ellen smacked her lips after the first bite of dessert. Then with her
usual stern pose, she said, "See here, sister Laura! Mince meat's
got to have a lace of brandy! . . . But don't tell anyone I told her
so," she said in an aside to the children at the table.

Through Henry and Laura, Ellen met the Howes. The patriarch
and matriarch of this brilliant family made deep impressions on
the malleable mind of their daughter's friend. In Samuel Gridley
Howe, Ellen had access to the mind of the man who founded
America's mental health movement. Howe's work with the
feebleminded, the deaf, and the sightless was world famous. His
enlightened treatment of Laura Bridgeman—the Helen Keller of
an earlier era for whom his daughter was named—became a
"classic in the world's psychological literature." His cottage system of caring for the handicapped and retarded has hardly been
surpassed in the years since.

From her conversations with Howe, Ellen formulated basic
concepts about education and environment. The cottage system
she saw as an environment designed and operated to educate its
inhabitants to their surroundings. By learning that simplified
environment, the occupants grew more in control of it and thus
themselves. On this premise, Ellen built new principles of education in general; environmental education in particular.

Then there was Julia Ward Howe—artist, activist, and humanist in search of causes on which to expend her talent and prestige.
Ellen joined several of these efforts. Perhaps the first, shortly after
her marriage to Robert, was the campaign to open the Boston
Latin School to girls. When that failed, the group succeeded, with
the help of William Fairfield Warren, in opening Girls' Latin.
But they were forbidden to call it Boston Girls' Latin for fear
they would ruin the reputation of the boys' school.

Others, outside the family, were drawn to the warmth and
vitality of the Richards's home. Here Ellen talked with William
Barton Rogers in his last years. "The man who could see the
statue in the marble," she called him. Besides Rumford's heady
ideas on art, agriculture, and applied science, she listened to
Rogers tell about Virginia's "Malaria Districts," where undrained
swamps and disease were changing the Virginian image, born at

Jefferson's Monticello. Rogers must have been impressed by the emerging scientific investigations of this petite woman opposite him in the parlor. She told him of her interest in food. Perhaps, Rogers may have thought, agriculture is not gone entirely from "Tech's" curriculum.

After Rogers's death in 1882, Ellen's friendship with his widow, Emma, continued. The sunny Rogers's estate at Newport, within sound of the Atlantic breakers, became a favorite place to relax, reflect, and regenerate.

On the evenings the Rogers came, and later his successor, Francis Amasa Walker, the venerable Edward Atkinson was likely to be there, too. The founder's long-time friend and fund raiser and a director of the MIT Corporation, Atkinson was a high school drop out who won honorary degrees from Dartmouth and the University of South Carolina to go with his honorary Phi Beta Kappa key from Harvard. He was one of the most colorful and controversial men in America.

From bookkeeper, he rose to the top of the textile industry. In the 1870s, he founded Brookline Savings Bank. By 1880, he was head of an historic insurance company. But these were only a small part of many activities that gave him the reputation of "a raving liberal" and "champion liar" to go with his incredible record of humanitarian ventures. Money, Atkinson preached, had most value when it contributed to human improvement. Articulate and literary, he spoke, lobbied, wrote, and published his views on the most sensitive issues of the time.

Atkinson—a financier of John Brown's raid—had promoted abolition before the Civil War. During the conflict, he financed a school to educate escaped and liberated slaves. After the war, he became a leading figure in revitalizing the South's economy. He introduced cotton grains from Egypt and China along with the soybean. He proposed the world's first industrial exposition in Atlanta, an event southerners credited as the industrial rebirth of their land. In the North, Atkinson was criticized by his former fellow textile friends with aiding the enemy.

Ellen was quite taken with this massively built man of full silver beard who thrived on controversy. She was impressed that he had been an advisor to President Lincoln and had continued that role with five other presidents. Well connected with government and industry—Andrew Carnegie was a good friend—Edward Atkinson was to become Ellen Swallow's closest collaborator. In the 1870's, he was still smarting over his inability to get the legislature and railroad lobbies to connect the many independent tracks coming through the Hoosac Tunnel to the Port of Boston. Linking those lines, he believed, might help preserve Boston's competitive standing as a port. The city was 300 miles closer than New York was to Europe, a fact that gave the Hub its high rank in the eighteenth and nineteenth centuries. But Boston was also 300 miles farther away than New York from the Breadbasket growing up in the Midwest. The Hoosac Tunnel through the mountains to these supply sources notwithstanding, he saw the city losing ground to New York.

Great minds wrested with great issues in the Richards's parlor: Dr. Samuel Eliot of the Blowpipe Conspiracy, Dr. T. T. Bouve of the Boston Society of Natural History, and his successors, Alpheus Hyatt and Samuel Scudder. There was Lucretia Crocker, educator; George Tichnor's daughter Marie, founder of "the first University Extension School"; Arthur D. Little, an interior decorating consultant to the Woman's Education Association, who became a student, friend, and follower of the Richards.

There was Cora Pike, one of many for whom Ellen designed science laboratories, at Wheaton Seminary; Mary Hemenway, who had opened a new kind of school in Boston; Mrs. Louis Agassiz, widow of the famed scientist Harvard had imported from Europe. And then there was the Woman's Education Association distinguished membership—the Lodges, the Cabots, the Lowells, et al. Julia Lathrop, on her way to becoming the first woman in the federal government, as chief of the Children's Bureau of the Department of Labor, came all the way from Jane Addams's Hull House in Chicago to consult with Ellen. Alice Freeman, Wellesley president at twenty-six, came. So did her husband-to-be, Harvard's ethical philosopher, George H. Palmer. As husband and wife they would help reorganize the University of Chicago. Dr. and Mrs. I. T. Talbot of Boston University and leaders in many civic causes came with their daughters Marion and Edith. Heiress and Vassar classmate Florence Cushing, who with Alice Freeman and Marion Talbot would become primary instruments in Ellen's crusades, came often.

There were many "instruments" shaped in that home. No few

of them were students, young men and women. ". . . some hundred of each . . . now like to come here each week," Ellen noted. During the week and at every Sunday open house, students mingled with faculty, philosophers, and friends of friends from all over the world. The Richards weren't wealthy. "I like to show them what they can do with small means," Ellen said.

"I have a vivid recollection of that charming house to which we were frequently invited—its plants and flowers, its embracing atmosphere of hospitality, its abounding cordiality, and, to hungry boys living in boarding houses, What Food!" a student remembered fifty years later.

Not only the student body but the mind was well fed. With the likes of James Phinney Munroe, Edwin Jordan, C.-E. A. Winslow, Augustus Gill, Alice Blood, Alice Bryant, Caroline Hunt, and hundreds of others, Ellen Swallow found her way to the reforms of a new century. The house was a place to stimulate, educate, and inspire; to enlighten as well as entertain; to persuade, recruit, and plan the humanistic plots of science hatched over the next forty years in the fertile mind of its hostess. In nearly all of these she would remain anonymous. While others were given—or took—credit, she was content to see the work done.

There was a lighter side to those gatherings. Minnie Glover and Professor Silas Holcomb quietly pursued their secret courtship across the crowded parlor. So did Professor Ordway and Ellen's student, Evelyn Walton.

The house was always active, always open, even if its owners were out of town. "Mother or someone will be here to let you in . . . make yourself at home," she wrote when she heard a friend was coming to Boston. If she was at home, "We always found our day well planned for us," Anne Mineah said. "There will be plenty of work to do if I'm around. You know me well enough to know that for a certainty," the hostess warned.

Up at 5:30 AM, Nellie put on the coffee and woke The Professor for their daily walk around Jamaica Pond's one-mile shoreline, two blocks away. "Fair weather or foul," Ellen used to say. "I can still see them from my bedroom window when I was allowed to stay over for the night, walking arm and arm up the street to the pond," Laura Wiggins recalls.

Sometimes there were more visitors than beds. When that

happened, a guest would be ensconced unknowingly in Ellen's bedroom. When everyone had retired and the house was quiet, she'd take Dutchess and slip into town for the night at the College Club, which she helped found, or go to a hotel. At 5:30, she was back, her routine unbroken. Guests arising upstairs could smell the aroma of "those wonderful breakfasts."

Breakfast was a cornucopia of nutritious foods: juices, fruits, unprocessed cereals with nuts and honey, homemade bread and biscuits, and fresh milk.

"There is a FEAST of Life," the scientist wrote—an acrostic of "Food, Exercise, Amusement, Sleep, and Task. We must take the FEAST of Life daily as 'habit' to live full and healthy lives."

In later years, when her puritanism subsided, Ellen's taste in amusement extended beyond the combination of her husband's hobbies and her own avocational activities to include the theater. Every Thursday evening Robert and Ellen were in their usual seats at the small, legitimate theater off Boston's old Castle Square behind Back Bay Station. She also grew to love the opera and once even shortened a not too important meeting to hear a favorite tenor in a favored role.

Their friends knew her habits and reserved seats nearby so that they could visit the busy couple before the curtain and at intermission.

Ellen also looked forward to Robert's annual performance with the Handel-Haydn Society and to less formal musical evenings with Atkinson's active family at their home, Heath Hill, in Brookline. Robert's deep, rich bass voice augmented Atkinson's "three and only bass notes."

In an evening at the Richards's, a tasteful, nutritious dinner— "there were never fewer than four" people present and more often so many that a buffet was prepared—was followed by "adventures in conversation," usually about important matters in the lives and times and work they shared. As the hour grew late, The Professor would tell a story—like the old chestnut of the Irishman during Lent ordering fish in a diner that had none. "Well, then, give me the pork chop, lamb pattie, beefsteak, and veal roast. God knows I ordered fish!"

As his wife watched proudly and explained the craft, Robert would conclude the evening with a demonstration of glass blowing, making a water hammer to auction off to the delight of guests.

This was their home. Each morning Robert and his Nellie made the four-mile trip to the Institute together, returning in the evening; talking, planning, and working on the way. They made the trip at first by a horse drawn omnibus that went past the house, "a funny thing on wheels in the summer, runners in the winter." Later, a horse drawn trolley and later still, an electric trolley, and then America's first subway system took them back and forth.

Boston was indeed the capital city of science and technology in America. Robert Richards and Ellen Swallow and their home and friends were at the center of the wheel that made it go.

EIGHT

A New Laboratory

When she picked out the Jamaica Plain house in 1875, Ellen Swallow set out to make it a home. A year later, after the Women's Laboratory opened, it became apparent she was making her home into something else again.

The environmental scientist had become a zealot in her campaign for pure air and water. Using new knowledge developing in the laboratories of science and technology, she overhauled the house, tearing out, redesigning, and rebuilding its circulatory and respiratory systems.

The Richards had no municipal sewer or water systems for their Jamaica Plain home. She tested and found pure water in an old well under the porch. She checked the house drainage to make sure it wasn't headed in the direction of the well, a common fault in those days. To make sure, she extended the drain pipes farther away from the well. She had the level of the ground surveyed, and she took extra steps to protect and separate its water from its waste.

She checked and adjusted the plumb and fit of pipes through the house, replaced most with modern-seal joints, put in traps and other precautions for waste water, discarded the old lead poisoning water lines. A hand pump in the kitchen pulled water up from the well into a storage tank on the second floor for bath and toilet. None too happy with this arrangement, she had no choice, given the technology available at the time. After improving what she knew were the worst features of an unsatisfactory system, all she could do was subject these arteries to close surveillance while she, Louisa Hewins, and others in the neighborhood tried to speed up action for a link to Boston's system. When the mains were laid, she watched her house tapped into the municipal water and sewerage systems. Taken for granted today, it was major progress and protection then. No one knew it better than the woman who was constantly studying the problem.

Now, with her engineer husband, she overhauled the vital organs of the house. She redesigned an inefficient water heater in the basement, replacing its input pipe and burner so that water would heat faster with less fuel. She put a "water back" on the furnace, using the heat from it in the winter and the water heater itself in the summer. At a time when most homes had no hot water when there was no fire in the stove, theirs had it all year round.

These devices became industry standards, but neither Robert nor Ellen tried to patent them. Robert said he felt it was his "duty to humanity" not to patent them. Ellen may have been more accurate when she recalled years later that "applied scientists" were not allowed to take out patents on their work then for fear the "pure scientists" would brand them opportunistic and unethical.

Satisfied with the safety and efficiency of the water-sewerage systems, she turned to the home's equally important respiratory system. The building itself she'd chosen for its "access to air and sunlight" on all four sides, a benefit made possible by the diagonal placement of the house on a half-acre lot. Other houses on the street—any city street then—were crowded together side by side. Streets and homes were not given the consideration of air and light by the architects and builders of the day. Accidentally, the Richards's received both all day long.

Windows in the house were torn out and rebuilt so that they would open from the top, as well as from the bottom. Warm air, Ellen knew, is polluted air. It rises to get away from the life that has used it to clean itself and return. Opening a window from the bottom only pushes used air up against the ceiling, filling the room downward, slowing the entry of a fresh supply. Top-opened windows let warm, polluted air escape, making room for fresh air from below.

In those days of fossil fuels—coal and wood for heating; coal, wood, and oil for cooking; gas, oil, and coal oil for light—lack of pure air was a serious if largely unrecognized problem. Normal combustion of open flames burned up the oxygen in an airtight room and trapped fumes in the house. As living room fireplaces with chimney ventilation were replaced by cellar furnace systems, homes became more airtight, and subnormal combustion of fuels and more harmful fumes became a problem. So did tuberculosis in the nineteenth century, although the relationship between foul air and respiratory disease was not fully recognized.

Working with new knowledge of air analysis gained at the Institute, the Richards designed and installed a mechanical system of ventilation and circulation, a radical innovation in homes or any structure of their day. The engineer and scientist had holes cut in walls, in ceilings over lamps, and above heaters. They installed a large master vent in the skylight at the top of the house. Fans were put in to pull out dead air and give a life-enriching atmosphere inside.

The kitchen stove was hooded; a fan was put there, too, another innovation. But nature was also given a place in this house. Under openable windows of hand-made glass that did not filter out all the sun's beneficial rays, miniature botanical gardens thrived on sunlight, their own reservoirs tapped into water lines. So also thrived the people who breathed the rich air circulating in the house.

There were no curtains on the windows except short, washable ones in the bedrooms and baths; nothing to catch dust, soot, or soil that couldn't be easily, quickly, and inexpensively removed for cleaning.

Twenty years before the twentieth century, Ellen tested in their home the scientific and engineering principles for the air, water, and sanitation systems she would fight to introduce into America's schools, hospitals, factories, and public buildings. They were only some of the innovations used to design the modern healthful home, for which hers was the prototype. Always working to improve the air and the water supply, she next turned her attention to another important environmental element: food.

MIT's Women's Laboratory had been conceived as an educational medium—a place to teach women to teach science. By 1877, however, Ellen focused on another potential.

"Minnie Glover has been put in charge of a new course in the laboratory," the scientific investigation of food, Ellen Swallow wrote. It was ". . . a natural subject for woman's study . . ."

Four miles away from the Institute another laboratory began to take shape, also the first of its kind. In her home at 32 Eliot Street, Jamaica Plain, Ellen Swallow created the first consumer home testing laboratory, forerunner of thousands in existence today. Bringing in selected students from MIT, she traded off board and room in return for their work on her experiments in this new field. Home Chemistry, she called it at first.

Here she directed Minnie Glover, Sarah Wentworth, and other women students in putting man's science to work in the home environment. Here she measured, checked, compared, and revised data drawn from the Institute's sterile beakers and microscopes. Here clinical theories came alive in actual performance in the Center for Right Living, as she called her home laboratory.

From this three-story building came the most advanced— often the only—proven science knowledge of products and processes for American consumers. Since industry and government hadn't bothered, her home laboratory introduced product and process testing and regulations for them, too.

Everything from furnishings to foods, utilities to utensils were examined; gadgets and myths from the marketplace were tested, approved, or exposed. She used science to determine their true values; controlled studies to test their efficiency. What didn't measure up was discarded and discredited. Improvements were suggested, such as putting the lip on the other side of the saucepan for left handed people, or better yet, on both sides for all. She replaced carpets with rugs as more efficient and healthful in those pre-vacuum cleaner days. She substituted gas for coal and wood and oil fuels for safety, economy, and health in cooking and lighting. She installed a telephone soon after Alexander Bell introduced his invention in Boston in 1876. Electricity was added as soon as the lines were run, ridding the house of fumes and flames of gaslights. Testing these utilities at a time when even their suppliers did not, she meticulously measured pennies against minutes; quality against convenience and health. When cost was arbitrary, quality was a constant, inflexible factor in her research.

For greater precision, she moved the gas meter from the cellar to the kitchen to watch its dials and tabulate its volume. She calculated to the closest cent, second, and cube, the fuel, time, and money used for individual tasks. Adjustments were made; optimum times found in cooking; exact balances between economy and nutrition. Health was the inflexible factor here. But in all her experiments, she was always impressed by how cost and quality compared so favorably with health and efficiency. Comfort and convenience, the Yankee found, tended to corrupt health and eventually economy.

She knew the precise cooking time and cost per dish per person and evaluated these against food value; she computed how long it took to heat, clean, or ventilate a room and how best to do it. If these things seem superfluous today—crises in costs of living and energy resources suggest they are not—they were virgin knowledge then, and not just in the home. Waste and inefficiency were unknown cost factors in industry and government as well.

"She had mastered the principles of scientific management long before they became the subject of discussion in the industrial world," wrote one prominent graduate of the Institute of Technology. A follower of the consumer and environment paths opened by the mistress of this unique home, recorded her observations:

> The house was not strikingly different in appearance from other well conducted homes . . . [but] it was free of fads, rich in comfort, health, safety and efficiency. . . .

> It was like breathing cleaner air to come into the house. The dust of non-essentials had been swept away and the supply of oxygen seemed greater here than elsewhere. One breathed an air at once restful and invigorating. Persons leading . . . a complex city life, beset with undertakings overtaxing their strength and time, came here as to a refuge, not only for affection . . . refreshment and rest . . . but for actual strength.

If the air and water of that environment stimulated human euphoria, so did its food.

> . . . food served at her table was always determined with reference to its effect upon efficiency in work. If, after a fair trial, a given food seemed to leave the brain dull and the body unfit for labor, it was rejected. This process of elimination disposed of, in the course of time, most of what are known as "made dishes." There were few rich gravies in her bills of fare, few complicated salads and little pastry . . . [meals] were made up chiefly of meat, never in large quantities . . . good home-made bread, fruits and vegetables. Fruit or simple home-made ice cream constituted the dessert.

Many others have written about the unique laboratory Ellen Swallow fitted into her home to extend her work with air, water, and food, and all their related systems and equipment; even more of her pioneering work at the MIT laboratory. But for all the topical interest given to saucepans, fuel supplies, and sanitary science, there was a much greater significance to her work in the late 1870s and early 1880s.

Ellen Swallow was developing a new body of knowledge for the basic units of physical and social environments: the home and the family. The former Yankee farm girl was building modern environmental science from these roots out into the community at large.

NINE

The Environment: 1870-1900

The unhealthy physical environment of the second half of the nineteenth century was a healthy influence on the career of Ellen Swallow. It was a time when science was beginning to unravel the mysteries of nature and a time when technology was putting them back together in man's "great design." Science and technology grew closer to government and industry in the process. In the Public, Profit, Power triumverate for environmental management, the public interest very often seemed to come last. Instead of being the beneficiary of the economic and political systems that resulted from science and technology, a great deal of what resulted in that environment was harmful to human health.

As science and technology and government and industry grew together, so grew the cities—economic and political centers that became a perfect culture for disease, as people crowded together to share the use and abuse of common air, water, and food supplies. As more people were drawn to the cities, more industrial and municipal wastes were flushed back into the environment to be used again. And again and again.

There was nothing to prevent the practice. There were no laws to slow the tide of filth spewing into streams, rivers, and well waters; rising thick and dark into the air; laying undrained and uncollected in the streets and yards. There was little knowledge of rudimentary sanitation and less concern for its effects. Men, women, and children as young as eight years worked in or lived near factories, sweatshops, and mines. They lived hard and died early, victims of obvious maladies such as "black lung" or "careless accidents."

Less known and less obvious were the causes and preventions of pneumonia and tuberculosis that ravaged population in winter, malaria and typhoid in summer, diphtheria, scarlet fever, cholera, and smallpox all year long. Bacteria and germs were largely unknown or unidentified, as were their means of transportation into the human system.

These air, water, and food borne invaders found the contaminating procedures of the day a healthy environment for their own growth. Millions of people were sick and thousands died yearly not knowing of what, let alone why. Modern medicine's miracles were still far off. Sterilization was only a few years old and still the subject of professional controversy. Joseph Priestly had discovered oxygen 100 years before, but man had yet to realize the full role of this basic element.

Bad air, water, and food were recognized by some scientists as having some relation to human health. But it was not really known what bad air, water, or food were. Many scientists insisted that sickness and disease, like crime and poverty, were inherited. Either way, little was done to improve the environment. New generations grew up sick, diseased, poor, and ignorant to support the hereditists' prognosis.

Mostly, illness and disease were accepted as "occupational hazards" at work, fatalistically at home, necessary evils in the struggle to stay alive and raise a family in the industrializing world. Only when air or water killed outright or caused acute sickness were they judged unfit for consumption. The long-term effects of pollution went unrecognized.

The assault on life by a poisoned outdoor environment was aided and abetted by poor environmental quality indoors. Often the home was as deadly as the factory or mine. Contamination outdoors was bad enough; pollution under the roof was almost universal.

Stale air, poison fumes in airtight buildings, improper plumbing, if any at all, foul water, and the ignorant handling of sewage added to a family's infirmities. Compounding the problem was the universal acceptance of available foods and their unsanitary handling or their deliberate adulteration.

The spurting growth of cities made it necessary to transport perishable goods over greater space and time. There were few safe preservatives. Food spoiled on the way from the farm to the table as it was carried and displayed in uncovered and unsanitary vehicles and stores, gathering filth and germs from the streets. Poor refrigeration accelerated bacterial decomposition.

With every meal, every breath of air, every swallow of water, every walk or ride through town, every visit inside an unventilated building, the odds in favor of illness went up. Industrial practices, government apathy, and public ignorance stimulated the spiral. As more people came in contact with more people in ever unhealthier environments at home, work, store, play, or school, the odds multiplied.

This was the physical environment of the mid-nineteenth century; a time, too, when the social environment began polluting.

This was the era that saw the nation spurt forward with the peculiar mix of genius, greed, and gumption that became known as the American way. It was a time when fortunes were amassed by Carnegie and Gould, Astor, Rockefeller, and others; when James Duke's cigarette-rolling machine helped tar the lungs, fetter the breath, and constrict the arteries of millions yet unborn.

Less than ten years after the first railroad spanned the continent, three more opened the West to earnest development. Thanks to the cavalry and the cowboy, America's native ecologists were safely confined to the reservation. Sitting Bull, who had served Custer at his last stand, found a home with Bill Cody's Wild West Show, giving away his earnings to homeless urchins who begged outside the show grounds.

Buffalo were slaughtered from train windows by "gentlemen sportsmen" and by "professionals" who skinned the native animal and left the Indian's meat to rot in the sun. Commercial cattle replaced them. Meanwhile, off the ranch, Butch Cassidy and his "wild bunch," the Coles, the Youngers, and the James Brothers were declared public enemies for the new business opportunities the railroads represented to them.

More than half of the United States population of 40 million in 1870 lived on farms. But the cities were growing. Half a million immigrants came in a year's time; five million more before the turn of the century. Most of them settled in cities. Chicago's population doubled in a decade. The cities swelling size—with people foreign to the language and the life style— gave impetus to new environmental sickness.

Urbana was not Nirvana. It was the hothouse for crime, corruption, and violence. The crime rate in the 1870s was "perhaps twice that of today," according to *Smithsonian Magazine.* Insects were so bad—collecting in the urine, spit, and garbage in the streets of New York—that the merchants organized an association to fight flies, while Boss Tweed cleaned out the city treasury. Chinese chopped heads in San Francisco's Tong Wars. Negroes rioted in the South; the Irish rioted in Boston. White frocked Ku Klux Klans "whipped, tortured, and murdered hundreds" of blacks and their sympathizers in the East, North, and South. "Labor negotiations" in Pennsylvania's coal and steel industries were conducted in collective brutality.

In Washington, the White House dipped into the little black bag of payoffs, while organized crime made its American debut with the Society of the Blackhand in New York. Police corruption, too, reached scandal proportions. And New York, "that wonderful town," reached the rate of "a murder a day," an urban achievement that would set its own self-destructive record in the years ahead.

Edison was the man of the hour; electricity, his power to the people. Toward the end of the century, trolleys began to replace horse power for public transportation; the always hungry family Dobbin gave way to the bicycle. New ground was gained and new weaponry was found for man's escalating war on time and space. Tunnels bored through natural barriers, dams revised and rerouted the flow of inland water. Steel bridges went up. In Chicago, so did the first "high-rise building." Chewing gum caught on. The Otis elevator rose in popularity, shaking all the way up and down. Prices and productivity went up, too. Wages followed slowly. Consumption—all kinds—went up faster.

The Republicans ruled the White House for twenty-four years. When a Democrat, Grover Cleveland, at last came in, the sensational interpretations of Joseph Pulitzer's *New York World* and Hearst's *Journal,* began the circulation war that was said to cause the United States war with Spain in Cuba and the Philippines. They also gave the profession a name: Yellow Journalism.

Although less than two of every 100 people in America were about to enter college, public education through high school was available, if not mandatory, for those who would or could go. Once there, young people learned not much more than the three R's, and no less than the rote philosophy summed up by the common school poster of the day:

> It is better to do One Thing One Hundred Times Than do One Hundred Things Once.

Truly, this was an education to become the heart of industry's technological use of human creativity.

Women's status progressed rapidly—for awhile—though books, like students, were still segregated by sex, and a husband legally owned the valuable gifts he gave his wife.

It was a time when the Three R's were joined by another initialed trio to stimulate the American spirit: Advertising, Almanacs, and Alcohol. The Three A's school of commerce was not as far from education's Three R's as it might seem.

A deluge of patent nostrums in the 1870s became a flood tide of consumer abuse and corporate irresponsibility by the 1880s. Thousands of patents for medicines, devices, and gimmicks boggled the mass mind and undermined the body. Merchandising products in a way that confused copyright and copywriting, manufacturers advertised claims to improve health, beauty, sex, and salvation to the cash registered tune of millions.

Patent medicines also registered with an unknowing public. "For man, woman or child . . . a Wonderful Discovery . . . one of Nature's Remedies to cure neuralgia, dyspepsia, rheumatic troubles, stomach disorder, colic, bilious affection, kidney disease, torpid liver, aching back, depression, blues and languidity, cold hands and feet, nervous debility, despondency, melancholy, weakness of mind, body and its parts."

One such miracle product was an electric battery to "infuse electricity into your system; invigorating, stimulating . . . purify the blood, give vitality and strength to the nervous system, cure you, cost you little and do no harm . . . is certain, pleasant and positively the only safe and certain cure for all Stomach, Blood and Nervous complaints of whatever nature." Still other nostrums promised the blind they could see.

Nearly all these products carried the Madison Avenue forerunner's standard footnote for a gullible consumer. "Accept no substitutes or explanations."

For symptoms of pain and depression, that footnote was unnecessary. America's drug culture was born. "Florida, Texas, New Mexico, Vermont, and New Hampshire . . . grew poppies . . ." for a flourishing domestic opium industry, though most opium was imported; for patent medicines; to smoke in opium dens like those on New York's Pell Street; or to sell over the counter in neighborhood drugstores. The friendly pharmacist also had a large jar of Cannabis (marijuana) on hand, prescribed in at least one "medical journal" to treat masturbation.

Opium was "the base of more than one great family fortune." It was also the base of children's cough syrups. Cocaine, too, was widely available, and Americans drank "more alcohol in patent medicines than in all licensed beer, liquor or wine sold in the country." In those do-it-yourself days, much of the alcohol needed for a growing national habit was unlicensed—made at home or on the farm. Millions of men, women, and children, raised on these daily cure-all cocktails and family fixes, set the stage for movements such as Frances Willard's Woman's Christian Temperance Union, later organized in Evanston, Illinois.

The Generation Gap was there, too. Young men shaved their cheeks and lips to protest the ways of their elders. Their elders in turn worried about "the excitement . . . produced from the comingling of sexes in warm rooms where the mind is unbalanced by the wild delirium of the waltz."

It was delusion, deception, and degradation on a grand scale, perpetrated by advertising in newspapers, posters, and, most of all, in the ever-present, always "reliable" medical almanac, second only to the Bible in home use and public popularity in late nineteenth-century America.

This was the environment—physical and social—Ellen Swallow saw 100 years ago. In it she saw incubating a far worse future environment. From her feminine perception of science, she felt the condition of physical environment was relative to the condition of social environment. Each was an influence—however subtle, however disputed by the hereditists of science—on the other. Together, these conditions set off a degenerating chain reaction by which the total environment regressively worsened at a time when the knowledge was becoming available to correct it all.

The strongest link in that chain was public ignorance, a common pattern woven into a whole cloth of human and environmental liability. Once again, Ellen Swallow saw in the weakened weave of society a common thread that, if strengthened, could overcome ignorance and improve the quality of environment.

The chemist analyzes the parts and substances of a given matter, breaking it down and adding it up to identify and understand their interactions. Chemist Ellen Swallow followed the same process to analyze the environment. There was nothing wrong with the environment other than what man was doing to it. She traced this overactive ingredient to its source. Home, she concluded, is the root unit of physical environment; the family within that home, the basic unit of social environment. Total environment is a macrocosm of these parts. If total environment was to be improved, corrections must be made in the beginning with the home and family.

Swallow was more than a chemist. She was a student of the history of human evolution at a time when the theories of Darwin and Haeckel were still controversial in science. Whether she was aware that woman was the source of the common cooperative culture that marked an animal's evolution to human status, she was well aware that the first environment of man is woman, that man and woman beget child, that together, for more than 10,000 years, men and women had educated children to become men and women who would pass on again the knowledge and values necessary for survival in civilization's environment.

With the Industrial Revolution, this traditional pattern had undergone a radical change. Man left his home and farm for the factory. Son was no longer educated by father. He needed new knowledge for a changing world. So sons, too, left home for schools to secure knowledge they previously obtained at home. The traditional information functions of home and family were seriously, basically altered.

Woman alone remained at home. And in the nineteenth century, with its accelerating changes, woman was the worst off of all population. A few—the Julia Ward Howes in America, the Faithful Beggs in England—escaped and adapted to the change. Then they, too, left the empty physical confine to enter a newer, larger environment: the community at large. But for all the reforms a few women perpetrated in the mid-nineteenth century, the vast majority of their sex were left behind, isolated in the less functional environment called home. Once the center of creative, constructive family activity, home had become less. creative, less meaningful, a four-letter word for drudgery.

Home and hearth and the woman who kept them together were by-passed by the Industrial Revolution and its new ways. She was kept from and subordinated to a rising tide of new information about a world she comprehended little and participated in less. Outstripped by new knowledge, she was less able to cope with what it produced. A new culture was emerging—a cosmetic, mechanical culture created by man's exploitation of advancing knowledge. By detaching woman from its new processes and functions, he was creating a new environment with new human values in which the female's point of view was missing. It would be missed even more in the future. Less informed and less involved in the human enterprise, it was not coincidence that woman was less stable and less healthy than man.

Ellen Swallow saw this situation. She understood that woman's "psychosis of negation," as their widespread infirmity was called, was directly parallel to their lack of function in the new environment. And there were, she knew, two edges to that function.

For population to live in harmony with environment, population must be fully represented at the point of contact in order to balance population's response to environment and environment's response to population. To Ellen Swallow, the interface between organisms and their world were neither mystical nor mythical. It was hard to see, but it was very real and very important.

The human-environment interface could be seen most clearly at its source: in the home and in the family. If the human organism is to live in harmony with environment, it must be learned at the source. To do that, it is necessary to educate the largest half of the population: Women.

TEN

Organizing Women

It was in 1879, the year the first woman was admitted to practice in the United States Supreme Court, that Ellen Swallow activated her campaign to rejuvenate the retarded cell of the environmental microcosm: the home.

Maria Mitchell, Vassar astronomy professor, wrote to her now prominent former student. Would Ellen address a group of Poughkeepsie women who were organizing one of the many women's clubs springing up around the country? A firm critic of feminine separatism, Swallow saw women's clubs as self-help programs designed to inform and educate, to make women more useful to the changing American community.

Her speech to 300 women was a milestone that sounds strangely current today. An enthusiastic audience heard her attack "irrelevant education" in an educational system poorly structured; false advertising and product labeling that took advantage of consumer ignorance, which resulted from poor schooling.

She condemned inferior merchandising, unfair pricing, and profits for products unfit for consumption. She showed how it all contributed to the higher cost of living and lower environmental quality. She said science and technology were outstripping the home and human values to set up more serious human and environmental problems in the future.

Above all, she singled out women's ignorance as an inherent cause and cure for unsanitary living conditions, polluted air, contaminated water, poor nutrition, and health in the homes and families that made up the community.

> Our educational system unfits girls . . . for their life. It can not be knowledge which unfits the young . . . it must be that some sort of false logic has crept into our schools. . . . Scientific facts are taught, but [too often] in the same way . . . by the same teachers . . . as historical facts are taught . . . without relation to everyday life.

She was against "rote" learning. She also said not enough was being taught in the schools.

"Can a railroad engineer . . . a cotton manufacturer . . . know too much about what they work with? Can a woman know too much about the composition and nutritive value of the meats and vegetables she uses . . . the effect of fresh air on the human system or the danger of sewer gas or foul water? Yet . . . the people I have seen [tending the home] know nothing about botany or chemistry and the people who know botany or chemistry do not [tend the home]," she observed.

> We must awaken a spirit of investigation in our girls as is often awakened in our boys, but always, I think, in spite of school training. We must show [that] science has a very close relation to every day life . . . train [women] to judge for themselves . . . to think . . . to reason . . . from the facts to the unknown results.

The living environment, she warned, is being outstripped by the father of technology—mechanics—and by the mother of science—chemistry.

> The improvements that affect our daily lives have resulted from Mechanics and Chemistry . . . the mechanical devices which render travel [and] communication . . . comfortable, easy and rapid . . . methods that make possible things that seemed impossible. . . . Chemistry has given us self-raising flours, bread powders, washing powders, glove cleaners and a hundred other patent nostrums. But where are the advantages [in the home] commensurate with manufacturing?

The home is no better, Ellen said. It is worse because these advances are "alas! rendered almost useless by the ignorance of those into whose hands they are put."

In spite of advancing knowledge, she went on, ". . . our cooking, ventilation and drainage are still bad. Why [can't] the home keep pace with industry? Why has not the knowledge of sanitary laws filtered down through the community as rapidly as mechanics?"

In the country towns, there are "the same poor conditions as there were . . . 30 years ago. In the city, how much better, rather how much worse is it?" The woman is the "one person in the position to improve the basic environment for population," she said.

She criticized products, labels, and advertising that deceive and mislead. In the end, however, she said woman's ignorance permits deception as much as manufacturers' intent. She showed how the women in that room could purchase the same goods for four or five cents, rather than pay twice to ten times that amount for manufacturers' and advertisers' "ingenious manipulations."

Then, to that 1879 audience, she foretold not only the consumer groups of the 1970s, she forecast the prototype organization she would form in the waning years of the nineteenth century.

Perhaps the day will come when an association will be formed in each large city or town with one of their number a chemist. Some similar arrangement would be far more effective . . . than a dozen Acts passed by Congress.

The power of knowledge is appreciated by manufacturers. They take advantage of every new step in science. The woman must know something of chemistry in self-defense. If the dealer knows his articles are subjected to even the simple tests, he will be far more careful to offer the best.

The housekeeper should know when to be frightened. If women in general understood mechanical and physical laws, would they long endure the . . . life style . . . that requires coal to be shoveled down cellars only to be brought up again to the kitchen range, [then] carried back down again as ashes only to be brought up again for disposal?

It is for women to institute reform. The chief reason why American inventions [are] coming upon the world with such startling rapidity and perfection [is] that a better class of working men are

in command here. If American men can have perseverance, energy
and ingenuity . . . shall American women be less successful . . .
[in improving their environment]?

It is not an easy task we have before us. So long as we are content with ignorance . . . so long we shall have ignorance; but when
we demand knowledge, because we know the value of knowledge,
then we shall succeed.

Stepping down from the podium, she had just launched the
consumer-environment movement of the nineteenth century.

Movements need armies: troops, officers, and organization. If
Ellen Swallow was right—if women held the key to heal the
nineteenth-century's physical and social environment at its roots
of home and family—then women needed information and education. A hundred years ago, that meant more than simply
getting more knowledge to women. It also meant getting more
women to where knowledge was kept and where most women
were kept from: college.

The higher education of women was a complex problem. No
one knew better than a determined farm girl who had defied
the odds and worked her way through. If the great mass of
women were isolated in "less meaningful homes," the few who
aspired to college had another reality to overcome.

"My mother used to write me that my name was never mentioned to her by the women of her acquaintance," wrote a college
educated woman years later. "I was thought by my family to be
a disgrace to my family."

Family fears were supported by medical opinion. The distinguished Dr. Edward H. Clarke wrote in his 1873 book, *Sex
in Education*, ". . . the identical education of the two sexes is a
crime before God and humanity that physiology protects against
. . . and experience weeps over. It defies the Roman maxim . . .
mens sana in corpore sana!"

The good doctor described gruesome examples of educated
women he had seen. He told how their reproductive organs
were damaged by the ordeal.

One young woman who aspired to college wrote:

I was always wondering if it could really be true, as everyone
thought, that boys were cleverer than girls. . . . I dared not ask any

grown-up person . . . the direct question, not even my father or mother because I feared the reply. I remember praying . . . begging God . . . if it were true that I could not master Greek . . . and understand things, to kill me at once.

We were told [our] brains were too light, foreheads too small, reasoning powers too defective. . . . I had seen only one college woman. I had heard . . . such a woman [a Vassar graduate] was staying at the house of an acquaintance. I went to see her with fear.

In spite of fears instilled in childhood, some young women dared defy the dangers of college. For these, there was another obstacle: where to prepare? Special schools prepared boys for the classical requirements of college. Segregated lower schools for girls, however, gave the weaker sex an even weaker course of study. It all worked hand in hand—medical opinion, family fear, economic pressure, and the girls' "awful doubts." College entrance examinations confirmed the chain. Drawn up by the dedicated men of academia, college requirements were a kind of sexual poll tax to eliminate women who wanted education.

For the extraordinary few women who managed to enter and go through college, one final and bitter indignation waited: social ostracism. In the Sewing-Circle-Spelling-Bee-Card-Party-Taffy-Pull ladies society of the 1870s ". . . there was no Junior League or . . . Vincent Club . . . that wanted a young woman so different from their own. . . ." The educated woman was a freak; the object of whispers or embarrassing questions if she was present; subjected to jokes and gossip when she wasn't. Even in her old neighborhood she was an outcast, a social "mariah" facing a new kind of isolation.

The "old maid" or "spinster" stereotype of an educated woman was well founded. Uneducated men feared her; married women shunned her. Educated men weren't sure. More than was credited, though, educated women of the time also had a part in the decision to stay single. It was often the wiser course—rather than revert to the subordinate status her education had overcome.

"Every college woman owes an enormous debt [to her]," Dr. Alice Bryant much later eulogized Ellen Swallow. No woman of the time knew the problematic progress of the female better than she did. Her old diaries show the pains of frustration and depression. At her own incentive, she left the family to pick up in Worcester the education she couldn't get at home or at Westford Academy. Prepared, she had put herself through Vassar, graduated, and then gone through it all again at MIT. Afterward, she avoided ostracism by making her home a center for educated and enlightened men and women.

In 1870, "one could count on one's fingers the number of college educated women." Ellen Swallow was not just one of those fingers. She became the thumb on the hand that took hold of the problems of educating women. Not content as the first woman science school graduate, she put her vulnerable position on the line to pull others through the door she had opened.

In the five years after the Women's Laboratory opened, she increased the depth and scope of her activities. In 1881, she pulled together the many strings of her varied experiences to structure an organization that would become the most significant breakthrough in the higher education of American women.

The Association of Collegiate Alumnae—now the American Association of University Women—had its genesis in numerous Ellen Swallow projects. In 1876, she organized the Boston Chapter of Vassar Alumnae. Under her direction, it was an organization in which educated women could meet each other and a means of encouraging bright young women to attend her alma mater. If deserving candidates could not afford the luxury of education, she helped raise funds. These weren't the first college scholarships for women in America—the Woman's Education Association's were earlier—but Ellen Swallow was involved in both.

In 1878, she helped open Girls' Latin School to prepare girls for college exams. And at Julia Ward Howe's Saturday Morning Club—as in her own home, the Vassar club, and in an increasing number of lectures and articles—she exposed young women of the day to the great future to be achieved through education. In 1881, nearing forty, Ellen Swallow was a preeminent woman in Boston's educational circles and a scientist of rising reputation. In her first ten years in the city she had seen and helped make changes that came grudgingly. But for the purpose of her crusade, it was not happening fast enough.

Girls with brains, money, perfect references, and immaculate reputations could enter a few colleges. Vassar, Smith, and Welles-ley were open. Though, Ellen replied to an inquiry, "I couldn't recommend Wellesley under its present management." But these were women's colleges. The overwhelming cache of knowledge was still held captive in all-male bastions. Cracks were appearing in those walls, too.

In 1876, the University of Michigan had admitted a dozen petitioning women. One member of that class, Alice Freeman, she heard, had just been hired to teach history at Wellesley. Cornell and the University of Wisconsin had been breeched; Boston University had admitted a few women. The daughter of Mrs. I. T. Talbot, a cohort on the Girls' Latin School project, had tried to enter Boston University but had been unable to pass the entrance exams. Her mother was not as easily put off, and her father, a faculty member of the medical school, interceded. Marion Talbot had entered and gotten her B.A. in 1879.

Harvard, of course, was still an important holdout. The Woman's Education Association had long since given up its 1872 plan for ". . . a course of study for girls whereby they might get a degree equivalent to that of Harvard College." As Ellen put it, "I hope no Vassar girl has thought it necessary to pass the Har-vard examinations . . ." But there were cracks appearing in Harvard's shield, too. In 1879, some of the faculty formed "A Society for the College Teaching of Women by Professors and Other Instructors at Harvard." It would take almost twenty more years for Radcliffe—first as "the annex"— to mature. Even then the Overseers would see to it that the women were classically segregated from the men.

In the autumn of 1881, Ellen Swallow was busily immersed in many projects when she received another invitation to Julia Ward Howe's famed Saturday Morning Club.

Mrs. Howe organized these weekly gatherings of intellectual women in the 1860s as a cultural stimulant for her daughters. When the girls were grown, the sessions "formalized" into a kind of weekend school. Ellen Swallow, scientist, educator, and fam-ily friend was a popular attraction.

Most girls enrolled in the club were younger than college age. But on this morning, Mrs. I. T. Talbot, there to enroll her younger daughter, Edith, had brought along her eldest daughter, Marion.

The older girl listened attentively to the scientist. Afterward, they talked. At twenty-three, Marion Talbot was facing the problem of finding intellectually equal friends. Out of college two years, she was, with her mother, searching for something to do with her life and education. Much like the aggressive Mrs. Talbot, Marion's energy appealed to Ellen Swallow. She suggested a visit to the Women's Laboratory. On October 20, 1881, Marion Talbot enrolled. She was to become a very "special student" in Ellen Swallow's educational schemes.

The official record of the birth of the Association of Collegiate Alumnae—an organization that made possible the higher education of millions of American women—was written fifty years later from the recollections of the only survivor of its conception, Marion Talbot. The scene is the family residence at fashionable 66 Marlborough Street, Boston.

> One day the doorbell rang and a young woman asked if she might speak with Mrs. Talbot. When Mrs. Talbot entered the room, the young woman apologized for presenting herself so unconventionally and without formal introduction and added the information that she was Alice Hayes . . . graduated the previous June from . . . Vassar College. Knowing Mrs. Talbot's interest in women's education and in college training especially, Miss Hayes . . . had ventured to call to see if she could get advice.

The circumstances are very much like those of the old Blow-pipe Conspiracy. How did a new Vassar graduate find her way to 66 Marlborough Street, the home of a family she'd never met? What prompted her to seek out at this socially prominent residence the very proper *mother* of a girl near her own age and to lay her case before her instead of the daughter? A Vassar graduate new in town would be inclined, if not advised, to check in first with the school's most prominent graduate in the city, the founder of the city's Alumnae Club. In any event, the official recollection goes on:

> Mrs. Talbot . . . as if by inspiration . . . saw as if in a flash of light . . . an association of educated women. . . . At once [history says], Marion Talbot consulted her friend and teacher, Ellen [Swallow] Richards, and together they issued a call to all the

college women they knew . . . to meet on the 28th day of November, 1881, in the hospitable halls of the Massachusetts Institute of Technology.

Very probably, Mrs. Talbot and her daughter had "consulted her friend and teacher" before that "flash of light" without knowing it. In any event, if Mrs. Talbot saw the organization as "an extension of the Saturday Morning Club," the forty-year-old scientist-educator who chaired that first meeting at MIT saw it as something more. And if Marion Talbot recalls inviting "all the college women we knew" to that first session, Ellen Swallow invited far less. Seventeen college graduates attended.

"If the Jews had been led out of Egypt by a large committee, they would be wandering across the sands still today," Ellen said. A practical organizer by now, she meant to structure a viable body. She wanted a small, controllable meeting; a meeting where the right foundation could be laid. In fact, her Vassar Alumnae Club alone could have delivered more than seventeen women. (It had twenty in 1876.) That would have been too many. Worse, to unbalance the group in Vassar's favor not only might inhibit other representatives but too many Vassarites would draw too much attention—and support—to her. She took pains to avoid this problem for good reason. Only Miss Hayes, herself, and two other women represented Vassar. Ellen Swallow's intent— her lifelong pattern, in fact—was to conceive of and circulate an idea for others to develop. She was successful in this modus operandi most of the time. But there were times she must have regretted it. There would be one time, certainly. But only after that disappointment would she allow herself the prominence of leadership.

At the first gathering of what would become the Association of Collegiate Alumnae, the chair, Ellen Swallow, immediately appointed Marion Talbot to take minutes of the meeting and to follow through. For the next ten years, with Marion Talbot secretary, the organization's address was 66 Marlborough Street, where mother and daughter together could pursue the "vision" that had come to them there.

Next, the chair, with due homage, recognized the senior woman present—veteran of women's causes, Lucy Stone, Oberlin, class of 1846. Lucy Stone was tired of woman's wars. Perhaps defeated. She saw no need for such an organization and, saying so, bowed out. That left Ellen Swallow, forty in a few days, ranking in age. She was also one of only two married women there. Some might feel a married woman as president would take some of the sting from the stigma of an association of "sexually damaged" educated women. But Ellen Swallow did not want that office; she supported the other married woman, Jennie Bashford, University of Wisconsin, 1874, for president.

Florence Cushing, Ellen's student, was elected first vice president, and the remarkable young woman from the University of Michigan, Alice Freeman, who was reorganizing Wellesley, second vice president. Assured of continuity, energy, and intelligence, Ellen Swallow took a seat on the executive committee from where she could subtly exert her guiding influence on the younger women.

The A.C.A's first three activities reflected that influence. First, they had to refute the widespread myth that education damaged women. Only science could do this. The only scientist in the group arranged for a scientific survey of the health of college educated women.

About one-half of the college alumnae in the country received a questionnaire. Then, calling on Edward Atkinson's statistical connections and her own good standing with the State of Massachusetts, Colonel Carroll D. Wright, Chief of the Massachusetts Department of Labor, tabulated the figures and "deemed the inquiry to be one of great value." The Commonwealth officially published the findings:

> In conclusion, it is sufficient to say that the female graduates of our colleges and universities do not seem to show, as the result of their college studies and duties, any marked difference in general health from the average health likely to be reported by an equal number of women . . . generally, without regard to occupation. . . ."

By official government document, medical myth was shattered. To help spread the word, the published study was mailed to media, including leading medical journals. Women could breathe a little easier.

Out of this early work, the A.C.A. built a program to help

women breathe better, agitating for physical conditioning for girls in the nation's schools and colleges. On this project, Swallow came in contact with another pioneer, Dr. Dudley Allen Sargent, head of the Harvard Hemenway Gymnasium and founder of Sargent School for Physical Education in Cambridge, a leader in developing the scientific disciplines of physical and occupational therapy. Not coincidentally, these became scientific specialties for women.

Next, the matter of "The Industrial Training of Women" was put to the association. Ellen knew the need to broaden women's education to equip and involve them in the changing environment. For this, she selected another former student, Evelyn Walton. Miss Walton had time, inclination, and access to this subject matter in her romance with an industrial chemist, John Ordway. Under the A.C.A., industrial training followed the same path cut by physical training for women—into the public, normal, and specialty schools.

The third original A.C.A. project was indeed close to the founder's heart: hygiene. Through her particularly broad view, hygiene could be and was applied to every early A.C.A. function: physical hygiene, social hygiene, and mental hygiene. They covered the home, the individual family, the community, and education. In Swallow's mind, all overlapped.

As the A.C.A. followed her interpretations of hygiene up and down the human and institutional scales, the foundations were laid for the nation's early preschool and child development programs, along with many other social and civic reforms.

She organized a sanitary science club within the organization. Under her personal supervision, its college educated women made environmental quality and efficiency studies of homes, communities, and schools.

One other important principle had been fused to the organization at the outset—important to the original purpose of improving women's higher education. By basing membership in the A.C.A. on institutional rather than personal grounds—that is, only women graduates of colleges that met the A.C.A.'s high educational standards—the small but growing group was able to wield a power far beyond its size. As the organization grew, Ellen Swallow never revealed her full role in its founding. Neither did anyone else, including Marion Talbot. Probably they weren't aware of what they hatched, or how, anymore than Robert Richards or MIT had been aware of what they'd "gotten into" earlier in the Blowpipe Conspiracy.

By 1882, when Ellen Swallow had organized an elite officer corps for her consumer-environment crusade, she had already begun to recruit its rank and file.

The Society to Encourage Study at Home was started in 1873 by Anna Ticknor, daughter of George Ticknor, Harvard's great language scholar. It was first a correspondence school—perhaps the first—at a time when Aaron Montgomery Ward was developing a new consumer market through the United States mails.

After Ellen Swallow joined the society, it became an experiment in adult education cited as "the first university extension school in America."

"The purpose of this society," the catalogue read, "is to induce ladies to form the habit of devoting some part of every day to study of a systematic kind." Ladies "at least 17 years old . . . for Three Dollars a year" could take any number of courses "after the first term." Groups of women, "Study Clubs," could join as "individual" members for the same rates. Many did. The thousands of students enrolled were actually many more, since each club counted anywhere from six to dozens of women studying under a single name. The society had a "lending library" of more than 2,000 volumes, a considerable asset in the days when there were few libraries in reach of the average citizen. Andrew Carnegie had hardly started his legendary endowment of these facilities. The society did much to fill the information vacuum of the age.

The society's curricula were divided into sections—five of them at first: history, fine arts, French literature, German literature, and English literature. Each category broke down into numerous subdivisions. In an afterthought that turned out to be a stroke of marketing genius, Marie Ticknor included a small science section under the management of Lucretia Crocker. In 1876, when Crocker was made a supervisor of Boston schools, Anne Ticknor asked Ellen Swallow to fill the little void in the struggling enterprise.

By 1880, the science section was second only to history and

climbing. Miss Ticknor was amazed, since science "was only partially recognized as an element in liberal education" in the normal schools and colleges of the time. Laboratory science— science instruction by experimentation—was all but nonexistent beyond professional circles or, of course, in schools where Ellen Swallow's former students were teaching.

In an age when there were no radios, televisions, cars, airplanes, or satellites, when daily newspapers were more easily available at newsstands than as home deliveries, Ellen Swallow had the audacity to put science laboratories—microscopes and all—into homes so remote that electricity was still unknown. For a time, many rural and city homes to which her courses were mailed were ahead of most public schools in science. When schools caught up, it was partly her doing, too. But even when they did, they were hard pressed to keep abreast of new science developments Ellen Swallow digested in mailings to her students.

With Charles Dana's help, she structured a course in geology, still an infant science. She added physical geography, zoology, botany, mineralogy, mathematics, archeology, and the all-important chemistry. As the volume of materials multiplied, so did enrollment. Then she added a new course that pulled environment together for home and community study—a composite subject, including botany, zoology, geography, mineralogy, and geography called *sanitary science,* a forerunner of Swallow's environmental science.

By the mid-1880s, the society's Faculty of Correspondents, those who dealt individually by mail with the students, had grown to more than 200. In the science section, except when she allowed one of her MIT or home lab students to structure a lesson for society students, Ellen Swallow did most of her work alone. At times, though, it seemed she had added the other faculty members to her student roster, sending them promotional circulars on science to include in the mailings to their students. For her, the volume was always increasing.

Convinced that books and papers weren't enough to win student involvement, she began mailing specimens along with the microscopes, texts, and lessons.

"Unclasp the book of Nature," she urged.

As more took her advice, it is interesting to see that only the science section of the Society to Encourage Study at Home offered special courses for "Family Study." It was this early preschool technique by which she sought to expand the woman's traditional role as a teacher in the home. To Swallow, "innovation" was simply a return to tradition that multiplied the reach of her instruction. "You might as well do it to a nicety while you're about it," she recalled.

"Look at anything that interests you," she wrote. "Once you see it under the microscope it will [interest you] for certain."

She suggested the family begin their own "herbariums" and suggested design and content. She coaxed others to examine plants and fossils in the woods or yard, food from the garden, and water from the pipe or well.

"Compare them . . . See what you are putting in your bodies."

She also taught the basic physics of heating and ventilation, house placement on a lot, how to check terrain and drainage, how to test furnishings and appliances, how to decorate and dress. All her courses were designed and taught from the consumer-environment point of view.

As enrollment grew, so did her personal involvement with her students and her students' involvement with their environments, natural and man-made.

"Now every little twig has meaning to me," wrote a student from a large city. Another who, we're told, later "contributed much to the public health movement," wrote ". . . just what I wanted and needed . . . I only hope some day to know enough to help some girls as you are helping me."

One unfortunate but not uncommon woman of the day, who, "because of the unconventional mode of her family's life style was 'ostracized' during her youth" wrote, ". . . your course was my mainstay through the most difficult years of my life."

Many more shared the feelings of the woman who wrote ". . . I have eyes to see what I never saw before."

The source of this ever-expanding awakening worked at it nights, days, and holidays. She drew charts, diagrams, and designs for individual students. She helped others plan their room decor, gardens, and menus; asked all to analyze their homes from the drain to the ice box and cupboard, even their habits of dress. "If it is a relief to undress at night . . . be sure something is wrong. Clothes should not be a burden [but] a comfort and protection," Ellen said.

So many letters came from sick and depressed women, she noted, trapped in their lives with little will to go on, but the need to tell someone about it. To these she gave her imagination and encouragement. Together, by mail, they planned new activities. Most important, she wrote to them, a distinguished scientist who spoke to them about their problems and dreams, not just as students or names on a mailing list, but as individuals—persons.

"Occupation of the mind helps the body . . . I know we cannot always overcome physical weakness (as she had) . . . but we can avoid many troubles by a proper mental attitude," she told one faltering spirit.

From her home, at work, or enroute, she "talked" to the thousands of faceless names across the United States and Canada, from Boston to the West Coast, and as far away as Europe. When she learned of a student planning a trip to Boston, she invited her to stop and see MIT's laboratories.

It was not all one sided; not all giving or teaching on her part. The countless dispirited women who wrote back were a part of Ellen Swallow's continuing education. She received as much as she sent; asked as much as she answered. Almost always she corresponded by hand without the help of a stenographer or typewriter.

When women succumbed to pressures in their lives and "begged off," their resignations from the study course were often refused. "Don't give up the fight yet, Mrs. ————. We've only started with you." or, "I'm glad you told me about it. . . . Our little effort is made just for people like yourself, you know." Persuading, cajoling, scolding, pleading, and encouraging, she held on to their involvement, restored their interest, and gave them confidence and self-respect. She felt it deeply when she failed. So she made it a point to fail very seldom.

She was heartened by those women who stayed with it; gearing down the pace when necessary, picking it up when she felt they could stand it. She was pleased when together they could find and hold their best level.

She was amused by the constitution and spirit of one hardy correspondent who wrote, ". . . I opens the book, props it up and reads to myself while scrubbing the floor." She was touched by another woman who told of her child's explorations with the microscope: "Mother, come and see what God has made," the student reported. And she would always remember the invalid girl who found in the science lessons and equipment the desire and purpose to go out doors ". . . to study all I can reach."

This two-way communication, though taxing, gave Ellen Swallow contact with every walk of life and most of its problems. She was ever more impressed by the high frequency of women's illness, poor health, and depression—"the psychosis of negation." Finally, she wrote for these thousands a book on "right living" called simply, *Health*.

Health explained Ellen Swallow's standards for individual, family, and home life. For depression, in addition to books, poetry, and other mental stimulation, it advocated that free, abundant Rx that had cured her: "Fresh Air, Pure Water, and Good Food with Sunshine."

In 1885, she asked the society to add a "post-graduate course" in sanitary science. The Association of Collegiate Alumnae was growing but not fast enough for her purposes. Its narrow criteria for membership bypassed many college women in the South and West. Unreachable through the structures of either the A.C.A. or the Society to Encourage Study at Home, she nonetheless needed them in her work. And they, she felt, needed her knowledge, too.

She wrote and visited many colleges in the South and West and those in the North and East, too, that had not passed A.C.A. muster. She compiled lists of graduates from these schools and tailored a special course for them. Many had married, settled down to raise families, and manage homes. If their schools weren't up to A.C.A.'s standards, all the more reason to suspect they could use the information she published in the course, "Sanitation, Hygiene, and Nutrition."

The incredible, tireless efforts of Ellen Swallow were all the more remarkable considering she got little if any money for expanding her work. What she did get, though, was ever larger support for the campaign her life had become. Women were the mainstream of that movement, but now some men were able to liberate themselves emotionally toward women—and professionally toward the environment Swallow was trying to improve rather than just overcome.

As sexual myth and prejudice about educated women declined, their prestige and influence in their communities increased. Now they, too, were given a book to help spread the word: *Home Sanitation.*

Home Sanitation was a compilation of the environmental quality studies Ellen Swallow had assigned the A.C.A.'s Sanitary Science Club, edited by Marion Talbot. With their personal and professional work between hard covers in published form, the women had an even greater motivation to recommend the book and show it to their friends and neighbors. Spreading the credit around as thoroughly as possible, it was one more idea conceived by Ellen Swallow for others to develop as their own.

Through the 1880s Ellen Swallow informed, educated, and mobilized women in large cities and remote towns and villages across America—educated women, housewives, women's and study club members, and educational organizations—into a growing legion of citizens concerned for a better environment. She was well aware they were but a fraction of the total. But fractions, she knew, when organized, informed, and directed, carried weight far greater than their size. And she had organized well.

Then, in 1882 she opened her campaign for public involvement with her own first book: *The Chemistry of Cooking and Cleaning.* This one had something to offer every woman, to reach out beyond the A.C.A. and the Society to Study at Home, although the members were the first to buy and recommend it to their friends.

The Chemistry of Cooking and Cleaning was a new kind of book. It took the ponderous, fragmented knowledge of science, pulled it together, cleaned it up, and boiled it down for popular consumption in the home. It remained in print for more than a quarter century and became a model for others that followed and still come off the presses today, if not as ambitiously as hers. The book filled the gap between educated women and insolated housewives, who were charter members in her consumer-environment movement. And as the public signed up for the movement, they also stimulated a rise in the host of "home" and "shelter" magazines soon rushing off the presses into stores and homes across America.

The crusade was under way.

ELEVEN

Matrix

With the same depth of perception that Ellen Swallow saw environment as something to be improved from inside the home and family out, she saw environmental science as something to be built from the ground up. This was the right architecture for a science of "everyone's house," the truest form for Oekologie. In concept, it was a remarkably simple, natural structure. It was much more complex to put together.

In her first years at MIT, her studies of air, water, and earth laid the base. Frank Storer had begun MIT's examinations of air, reporting his carbon dioxide studies in the board of health's second annual report. On her arrival and ever after, Swallow took seriously the study of this vital element. She knew chemical changes occur when air is taken in and exhaled from the life systems of plants and animals. Life changes air just as it does water and other environmental elements. So devout in her regard for this element, in 1874, she made a pilgrimage to the Cumberland, Pennsylvania, grave of England's Joseph Priestley, discoverer of oxygen 100 years before.

In water science, Ellen Swallow had no peer. Pure, fresh, used, and contaminated, she studied water from its fall from heaven to earth and in its journey into springs, streams, lakes, and rivers and along the water table to man-made wells and reservoirs, into the pipes of city, home, and factory, through the human and industrial processes, and back out into the earth again.

Earth, of course, was a familiar field to a Yankee farm girl. Beneath the surface soils and fossils she had known as a child, the scientist learned deeper secrets. She became an internationally renowned mineralogist, prominent for her laboratory studies of samarskite, lead, copper, vanadium, and titanium. In the field, she visited mines and refineries with her husband, developing new methods and equipment to test on the site what would take weeks to get back from a laboratory. Her work was more than expedient. It was uncommonly thorough.

David Browne, a Canadian miner, sent copper from his Coppercliffe lode to assayers. One copper sample went to Robert Richards, who turned it over to his wife. "There is five percent nickel in your copper ore," she advised Browne. "She discovered nickel in Canada from Boston," the delighted Browne said. Coppercliffe became the center of a large nickel industry.

At the huge Calumet Mills on Lake Superior, management credited Robert Richards with "savings of $200,000 to $300,000 a year." He said it was due to his wife's expertise. When the company offered them stock, the Richards declined. It might detract them from other service.

In 1877, Ellen Swallow's paper, "A New Method to Determine Nickel in Pyrrhotites and Mattes," made her a leading referee in mineralogical disputes. Two years later, the American Institute of Mining and Mineralogical Engineers elected Ellen Swallow its first and only woman member.

Hippocrates had emphasized life's need of pure air, water, and soil. Studying them 2,000 years later, the female chemist saw what that first scientist had seen: the life these three interacting environmental elements produce, sustain, and evolve. In each, she found the same chemicals but in different arrangement. In all she found evidence of life. She felt "called" to the study of this miracle. But she was a chemist, not a biologist; an applied scientist, not a "pure" scientist. More, she was a woman. Biologists and medicine men were the high priests of life science. They alone were fit to wear the robes. Yet the more Ellen Swallow studied environment, the more she was seduced by its inevitable relationship to life.

"We sail to Europe in 48 hours," she wrote to Anne Mineah in June 1876. "You will have more knowledge after we come back."

There was an unintentional prophecy in that promise. The

journey was an extension of the Blowpipe Conspiracy. Its three principals, Richards, his wife of one year, and cohort Bea Capen, were now assured the Women's Laboratory would open that fall. Through it, women would be able to enter the temple of science. If Swallow's plan succeeded, they would study life science at MIT too, something even the men at the school could then study only guardedly.

Ellen charted the itinerary: Robert would visit the mines and smelteries; "Miss Capen and I plan to see the Universities." There they would see the laboratories. The trip was, in effect, a survey of the world's best laboratories. They visited twenty-five cities in twenty-four days, a tight travel schedule even after the automobile and the airplane.

"There were certain things Nellie had read . . . and wanted to see . . ." Robert said. "We went from city to city." By boat, buggy, and train they made a whirlwind sweep across Europe: Scotland, England, France, Switzerland, Belgium (where they took time out to see the International Health Exposition), and Germany—Cologne, Leipzig, Dresden, Berlin, and Jena.

"We visited many of the German schools," Ellen wrote. But she had saved Jena for last. This rustic mountain village of cobblestone streets and ancient houses was the crown of Europe's knowledge, especially in science. Napoleon fought a famous battle there in 1806 in an effort to subordinate the German intellect, as well as to conquer people and territory. Seventy years later, in the shadow of the graves of the French and German soldiers who died in that battle, the University of Jena towered as a monument to Napoleon's lost cause. Swallow had paid homage to Priestly and oxygen. Now she made her pilgrimage to the laboratory shrine of Ernst Haeckel, the world's greatest living biologist, who had proposed evolutionary theories before Darwin.

Haeckel, founder of the "new zoology," in 1873 had coined one of many names for new sciences to be developed. So far, Oekologie had been ignored, even by him, as he continued classifying more life forms than any man alive and tracing them to a common source.

There was more to Jena's intellectual ecology that made it a fitting stop for the Blowpipe conspirators. Jena was the source of the world's finest industrial and scientific glass. Here, Carl

Zeiss was king. With men like Zeiss and Haeckel to reveal nature's secrets, Jena's famous printing press distributed the knowledge. Swallow knew; she had translated its material many times.

If Haeckel and Swallow met, no record of the meeting has been found. But she did meet his most ardent supporter and supplier, Zeiss. If Zeiss didn't walk her up the hill to the famous laboratory, he could describe it in detail to the woman fluent in German. Whether she met the man who named new sciences, the woman who founded environmental science was well aware of his work.

Zeiss, on the other hand, was impressed by hers. The businessman not only realized there was a lot of water in the world to analyze, he was amazed at the depth of this woman's knowledge of laboratory operation. He gave his personal attention to her selection of instruments.

"Nellie chose what she needed [for] the new work in biology," and the party sailed for America. They went directly to the American Centennial Exposition in Philadelphia. Robert was exhausted. While Ellen toured the educational exhibits, he ". . . simply sat down and watched the great Corliss engine wheel go round."

In Boston, the instruments arrived from Jena. And in the Women's Laboratory in the fall of 1876, Ellen Swallow and John Ordway began teaching the Institute's first course in biology, "though not by that name," she admitted years later.

Previously, the Institute's arrangement with the Society of Natural History allowed a little zoology and some paleontology in the classroom. Professor Kneeland, a medical doctor, added some physiology. But open instruction of life science in a school of applied science was a touchy matter. Ellen Swallow's role in making it a regular part of the MIT curriculum seems strangely familiar—similar to the decision under which a woman was admitted "without charge of any kind" as a hedge against responsibility of any kind.

Cultivating biology in the new Women's Laboratory gave MIT a ready disclaimer, if needed. The Woman's Education Association was paying for that facility, not MIT. What they taught there was their business. If Harvard or some lesser body objected, they could always complain to Mrs. Cabot and her well connected friends at the W.E.A.

This theory might explain why MIT never paid Ellen Swallow during those years. If she wasn't on the payroll, how could they be held responsible for what she taught? It would also help explain why she had paid from her own purse for some of the equipment she bought at Jena. The situation also explains what she meant, forty years later, when she said the first course in biology in 1876 "was not by that name." Ellen Swallow had learned to hedge a bit, too.

"Also at the request of the Woman's Education Association of Boston," the 1876 catalogue read, "new laboratories have been provided for the special instruction of women. Studies will be in Chemical Analysis, Industrial Chemistry, Mineralogy, and Chemistry as Related to Vegetable and Animal Physiology."

With "chemistry as related to vegetable and animal physiology," the blow was softened. In 1878, MIT's catalogue could openly list biology as a course under Professor John Ordway. If this was a milestone for MIT, it was an even more meaningful precedent for MIT's only woman scientist. The chemist had succeeded in making a junction between environmental and life sciences. She had begun the interdisciplinary matrix for the ecology called "the subversive science" today. Ellen Swallow was the subverter, and she had no intention of stopping there. She would add other branches of science to that matrix in the years ahead. But first she cautiously expanded her beachhead with chemical studies into less guarded life forms: dead life.

She trained her "special students" in chemical analysis. Just like the catalogue said. They analyzed coal, lead, copper, rocks in mineralogy—the pressurized life forms of eons ago. Next they studied industrial chemistry, analyzing organic matter used to make the man-made environment: leather, dyes, wood pulp, fabrics, oils, and more.

Then there was "chemistry as related to vegetable and animal physiology." From this base, they studied another form of former life, the plants and animals that make up the human diet: food. And in food science, Ellen Swallow felt closer still to the sciences of human life.

In the 1870s, food science, with few esoteric exceptions, was a vastly overlooked field and had been since Rumford, 100 years earlier. Not many paid much attention to it, including biologists. A few medical men did, but preventive medicine then, too, was more an after-thought than the mainstream for physicians who followed Villanova but not his prescriptions for human diet.

Once more backed by the w.e.a., Swallow approached the State Board of Health, Lunacy and Charity that succeeded the original board. Would they accept a scientific examination of Massachusetts's food supply? Approved, Ellen Swallow's corps swarmed over the state, border to border, visiting ". . . the very best . . . intermediate . . . [and] the very poorest . . ." stores in forty cities. They bought goods, interviewed grocers, and brought it all back to analyze in the laboratory.

> The object of this . . . is to show the general character of some of the staple groceries actually used in the State . . . especially those which have been suspected of adulteration with mineral substances: Flour, Sugar, Bread, Soda, Cream of Tartar and Baking Powders . . ."

The report exposed positives and negatives in the manufacturer-to-wholesaler-to-retailer-to-consumer food chain. Manufacturers and wholesalers were the worst offenders, it said. The grocer's guilt was of another kind. But consumer ignorance compounded and made possible the crimes.

> Few persons are in a better position to know the ignorance and superstition of even seemingly intelligent people than a grocer . . . These ignorant and superstitious notions must be accepted [by the grocer] if the trade of people is to be retained.

But, the report said, "Retail dealers as a rule sell what they buy. Whatever adulteration exists is to be found among manufacturers and wholesalers."

The study located the worst adulteration outside the packages —printed lies and defamations about theirs and others' products. "The country is flooded with the worst kind of trash," was the warning on one package. Its contents were no exception, analysis showed. Statements untrue, misleading, or destructive to public confidence in other goods were made about all items studied; ". . . selling catches for one and the same product," the report said.

The first scientific study of a state's staple groceries also found: Flour: twenty-five samples from eleven towns "in no case . . .

showed any evidence of mineral additions. In poor neighborhoods though, noting more sales of "store bread," the study
also noted the absence of ingredients and equipment for baking
bread at home.

Sugar: Analysis did not find the "tin flakes" as rumored. It
did find chloride, sodium chloride, calcium, and other additives
"up to eleven percent."

Soda: Chemistry buried the saleratus-soda debate forever. They
were one and the same despite claims and costs. Of ninety-three
samples from thirty-five cities, nineteen were "near chemically
pure;" forty-three "good;" twenty-five "not good;" and three
"very bad." But, it noted, soda was so cheap it didn't pay to
adulterate it.

Cream of Tartar: The "very worst evil." Of 160 samples,
ninety-four were "perfectly good;" forty-seven "mostly terra
alba;" others were "largely" or "wholly acid phosphate of lime."
One was almost all flour.

Baking Powder: Twenty-four of thirty-three samples were
good in that they "contain nothing injurious to the body" so far
as science knew then. However, nine samples had alum, five
ammonia, and twelve "a large excess of starch up to 45 percent."

As a rule, the report concluded, the grocer's own brands were
more reliable; price was not a measure of quality, but the
absence of manufacturers' identification on the packages was a
sure clue to the lack of quality inside.

Even more clear was the totally confusing consumer climate
that public ignorance, manufacturer's duplicity, wholesaler's
greed, and grocer's silent witness made possible.

Consumerism continued to grow at the laboratory. Other goods
were tested. Cinnamon that contained no cinnamon but had a
lot of mahogany sawdust, colored mustard with starch were
found. Results of examinations were always published when
possible. Some made the professional journals. Swallow preferred the popular magazines and newspapers that reached the
consumer. *The New England Farmer* was an early and frequent
medium for such articles as "The Spices We Buy" and "On Food
Adulteration." Other media and news magazines, sensing a trend,
picked up the pace. The work formally kicked off America's

pure food movement. In 1882 and 1884, with special reference to Swallow, Massachusetts passed the first pure food laws. But the movement was incomplete as far as she was concerned. She saw no sense to studying or publishing only the negatives. It wasn't enough to apply science to find what was wrong; science must also find ways to make it right.

The Chemistry of Cooking and Cleaning was a major part of the explosion of public interest in food, environment, and health in the home. A second printing came almost immediately. The book was followed by more testing of foods and cleaners, the results printed and publicized. Now another dimension of environment came under her scientific scrutiny: the household wares and goods that took the worker's wages and often his family's health as well. Now she examined papers, furniture, cottons, wools, silks, leathers, woods, and appliances.

If she found nothing harmful in 1870 lace, she found arsenic in wallpaper—food for the curious child. Some metals like mercury and fluids used in textiles and tanning were analyzed. Some were not just harmful to the consumer—they endangered men, women, and children working in the "manufactories." An interesting sidelight to this phase of her work is a letter she received from a Louisville doctor urging that she test stoves. Dr. J. Lawrence Smith was the same name and was from the same town as the man who read an earlier paper of Ellen Swallow's and devised tests that discovered gadolinium and samarium in samarskite.

Swallow was always careful to give others credit that might have gone to her. The crusade she originated, however, developed a larger base as a result of this practiced anonymity. Downplaying her part, she refused to be photographed (except as part of her husband's hobby) and declined personal publicity except when it served the movement. Even then she understated.

"My own work last year . . . was a little investigation of cleaning wool . . . by naphtha . . . published in *The Wool Bulletin*," she wrote. But in addition to the tremendous commercial profits brought about by the reduced cost of cleaning wool "by use of a quality called 'gasoline' . . ." this may also have been the discovery of modern spot remover.

By the mid-1880s, the consumer side of the movement was

well established. Swallow ordered an advance into still new territory. This was her boldest venture yet. With Atkinson's help —since the Atlanta Exposition, he was always sought as a consultant on trade fairs—space was secured at the prestigious New England Mechanics and Manufacturers Exhibit in Boston. Letting women into the men's affair was rationalized by their promise ". . . to show that men and women may and do work together . . ." to improve industry. Swallow and company kept that promise and then some.

"Various household articles of common use, with careful analyses of [products] from each manufacturer . . ." were tested for public view.

This was not merely a "first." Unfortunately, it was the kind of consumerism that didn't last. For those "tempted to ask what the practical result of all this expenditure of time and money has been, we may say that the fact that a circle of women exists who know the composition of the staple articles of household use which are sold in the centres of trade . . . and who know the names of the manufacturers as well as the dealers from whom they were purchased, is of itself a source of power the extent of which is not yet realized . . . but becoming more important as adulterations and substitutions multiply. . . ." How manufacturers felt about this "progress" apparently was not published.

Giving this power to women only, or only a few women, however, was not enough for Ellen. The public at large should have it, she said. People had a right to expect more from science and technology. Science and technology must mint the public side of the coin, too. In 1879, she took her case for the first time to the upper chamber of science.

"We have just been to the American Association [for the Advancement of Science] meeting at Saratoga. I appealed to the chemists there to help in this matter. . . . I seem to have gotten into that track now and must follow it out, whither or no. It is an open field but much study will be required . . ." The following year she presented a paper on food science to the "A₃S."

Many businessmen who had first looked down their noses at this "track" she was on were beginning to frown. But not the nonconforming Edward Atkinson. He joined her immediately. From this point on, their relationship would transcend the social stage on which it began, ascending to a high level of humanitarian collaboration.

The crusade grew larger; impossible to lead from Boston. For pure air, water, soil, and food—for nutrition, consumer, and environmental reform—the scientist became a professional traveler and lecturer. From Boston to California, Maine to Florida, and back and forth, and again to Europe, and to all the large and small cities in between, ever more away from home and laboratory, she taught, lectured, wrote, and organized. Through it all, she was adding more, newer knowledge to the interdisciplinary science she was building.

Wherever she went, she put samples of water into little jars to take with her and test. She asked someone in her audience to send others from time to time. She wrote her observations in letters, diaries, magazines, and journals. She expanded her network of correspondents and a growing number of followers.

From the study of environment, she had graduated to teaching it. Now she had organized a movement around its knowledge. But something was still missing from its official matrix; something very important if environmental quality was to evolve permanently, universally.

"We shall drown in our own work," she repeated wherever she went, "if it is not taken up." The knowledge science was accumulating—could accumulate—must be given greater distribution and use. She saw the problem and the potential wherever she went. From Virginia's coal fields, where she was conducting a "Moveable School of Mines," she wrote, "Virginia seems a nice place to live . . . but I should like to see it re-peopled or its children educated."

Education was the missing piece in her matrix. The home was no longer the information medium it once was. Schools had taken over the learning function, so they must teach environment, too. Even before Ellen Swallow founded the A.C.A. she was a much sought educational consultant, especially in science. She advised on curricula, method, texts, teachers—the economics and efficiency of it all—and apparatus. "It all depends on how the course is to be taught . . . to what end?"

As early as 1876, she was invited to a symposium on science training in Atlanta. Later, "I expect to take my vacation this year as a Juror on Education in Tennessee." She stayed in touch with educational developments in Russia, Japan, and Europe.

After an exhausting tour of European health and education exhibits, she took the long way home, by boat over the North Pole. On deck in the Land of the Midnight Sun—"the only place on earth where there are enough hours in the day for her"—she reflected on the world of tomorrow and the education of today with her companion, Alice Freeman.

"I feel we have a much better foundation [for education] here in the United States," Ellen Swallow reported on her return from one of these trips. "If only we can build on it [properly]. How to give young people that power of acquiring knowledge all their lives and not to stuff into their heads [in a few years] enough to last a lifetime! I am brought so close to this question in relation . . . to . . . the general educational scheme which I have more or less to do with."

It was always more. By 1881, she touched nearly every level of American education, from adult, post-graduate, and college, down through normal, preparatory, high, elementary, and primary schools. She may already have made her first contact during this period with the preschool experiments she would develop later—possibly in the School House Club Edward Atkinson had founded for his children in Brookline, or Camp Merriweather, which Henry Richards opened in New Hampshire. She was a constant consultant to Smith, to Wellesley, and to Bryn Mawr from the beginning. Her work at Vassar and at MIT only grew over the years, as did the list of other schools and colleges she worked with.

Ellen Swallow was the only woman awarded a degree at MIT until 1879. In 1880, she wrote, "Women can now take a degree" at MIT. "It is the great step . . . toward which I have been working . . . 8 years is not so long to wait for such a great step." She could be patient, but only when a cause was won.

Ellen Swallow believed education must be reformed, a recurring theme even when she addressed the other elements of her work. Education must become less rote and broader than the three

R's. Public schools should teach the modern environment, what it is, and how to live in it. In 1882, to help in this direction, she published her first textbook.

First Lessons in Minerals was a fundamental and human introduction to physical environment. It could serve as a basic text for elementary environmental studies today. To open the student mind to environment, the book taught mineral compositions of life as seen in air, water, soil. It traced these elements from the food, fuel, and materials required in daily living on into the body's composition. To make certain this knowledge took root, simple experiments for children were included at the end of each chapter by this believer in Comenius's principle that there is more to learning than seeing, hearing, or reading. *Doing* links the hand, ear, and eye to the mind, she said. A "new" school of educational theory, Manual Training, sometimes known as Vocational Training, or "the Natural Method of Learning," became part of America's public education system. Ellen Swallow was so identified with the movement as it spread across the country, at least one special school—in Chicago—would be named for her.

With education, vital to the environmental science matrix she was building, the parts of the science of the oekumenical "house" were falling into place. The most precarious parts of that structure still were the life sciences, however. The chemist knew it, and in 1881 she seized an opportunity to improve her relationship with pure life science.

Alpheus Hyatt, a paleontologist now teaching at the Institute, was an understudy of the late Louis Agassiz. Swallow and Hyatt shared an interest in several infant fields, "the Natural Method of Learning" for one, biology for another.

Swallow was also deeply interested in Hyatt's desire to resurrect a project begun by Agassiz just before his death in 1873: a marine biology laboratory.

Marine biology was an undeveloped discipline in America. Swallow had seen the world's best laboratories in Europe at Jena and perhaps Anton Dohrn's monumental facility on the Bay of Naples. Along with Hyatt and Agassiz's widow, Swallow urged the Woman's Education Association to underwrite the cost of a marine biology laboratory. Why us, they asked? Because women are now being accepted in science, if only on the fringes. They need a place for actual research. A place to learn by *doing*. This "Natural Method" was not new to the w.e.a. It was the basic concept behind the Women's Laboratory, the same thinking behind the large cooking school opened by the w.e.a. in 1879 in Boston with ninety-four students who heard Swallow's lectures on nutrition. The woman who lectured on food was, of course, careful not to compare a cooking school with a biology laboratory.

The w.e.a. agreed, ". . . not with the idea of permanent support, but with the hope . . . good work will result in its being placed on a more stable basis. . . ." In the summer of 1881, the pleasant sounding Summer Seaside Laboratory opened in Annisquam, Massachusetts.

"The purpose of this laboratory is to afford opportunity for the study under suitable direction of the development, anatomy and habits of common types of marine animals," Hyatt wrote in its charter. This was pure biology, but for Ellen Swallow it was also one more step further toward environmental science. Three years later, some forty students had completed the annual three-month courses. Some wrote "original treatises" in zoology. Importantly, more than half of those students were women. Biology had become bisexual. In 1882, Ellen Swallow wrote to Anne Mineah:

"Public opinion begins to become effective. They no longer sneer at women in science." Neither did they sneer any longer at Ellen Swallow. She was a scientist to be taken seriously. Ten years after becoming mit's first woman, things looked brighter every day to the first lady of science.

Then, suddenly, all her carefully built plans seemed to collapse. At forty-three, Ellen Swallow found herself unemployed.

Science had been undergoing rapid change, not just at her hands but universally. The day of the generalist was over. mit's original faculty had each taught a little of everything. Only a few had doctorates. A Ph.D. was not as necessary in those early days, as they had carefully explained to her. In the 1880s, this too had changed.

The accelerating accumulation of knowledge was forcing science into ever tighter specialties, a trend that ran counter to what Ellen Swallow was trying to do. The broad field of sanitary science had grown from the homeowner sanitary societies organized in England into the military sanitary commissions in America, and finally the scientific water pollution studies. This broad field to which Nichols and Swallow had contributed so much was beginning to fragment into new disciplines. Coming on fast was biology's youngest child, bacteriology.

Pasteur had linked microbes and fermentation in food in the 1860s. Between 1875 and 1878, a German physician, Robert Koch, proved at least one disease, splenic fever, was caused by a "bacterium." Then advances came faster. In 1882, tuberculosis, diphtheria, typhoid, and cholera germs were identified. The world of science, in which public health had been considered the domain of medicine, evaginated.

MIT felt the impact. Rogers was dead. Runkle was gone. Reorganizing under a new president, Francis Amasa Walker, MIT saw the chance to take the wraps off applied biology for good. Shopping around for a full-fledged biologist, they found one: William Sedgwick, a recent graduate of Johns Hopkins University. Ordway, never a biologist, although he had been assigned to teach it with Swallow, saw the handwriting on the wall.

In 1883, Swallow was overjoyed when she learned the Women's Laboratory would be consolidated with the men's classes. Then she learned her services would not be needed in the new arrangement. She was stunned. It wasn't a financial loss. Or was it? MIT had never paid her anyhow. At least, the W.E.A. was off the hook in supporting the Women's Lab. Then she learned Ordway had resigned effective the end of the year. Her main source of revenue had been from her work in his industrial chemistry practice. When word got out Ordway was going, she realized this work would dry up, too.

I feel like a woman whose children are all about to be married and leave her alone, so that she is to move into a smaller house and a new neighborhood. You see, it is quite a change for me . . . I cannot at once fit all the corners. My work is done and happily . . . but the energy will have to be used somehow. Our present Women's Laboratory will be torn down and my duties will be gone, as I shall not go into the new laboratory. Now I would not mind if I was away at the Lake and out of it all or if I knew where to store my apparatus, but everything is so unsettled owing to the uncertainty . . . I do not know that I shall have anything to do or anywhere to work. . . . Everything seems to fall flat and I have a sense of impending fate which is paralyzing. . . .

During the long year of 1883, she made herself useful—to Robert, naturally. He'd got a new mining laboratory in the re-organization. She helped Ordway until he left with his wife Evelyn Walton for Tulane. With Nichols, she hoped the state would come through with the long overdue survey of water and sewage. Characteristically, she was most helpful to the new man. The young William Sedgwick found this older woman "a great teacher." From her he learned of Europe's great laboratories. Sedgwick was deeply interested in the new field of bacteriology. She encouraged him and gave him the benefit of her valuable experience with water, sewage, air, and food analyses. She also encouraged his reorganization of MIT's spotty life science courses. In four years, they would become a full-scale biology department.

When 1884 rolled around, Ellen Swallow's professional crisis was resolved as suddenly as it had arrived. Edward Atkinson was there first. Now president of the Boston Mutual Manufacturers Fire Insurance combine, he appointed Ellen Swallow its chief industrial chemist, the first woman to hold such a position, a distinction she would make even more conspicuous.

The Institute's reorganization moved ahead. Reading the trend of sanitary science and public health, MIT gave Sedgwick approval to build a bacteriological program. Even more important, the Institute also opened the Sanitary Chemistry Laboratory, "the first of its kind in the world." Nichols was made director, naturally, but day-to-day operation of this unique facility was Ellen Swallow's charge. Finally, after twelve long years, she was officially named to the MIT faculty. Hired at last! She was forty-four.

I am Instructor in Sanitary Chemistry and have charge of the laboratory of the same—I have at present 7 young men (there are no girls in the graduating class). It is new work and all has to be planned and experimented upon.

For the next ten years this laboratory was headquarters for her persistent effort to bring together an accredited interdisciplinary science of environment.

> What am I doing? I think it would be easier to say what I am not doing. Monday . . . to Rice school for Lessons on Minerals. Before that, I weigh some nickel . . . and Sunday plan out some manual work for a Study at Home pupil who is visiting in town. . . . Tuesday I am at home and after a little house-putting to rights . . . work on [a new] book, *The Adulteration of Food* . . . also . . . an article for *Science,* and some lectures for the professor.
>
> Miss Minns came to the Lab and we discussed food adulteration and read over some of what I've written. . . . Afternoon not laid out but probably some chemical work will come in . . . Each day I go upstairs to the reading room . . . each evening [translate] two or three periodicals for report to the Professor . . . Letters by the dozen to write . . . Miss Peabody comes in to the Lab and we try tests on some of the things for [another] book . . . and read over how we should say it so they will understand. PM meeting of the ACA Sanitary Science Club. . . . Friday is not yet planned.
>
> Saturday morning I have been giving a course of lessons in minerals to 60 ladies . . . Sat PM for this month, lessons to the public school teachers . . . next week looks very leisurely now . . . but it will fill up fast enough. Some Home Study work [already] coming in and some ACA to be planned.
>
> One of the Sanitary Science Club goes to Lowell Saturday to talk to the Mill girls on ventilation. . . . I have got to get some apparatus ready for her and if she can't make it, I must go. . . . a very broken and varied life, but not an idle one as you can see. . . .

It is hard to believe that this incredible pace would go faster in the next twenty-six years.

"Don't you ever get tired?" someone asked.

"Yes, and then I go to bed," she replied.

TWELVE

The Christening of Oekology

November 30, 1892. In seven years and thirty-one days the twentieth century would begin. The complexities of a new era would replace the simple existence of the old.

Ellen Swallow had worked at an unbelievable pace to develop the interdisciplines of an environmental science she believed the next 100 years required. She knew work alone was no guarantee of permanence for the knowledge she had pulled together. If anything, the changing world—specialized, mechanized, cosmetic—seemed to take things apart.

The world is whole, like the environment. But in working with that world, the specialists of science and technology, government and industry were fragmenting it. Focused on their own individual fields, burying deeper and deeper in their respective niches, they seemed oblivious to the environment around them.

The First Lady of Science had gone in the opposite direction, putting sciences together to nurture the roots of environment. But to perpetuate her conglomerate body of knowledge and its applications, a permanent structure was required. Ernst Haeckel had been right when he suggested the name for a science of everybody's home. Ellen Swallow began to fill the void that accompanied Oekologie's 1873 proposal with her collection of old knowledge cross-fertilized with new to build "home science" for environment and life within it.

Since 1873, she had laid the foundations and aligned the interconnecting walls of that "house." Gradually, surreptitiously at times, she opened the structure—inviting, pleading, scheming—

for others to enter and occupy it. Now the time had come to open it completely.

In four days she would be fifty. The nineteenth century that had molded her was running out. The new one would be very different from anything mankind had ever known. She believed, since mankind had become both the provider and the product of his environment, he could meet the challenges of a changing environment by shaping it the right way. It was changing in any case. He must be prepared for that change.

At the end of the nineteenth century, the environment was still essentially held in human hands. But from her vantage point at MIT, Ellen Swallow could see that environment was being transferred to technology. It must not be turned over completely, she believed. *People* must retain some control over the shape and change of their environment. The only way they could, she saw, was to be equipped for that function—the man on the street or at work, the woman in the home or in the community, the child in school. *All* must have the knowledge required to retain their traditional relationship with environment.

If Ellen Swallow had learned one thing in her fifty years, it was the need first to know, to understand the substance one worked with. Chemistry was a good teacher that way. That's how she felt about environment. She didn't see environment always in the terms used to describe it today. It was a different environment then. But she believed if people would work with the environmental principle superimposed on their daily lives, they would grow more conscious of what the environment is and what to do—and not do—with it.

She intended exactly that on the November evening in 1892 when she christened the science she had nurtured through nineteen years.

It was Thursday, a crisp, chilly, early winter day in Boston. As the sun began its slow slide behind the trees and brownstones on the Boston side of the Charles River, a parade of carriages carrying well dressed ladies and gentlemen began arriving at the corner of Commonwealth Avenue and Exeter Street. In less than an hour, some 300 fashionable people climbed the ornate staircase to the elegant Vendome Hotel. This was the annual meeting of the prestigious Boot & Shoe Club, the *creme de la creme* of the footwear industry in Boston, industrial capital of the world.

Inside, the normally staid Vendome lobby hummed with activity. The crowd was so large—and so important—the hotel's State Suite of Chambers was taken over as a dressing room for the reception in the Main Parlor. The Banquet Hall, resplendent in blue and silver motif, waited. The bone china and silver service flashed with carats of light from the cut crystal chandeliers overhead. Even empty, the room was full of opulence, a dazzling jewel awaiting an historic engagement.

Ellen Swallow entered the hotel on the arm of her tall husband. They had walked the two short blocks from MIT. Now they moved down the deep-pile carpeted hall to where a reception was in process. Gentlemen and ladies exchanged greetings. Introductions were made. Voices, a mandolin, punch cups, and the rustle of expensive silks and velvets mixed in an elegance of sound.

This was the Boot & Shoe's second annual Ladies Night. The first had been devoted to a program entitled "Women in Higher Education," a topic Ellen Swallow helped make less controversial in 1891 than it was twenty years before. Still, as last year's program indicated and tonight's blushing condescension confirmed, the customs of several thousand years had not worn off for either sex.

Tonight, members, guests, and a few academic and science dignitaries who had accepted her invitation would witness what an educated woman had done and what she proposed: the public institution of environmental science.

Suddenly the gay sounds of the parlor grew louder. The colorful crowd gracefully made its way down the hall to the dining room. Filing in around the glimmering tables, gentlemen seated their ladies, then sat to be served. A musical chorale complemented the menu and aided digestion.

At each setting, an engraved parchment listed the characters in this drama, its theme captured by the words of the club's poet laureate, Ralph Waldo Emerson:

Is it not plain that not in the Senates or Courts nor in Chambers of Commerce, but in the dwelling place must the true character and hope of the time be consulted?

Then, after the liveried waiters had served a not too nutritious dessert, Club President F. H. Nazro "rapped the spoons into silence." Opening the program from the long, elevated head table, Nazro responded to Emerson's question:

"The days of the present are better than the days of the past. We are optimists, and we claim that the days of the future may be better than those of today." Even an optimist said "may."

As the nineteenth century draws to a close, he observed, humanity has not solved the problem of living. "Pray God, the twentieth century may." Then Nazro introduced the woman who would propose *how* the new century should solve *what* problems, another optimist: "Mrs. Robert Richards, Instructor in Sanitary Chemistry in the Massachusetts Institute of Technology."

Rising to face the distinguished audience, Ellen paused. This, she thought, is what it's all been about. Now is the time, the place. She began.

NEW SCIENCE, headlined *The Boston Globe* the next day. "Mrs. Richards Names It Oekology." Just below, "Tis the Art of First-Class Living." Either the word environment was too long for the typesetter or too abstract for a nineteenth century reporter. Perhaps his editor felt the concept too broad for the reader to grasp. In any event, "environment" was conspicuously scarce in the story that captured the more common interpretation of women's work, even for women of science.

The story did, however, take up the best part of the page, with its drawn illustrations of the evening, an account of the fashions, and a portrait of Alice Freeman Palmer, who had come all the way from the University of Chicago to attend the unveiling of Oekology. The former president of Wellesley was a dean at the University of Chicago.

"Speaking without notes and with convincing seriousness lightened by many touches of humor," Ellen Swallow threw open environmental science to the public.

> I would like to have the gift of mind reading for a while, for I think the very best speech would be to know what each one present expected to hear, here tonight. As your president has said, we have not come to talk over the science of domestics. A Domestic Science is something broader. It is a comfort to know [however] that you believe there [can be] a science for the home.
>
> But before there can be a science, there must be an art. The art

1

The Woman Who Founded Ecology

Ellen Henrietta Swallow, who one day would launch environmental science, was a frail and spindly child at six. Even then, in 1848, her black hair was pulled taut along her head, a style that with little variation became the style of a lifetime. The nosegay in her hand may well have been picked from the hills near Dunstable, Massachusetts, the small town where she was born.

2

When she was twenty-six, Ellen entered Vassar College as a third-year student. Two years later she was in the first graduating class. In 1871, she became the first woman to be admitted to MIT. At that time, "Tech" was housed in the Rogers Building, fronting on Boylston Street off Copley Square in Boston. In 1873, Ellen became the first woman graduate of a science school.

As Ellen Swallow was studying, Ernst Haeckel, a German biologist at the University of Jena, used the word Oekologie for a science he proposed to study: life's relationship to environment. But Haeckel went on to develop other life sciences. And a continent away chemist Ellen Swallow had already started the water, air, and mineralogical work she would use to develop an interdisciplinary environmental science that she would later christen Oekology.

Among Ellen's early work in the 1870s were her water pollution tests. In the photograph, she is shown with an unidentified assistant. The author estimates the picture was taken in the late 1870s. The scientist's hair is still black, although she grayed early. Her body, which permitted her to climb "hand over hand" up a rope for some thirty feet, appears still youthful.

5

7

A fighter for equal education for women, Ellen saw her planning bear fruit in 1876 with the opening of the Women's Science Laboratory at MIT. The world's first such lab, it occupied an old garage in a lot next to the Rogers Building. The building between Boylston and Newbury Streets was refurbished for women science students with funds raised by the Women's Education Association and by Ellen Swallow. There she taught science to women who went on to develop laboratory science instruction in America's schools and colleges in the late nineteenth century. The figure at the left in the photograph of the lab might well be Instructor Ellen Swallow.

In 1875, Ellen Swallow married Robert Hallowell Richards, the young MIT professor who discovered her mineralogical genius. "The Professor," as she called him, "revolutionized the academic instruction of mining engineering."

Ellen and Robert set up housekeeping at 32 Eliot Street, Jamaica Plain, a Boston suburb. In revamping the house, the scientist and engineer made it the prototype of the healthful home. Among many other changes, the dining room was enlarged and filled with plants, and with its adjoining kitchen became the first home testing laboratory, where Ellen furthered her food, consumer, and environmental sciences.

8

6

9

10

Over the years, famous personages in science, education, and humanitarian affairs came to counsel in the unusual house. Guests arriving to discuss great issues of the day were welcomed from an unimposing front porch.

A frequent guest was "the venerable Edward Atkinson," industrialist, economist, financier, and presidential advisor, who was one of the nineteenth century's most colorful and controversial figures. He appointed Swallow the first woman science consultant to industry, and as such she pioneered new health, safety, and environmental quality measures. Atkinson became her closest collaborator.

He also invented the Aladdin Oven—prototype for all modern ranges—to control the experiments Swallow made to give new impetus to food science.·

In her forties, Ellen Swallow's portrait was painted by Ellen Hale, daughter of Edward Everett Hale, theologian, author, and publisher. The painting was, appropriately, hung in MIT's women's lounge, the Margaret Cheney Room, for which Swallow was the chief fund raiser.

12

11

13

15

14

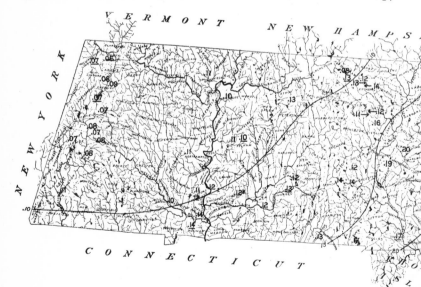

STATE BOARD OF HEALTH

MAP OF THE

STATE OF MASSACHUSETTS.

SHOWING

NORMAL CHLORINE.

EXPLANATION.

The amount of chlorine is expressed in parts per
100,000.

The lines represent normal chlorine.

The figures show observed chlorines which are
normal or nearly so.

The figures underlined represent chlorines of ground-
waters.

16

In 1881, in an effort to bring life science and chemistry closer together, Swallow took a leading role in opening the Summer Seaside Laboratory at Annisquam, Massachusetts. Six years later it was moved to Woods Holl in Hyannis and became the Marine Biological Laboratory. "Old Main" was torn down in 1970.

MIT opened "the world's first Sanitary Science Laboratory of its kind" in 1884. Three years later, when the picture was taken, Ellen Swallow was conducting the Great Sanitary Survey that modernized municipal sewerage treatment and gave the world its first water purity tables and America its first water quality standards.

The map of Massachusetts on the wall also was to provide a major new discovery: As Ellen Swallow recorded her data from the Sanitary Survey of Massachusetts water and sewage, the Normal Chlorine Map was born. It was an effective first tool in the war against water pollution, as it showed how much pollution in a given area at a given time was "normal" and how much was "man made."

19   20

21   22

During the years that Ellen put her scientific training to work for nutrition, consumerism, education, and industrial hygiene, as well as the environmental sciences and technologies she developed, she and Robert were surrounded with her co-workers and disciples at home and at MIT.

Among those whom she won to her crusade was Melvil Dewey, *right,* creator of the Dewey Decimal System of library classification and founder of modern library science and the American Library Association.

Marion Talbot, *below right,* often credited with founding the American Association of University Women, was, according to the author, more the instrument of her teacher at MIT. An early student of air and food sciences, Marion Talbot later taught at Wellesley College and went on to become dean of women at the University of Chicago.

Alice Freeman Palmer, *opposite top left,* who became president of Wellesley at twenty-six, was a close consort in Ellen Swallow's crusades to improve higher education for women and to reform public school education. Under Ellen Swallow's leadership, she and Marion Talbot were charter members of the Association to Advance Scientific Research by American Women, an organization that later set up the first international science competition for women.

From the work of Dr. Samuel Gridley Howe, *opposite top right,* "founder of America's mental health movement," Ellen evolved basic concepts for her second environmental science, Euthenics.

His wife, Julia Ward Howe, *opposite bottom left,* was a long-time collaborator in Ellen's causes. A leading figure in the woman's movement, in abolition, and in other reforms of the nineteenth century, she is perhaps best known today as the author of the words to "The Battle Hymn of the Republic."

Dr. and Mrs. Howe were the parents of Ellen's close friend, Laura Howe Richards, *opposite bottom right,* who, as the wife of Robert Richards's brother Henry, was Ellen's sister-in-law. Laura Richards wrote some seventy literary works and won a Pulitzer Prize for her biographical writing.

18

17

In 1890, Swallow opened the New England Kitchen. Although really a laboratory in which the "most nutritious food [was] cooked for the smallest amount of money," it was open to the public, first as a take-out restaurant.

Encouraged by her successes, Ellen Swallow publicly "christened" Oekology in 1892. But food and consumer sciences, not environment and education as she had hoped, dominated the movement. The result was that in 1893, at the request of the Massachusetts government, she opened the Rumford Kitchen at the World's Columbian Exposition in Chicago. The Kitchen was credited with the first public use of nutritional science information and for that and

25

26

other innovations won the praise of America's medical schools. Inside, all food and sanitary procedures were open to public inspection, a precedent for restaurants of the day. Quotations and slogans hung on the walls, and menus listed the nutritional content of each dish, computed to price and quantity of serving.

By this time, Ellen Swallow's reputation was such that when she returned to Boston she introduced the first "nutrition lunches" into schools, an innovation she repeated in factories, hospitals, jails, and asylums. In the picture, a group of Boston Latin School boys crowd the serving line "manned" by two followers of Ellen Swallow's Oekology movement.

27

28

29

But Ellen Swallow's reforms went too far and too fast. She was dismissed as an agitator, and the life sciences took over her Oekology for botany and zoology. Nevertheless, convinced that people respond to their environment, Swallow and her followers formed the Lake Placid Conference for what she called Home Oecology. Seated around their leader in the top picture are early members of the Lake Placid Conference: Annie Dewey, Maria Daniell, Alice Norton, and Maria Parloa. Maria Daniell was an early nutrition writer, and Maria Parloa was Swallow's choice to teach nutritional principles to Boston medical students in the 1890s.

By 1908, when the home oecologists voted to call themselves home economists, Ellen Swallow was at work on her second environmental science, Euthenics. Gathered around Ellen Swallow, first president of the American Home Economics Association, are, in the back row, Adelaide Nutting, Abby Marlatt, Emma Jacobs, and Helen Spring. In the front row are Annie Dewey, Helen Kinne, Caroline Hunt, Alice Ravenhill, Mary Abel, and Isabel Bevier.

Although busier than ever in the last eleven years of her life with her multitude of projects, writing, lecturing, and traveling, Ellen with Robert took time out for the tonic that the New England mountains gave them. The picture shows them outside Robert's family home in Gardiner, Maine, around the turn of the century.

Not long after that "Nellie" and "The Professor" found time to build their dream cottage in the New Hampshire mountains. She named it The Balsams.

30

La Follette's
WEEKLY MAGAZINE

"YE SHALL KNOW THE TRUTH AND THE TRUTH SHALL MAKE YOU FREE"

VOL. II, NO. 52.   MADISON, WISCONSIN,   DECEMBER 31, 1910.

ELLEN
HENRIETTA
RICHARDS

who received the honorary degree of Doctor of Science at Smith College, October Fifth, Nineteen Ten

"Bachelor and Master of Arts of Vassar College, Bachelor of Science of the Massachusetts Institute of Technology, and there for over quarter of a century Instructor in Sanitary Chemistry. By investigations into the explosive properties of oils and in the analysis of water, and by expert knowledge relating to air, food, water and sanitation, and the cost of food and shelter, set forth in numerous publications and addresses, she has largely contributed to promote in the community the serviceable arts of safe, healthful, and economic living."
—PRESENTATION SPEECH.

—The Caro Studio

32

33

By this time, Ellen's health was beginning to fail. And then in 1910 Smith College gave Ellen an honorary Doctor of Science degree, the doctorate that MIT had denied her. The influential weekly news magazine published by "Fighting Bob" LaFollette, featured environmental scientist Ellen Swallow for its December 31 cover story.

In contrast to Ellen in her academic robes is the picture that she and Robert posed for in a favorite wooded area near their home in Jamaica Plain.

A few months later Ellen Swallow Richards, First Lady of Science, was dead.

of living has been given a good deal of consideration, and for some time there has been formulating a science of living.

Perhaps no one is to blame for the fact that the science to teach people how to live [in their environment] has been so long in getting any attention. . . . Men built houses long before they knew how to live in them safely.

The implication was clear. Before people build a new environment, they had better learn to live in this one. Otherwise, the very base of what is built will be flawed.

She suggested, subtly, that perhaps the real reason why man built houses without knowing how to live in them was that woman, the traditional caretaker of that environment, had been denied the education that would have augmented man's knowledge. Rather, knowledge was imbalanced and "has created many victims," as well as progress, she said. Woman is man's balancing factor, especially when it comes to environment. Together, they can live right, in a right environment, she said. But first man would have to let his counterpart catch up with the knowledge creating a new environment.

There will be more "victims of science" in the future if we do not educate woman with knowledge that will allow her to manage space, time, and technology and to educate her children on how to live in a rapidly changing environment, Ellen warned.

In the words of the *Globe* reporter, ". . . she wittily reviewed man's endeavor to make life easier for women."

"To relieve women from drudgery, fathers formerly sent [daughters] to finishing schools and gave them lessons in the fine arts. But all of these semi-polite accomplishments turned to dust and ashes literally and figuratively in the crucible of life . . ." that is the home environment.

"They walled up the beneficient fireplaces and introduced airtight stoves and put washbowls in rooms to save steps, but they forgot to make the plumbing safe. The result has been to kill off all the delicate men, women and children . . . in greater numbers than any war has ever done," she said.

Then she "scathingly" attacked, not only the educational system that would permit this ignorance among men and women, but also the ignorance by which the learning environment itself was allowed to exist—"erecting improperly ventilated and un-sanitary buildings" in which children are supposed to learn. "They do learn, you know. But they learn to grow up and create more of the same kind of environment in which they learned.

"If that is the environment in which they learn, then that is the environment they learn to live in. How can we expect them to know, let alone teach or live a better way?"

Then she made her appeal:

And now I ask you here tonight to stand sponsors of the christen-ing of a new science and to give the same your fostering care and generous support. . . .

They nodded, applauded, and "rang" their spoons in approval.

Then Ellen introduced her protégée, Mary Hinman Abel, to discuss environment from the concept of "Cooperative House-keeping." The world is our common environment and it is changing, said Mary Abel. "It will do no good for one or some of us to keep it in better order. It is a task required of all who occupy it." Mary Abel deplored the resistance "by one man to another man's desire" for a better environment. It must be cooperative, she said.

"The next advance depends on a more thorough education" of the idea that a "better house" kept by everyone would, "like any other industry . . . show a decent return for its given outlay," universally.

In closing her part of the program, Mary Abel added a danger-ous thought: ". . . the solution that wealth buys is no solution." In fact, she said, when it comes to a healthy environment, wealth "in a narrow range . . . is often in defiance of laws." Whether she meant the laws of nature or those of man, they were harsh words to throw at the ears of nineteenth century capitalists.

After Mary Abel, the dynamic Alice Freeman Palmer took the stage. Identified by the *Globe* reporter as a graduate of "Swal-low's Laboratory (though in fact, another Alice Freeman seems to have been confused with the educator), she represented to the group the programs and support for this new science in the Middlewest, particularly at the University of Chicago.

She called for more emphasis on environmental education in schools and colleges, lamenting her own ignorance about "plumbing once it gets under the ground." She pointed to the reason there was not more such education: "There are so few to teach it."

"There are only three or four in the entire country" qualified to teach this new science, she said. Two of them were on the podium ". . . and another has just begun her work at the University of Chicago, Miss Marion Talbot of Marlborough Street, daughter of Dean Talbot of Boston University."

But women should not be the only ones to learn the roots of environment, Alice Palmer said. Men should "not be exempt from learning [it]. It is no less important that they should know when the plumbing is unsafe, the water polluted, or the air unhealthful," especially when it is men who design, manufacture, and install such systems.

She hoped the time was at hand "when along with everything else that is being taught in the colleges, this most necessary branch of science should have an honored place in the curriculum."

She outlined the University of Chicago's courses on "sanitary air, water and food," and referred to "the dread scourges of diseases that are terrifying the entire community and which would easily be overcome if sanitary living were better understood as it will be when there are people to teach and everyone appreciates the value of being taught."

In better syntax, much the same is being said in calling for environmental education in schools today.

Then this foremost educator acknowledged those higher institutions "dropping into line" to teach the new science: Brown, the University of Pennsylvania, and others. She congratulated Pratt Institute, New York, as the most recent addition.

The hour was late. Ellen Swallow had scheduled the right speaker to close—"the Honorable Edward Atkinson." Atkinson took the occasion to demonstrate his invention, the Aladdin Oven, a device that made possible the cooking of cheap, unpopular cuts of meats without destroying their taste or food value. Nutrition was a basic part of environmental science as seen by the Oekologists. To the delight of the audience, Atkinson opened "the contraption," and pulled out "a tough old hen . . . made as tender as Spring Chicken," the *Globe* reported.

Having presented the public purpose of her environmental science, Ellen Swallow announced:

For this knowledge of right living, we have sought a new name. . . . As theology is the science of religious life, and biology the science of [physical] life . . . so let *Oekology* be henceforth the science of [our] normal lives . . . the worthiest of all the applied sciences which *teaches the principles on which to found . . . healthy . . . and happy life.*

And, she might have added, to assure future environmental quality.

It was done. Acknowledging the comments and good wishes of the audience, Ellen and Robert thanked their friends and left the Vendome. Walking the quarter mile to Back Bay station for a train to Jamaica Plain, she felt satisfaction. She had invested the labors of nineteen years in her presentation of Oekology. Perhaps Robert Richards eventually prepared her for the great disappointment to come. But tonight he wouldn't spoil his wife's mood. Yet both scientists knew that no science had ever been made public property before. And that was exactly what she had proposed. She must have noticed that most of her friends in science were absent from the christening.

Right now, though, she was optimistic. Looking back on her achievements, she had good reason. One way or another, the many things she had started she had seen succeed. One way or another, she thought, she would see that environmental science spread out through the homes and schools of America to establish standards for peaceful coexistence for people and environment in the future.

People were the source of environmental quality and its pollution; individually and collectively. Government and industry, science and technology—all have a common human root. It was only logical, Ellen Swallow idealized, to go to the root of a problem for the source of a solution. She had seldom been wrong in the past. But with Oekology she was never more wrong in her life.

THIRTEEN

The Consumer-Nutrition Movement

The oekologists—years before they were so christened by Ellen Swallow in 1892—worked from her multiple matrix, which consisted of two main wings, each with two subdivisions: Consumer-Nutrition and Environment-Education. She drew no lines between them. In her comprehension, everything seemed to overlap.

America's consumerism began in her MIT and home laboratories and continued throughout her life. But in 1884, another dimension bloomed inside industry itself when Edward Atkinson appointed Ellen Swallow industrial chemist to the Manufacturers Mutual Insurance Company.

Manufacturing was crude then. Plants were hostile environments to the men, women, and children who worked there. Fires and explosions were as common as their uncommonly high costs in human health and property. Dismembering, blinding, and fatal accidents were "part of the job" for the fatalistic worker; they were "overhead" to the practical employer of the nineteenth century. In the rush for productivity and profit that followed the Civil War and led to the labor movement, worker health and safety was as incidental inside the plant as the increasing pollution outside. There were always more people looking for work. There was plenty of air and water. Such resources were expendable, natural bases to exploit for profit.

If the corporate conscience was undeveloped, so was industrial science. Mostly it involved the bolting down and loading of basic machinery. For greater productivity, more machines or more workers were added. When space ran out and demand increased, all were made to go faster or longer. These adjustments weren't always compatible with safety or profit. The strains presented hazards. None was more sudden, devastating, or costly than a fire or explosion that could obliterate a plant and its workers in minutes. Textile mills especially faced this problem.

In America's largest industry, textiles, Massachusetts was the capital. Railroads brought cotton north and wool east to the giant Merrimac, Amoskeag, and hundreds of smaller mills where mechanical looms converted them to cloth for New York, Chicago, and the world.

Insurance, too, was a young business, grown up in the need to underwrite risks of shipping cargo from place to place. Factory fire insurance was younger; the factory mutual system, younger yet. Fire insurance for textile mills had been prohibitive. The risk of fire in stagnant environments filled with inflammable cotton, wool, and cloth was too great. In Massachusetts, the mills mutually underwrote their own fire insurance. When Edward Atkinson became the second president of the innovative Manufacturers Mutual Insurance Company, he introduced the then new science of statistics (he was one of the founders of the American Statistical Association) to find that more than half of the mill fires came from friction and spontaneous combustion. He turned to science for solutions.

With Ordway, Ellen Swallow had worked on industrial problems for ten years before her 1884 appointment. An early and continuing aspect of that work was to create scientific apparatus that would allow experiments and study under identical conditions. In her new office, she was not just a designer or science consultant to a single company; through its policyholders, she influenced the entire textile industry. With her work, Atkinson could and did dictate new safety standards and factory procedures later adopted by other industries.

Machines make friction. They need oil. Bigger and faster machines create more friction. But they need more than just more oil. At that time they needed better, standardized grades of oil. They required new oils and new processes. Ellen Swallow learned that evaporation rates of oils used in factories ranged from 1½ to 25 percent! Prices of oils for the same processes varied from 29 cents a gallon to $1.05. The amount of lubrication used to make 1,000 pounds of cloth varied from 68 cents to $2.58. If a manufacturer could buy at 29 cents, why pay $1.05? If he could process 1,000 pounds of cloth for 68 cents, why pay almost four times that much? Science showed why.

Low-grade oils became gummy fast at high machine speeds. Friction increased; friction created sparks; sparks created fires and explosions. Some oils had lower ignition points than others. But they had the same potential danger from too much spark. Still other oils evaporated faster into gases, exposing bare steel to bare steel for better ignition, bigger explosions.

With Swallow's scientific data to back him up, Atkinson forced suppliers to improve their oils or to find new ones. For him, she pioneered the testing of oils for industry long before there was an oil industry as it is known today. To some extent, she helped spur the research and development functions so important in modern petrochemical industries.

When one oil man threatened a "suit of law" after Atkinson forbid his product in the mills, "I [Atkinson] immediately urged him to enter in court as I desired to publish [the scientific] facts . . . But I advised him . . . to change his oil instead."

Ellen won international recognition for her work in this branch of science, too—not by her name so much as by the names of her processes. Her Evaporation Test for volatile oils became a world standard. Her investigations into ". . . the recovery of wool grease . . ." not only won acclaim, it brought industry "enormous profits." Her study of cottonseed hulls "found great commercial value." She might have been a wealthy woman had patents not been denied the applied scientist.

The cost of mutual fire insurance dropped dramatically. "Several members . . . reported their savings in the cost of lubricants . . . had been more than the cost of their insurance," Atkinson noted. The savings from injury, death, lost time, damaged goods, and property gained by fires and explosions that never took place were much greater.

Spontaneous combustion was an even greater problem than

friction in the factories of the 1880s. The oil needed to reduce friction increased the hazard of spontaneous combustion. To Ellen, the solution was simple enough in theory. Execution was more difficult. After the chemist put in motion studies that would develop noncombustible oils, she turned to physics "to introduce the first systems of scientific air circulation in American factories." Ventilated, the textile mill was less susceptible to spontaneous combustion. Though these systems also gave fresher, cleaner air to workers, the plants were still unhealthy environments, she knew. She made a note to do something about that, too.

Meanwhile, Ellen Swallow joined in Edward Atkinson's expanding work for fire prevention. They tackled the problem of fires as an ongoing experiment to devise a fire resistant design and construction of factories that became known as "mill construction." This too was copied throughout industry. Chimney-like peaked roofs were eliminated for flat, less draft-producing structures. Floors were lifted, ceilings lowered to create space between them—vacuums to insulate against fires. "Hot spots" were removed from walls; pipes and flues were relocated and redesigned. New materials like asbestos cellboard, lathe and wire, plaster and sheet metal were tried. It was more than reminiscent of her undergraduate "dream house" and her work with "artificial stone." She grew obsessed with the idea that new building materials be found by science; that products be subjected to scientific tests in the factory and for the factory as she was doing in her home lab.

Atkinson did precisely that when he devised sprinkler systems, automatic firedoors, water hydrants on the roof for his factories, and insisted that suppliers come up with better, safer, more durable products. To reward the only supplier who made a better fire hose, Atkinson permitted it to be sold with the "Underwriter's Fire Hose" seal of approval. Swallow and Atkinson talked about establishing a laboratory for insurance underwriters to test products and processes and find new ones. In the 1880s, though, fires were Atkinson's main interest.

"Four fifths of all fires . . . in my judgment . . . are due to stupidity, negligence, carelessness or crime," he said. To his industrial chemist, this sounded a lot like the manufacturer-wholesaler-retailer plot compounded by consumer ignorance. Swallow became an authority on fires, holocausts that struck every large city at least once in its history. She also knew ". . . we burn nearly two hotels a day . . . a hospital or almshouse every two weeks. . . ." She hoped her work would be of some use to ease this suffering.

Atkinson was not a quiet man. He condemned "combustible architecture" and the "imbeciles and criminals" who allowed it. He wrote to the mayor of Boston:

> Jordan Marsh & Co., are putting up a very large building at Kingston and Bedford Streets. I intend to caution my family not to pass it lest it fall and crush them. . . .

Atkinson said its cast iron beams would allow it ". . . to stand [only] as long as it is not exposed to heat." He believed that the design, however, "is susceptible to fire." It is the architect's fault and the company's ignorance, he said, but the city is responsible.

A city inspector was dispatched. He found no violation of "The Acts," and the building went up while the architect, a Samuel Thayer, threatened suit—by that time old hat to Atkinson. On November 28, 1889, a Boston paper published the epilogue to the incident.

> The largest fire since the Great Disaster of 1872 broke out at 8:00 AM yesterday in the splendid block on the corner of Kingston and Bedford Streets . . . Twenty buildings . . . were destroyed. . . .

Surveying the city, Swallow and Atkinson found fire escapes on schools that wouldn't work even when there was no fire. The same was true of other public buildings. "I find hospitals in which the inmates are exposed to cremation before they are dead. . . ." he wrote.

As the massive, handsome Atkinson cut his outspoken swath through the established order, the small, plain woman constantly at his side quietly provided the truth of science for his arguments. They would be telling arguments in the years ahead. There was no insurance for public buildings, hence there were no standards of safety in design or construction. Schools would be the first to correct this terrible oversight. When that happened, Ellen Swallow would be responsible, but only at great professional sacrifice.

The industrial chemist took her findings from the factory and community back to her MIT laboratory, where she taught them to succeeding generations of students. It was during this period in the early 1880s when a young man she had first met on the interior decorating committee of the Woman's Education Association enrolled at the institute to study chemistry, particularly the brand of industrial chemistry taught so meticulously in her class. The particular attention to detail stressed in her classes is illustrated in a story told by another student, who, "making a large and careful experiment," felt the instructor's watchful eyes. Walking over to the desk, Swallow said softly, "You are wasting motions. Two trips to the scale are not necessary when one will do." Time and motion, not just substance—efficiency—was the industrial science she taught.

Arthur D. Little was not in that class that day. But this man who became a close friend and frequent guest of the Richards would go on to build the world's largest commercial laboratory for industry on just such principles of science.

Industrialist Edward Atkinson was interested in Swallow's scientific visions, too, especially in nutrition, ". . . when my attention was called to the quality of food the men [in the mills] were eating for lunch."

The year she became his industrial chemist, Swallow had begun another book, *The Adulteration of Food*. The book analyzed the second side of her pure food consumer movement. She discussed it with Atkinson. It is one thing to write about bad food; it is quite another to do something for good food, she said. Food science should develop this field, so overlooked since Rumford, 100 years ago. But like industrial chemistry, the lack of apparatus to test food preparation under identical conditions was an obstacle. This time Atkinson performed the role Ordway and Swallow had provided for him.

Pulling together Rumford's writings and the known physical principles of heat, Atkinson invented the famed Aladdin Oven. In addition to making possible the scientific study of food preparation, it was the prototype for today's modern home and industrial ovens.

"A rectangular outer case of wood about an inch thick, insulated by an inner lining of asbestos . . . over a steel oven core . . . [the Aladdin] had an air space to allow circulation around the oven internally. It stood box-like on four legs high enough to allow a kerosene lamp to be placed underneath. A hole in the bottom allowed heat from the lamp to circulate through the air passages around the oven." Food was loaded through a side door onto moveable shelves in the 18- by 12-inch interior. A thermometer outside completed the apparatus.

The Aladdin Oven permitted slow, controlled cooking, a process that also allowed tender, tasty preparation of cheaper, tougher cuts of meat. "An astonishing success in savings of food and fuel . . . over iron ranges and cook stoves," said one authority. Atkinson demonstrated his "contraption" to whoever would watch and listen. "It can do anything but fry; it can stew, simmer, bake and roast and can readily prepare 20 pounds of food a day [for] not more than two cents worth [of oil]."

The oven also allowed Swallow's experiments with ". . . the proper conversion of food materials" for maximum human nutrition. Accumulating data, she retained Dr. Charles Allen, head of the State Board of Education, and Dr. Augustus H. Gill, a former student, to prepare large charts illustrating the human body's chemistry in relation to materials found in food. With these impressive and instructional charts as backdrop, Swallow hit the lecture trail for better human diet. According to a prominent doctor, it was ". . . the first popular use" of such illustrations to show the mineral composition of foods and human needs.

Swallow's brand of food science did not depend entirely on popular education, however. She used the charts and other data in a second appeal—with the impressive Atkinson at her side this time—to the American Association for the Advancement of Science in 1885. Rapidly the movement gained momentum. In 1886, the American Public Health Association—organized in 1871 by Stephen Smith and up to now primarily a men's organization— invited Ellen Swallow to join. In recognition of her work in other aspects of public health and her scientific expertise, she was made a member of APHA's important Laboratory Committee. A year later, in 1887, Henry Lomb, of Bausch & Lomb Optical Company, asked her to judge the APHA competition for "the two best essays on sanitary and economic cooking adapted to persons of moderate and small means."

Studying the seventy papers submitted, she chose one by an American woman living in Europe who had seen the influences of Rumford in the Volkskuche and Fourneaue Economique public nutrition kitchens in Germany and France. "There is no second paper," Swallow ruled. In New York to present the Lomb Prize ($500), Ellen Swallow met Mary Hinman Abel. Neither woman realized how soon their paths would cross again.

Back in Boston, another woman was waiting to see Ellen Swallow about the nutrition wing of her crusade. Mrs. Quincy Shaw, Louis Agassiz's daughter, offered "a sum of money to study the food and nutrition of the working man and its possible relationship to the question of liquor." Just how, she left to the scientist. Sometime in 1889 Ellen Swallow got the idea for her Food Laboratory.

She spoke with Atkinson and wrote to Mary Hinman Abel. The latter agreed to spend six months as manager of the lab; Atkinson would donate the ovens and help raise additional money, some of which came from the Elizabeth Thompson Fund. On January 1, 1890, the New England Kitchen opened at 142 Pleasant Street, Boston. This was a different kind of laboratory in several ways, not the least of which was the fact that it was open to the public.

The kitchen was called "an interesting failure" by one critic. "A reconnaisance into unexplored territory" was a better description of America's first combined health food restaurant, poor people's kitchen, and nutrition laboratory. Its ilk has not been seen since, and its legacy to public health and food science is incalculable.

Swallow planned the kitchen as a place to perfect ". . . the most nutritious cooked food for the smallest sum of money." Paradoxically, the first response to it came from the city's rich. Doctors prescribed its food for their patients. One eyewitness reported physicians stopping by "to take a quart of nutritious and savory broth" along on their house calls. The well-to-do clamored for its "health giving foods."

Slowly, from no small effort, others came too. ". . . A feeble old man brings his pail . . . dainty looking young women . . . workers in shops . . . teachers . . . or students come [with] their shopping bags. Little children black and white [bring] pails, plates, bowls, and pitchers. Old and middle aged women appear, some apparently prosperous . . . others with the stamp of poverty and hard work fixed upon them. . . .

"Is this a charity or a money making enterprise? It is not exactly either. Its object is to cultivate [among the poor] taste for good, nutritious food scientifically prepared from the cheaper food materials. . . . Besides the many experiments made daily at the Kitchen, analyses of some of the dishes [are] made weekly or daily at the Institute of Technology. . ." Maria Parloa wrote in *Century Magazine.*

At first the kitchen was a take-out restaurant, open for daily lunch and dinner. But the poor wanted to leave as soon as they bought their food for fear of being seen there, while the rich who stood in line wanted to stay and be seen. An "eating room" and a delivery service were added for those either proud or shy of their patronage. "It was quite the place for us college girls," one patron remembers.

A poster in the window and circulars passed out in poor neighborhoods read:

The New England Kitchen, 142 Pleasant Street . . . is now prepared to furnish the following cooked foods:

Beef Broth for Invalids	12 cents a quart
Vegetable Soup	12 ” ” ”
Beef Stew	12 ” ” ”
Fish Chowder	12 ” ” ”
Potato Soup	12 ” ” ”
Tomato Soup	12 ” ” ”
Pea Soup	10 cents a quart
Pilgrim Succotash	12 cents a quart
Pressed Meat	12 ” ” ”
Corn Mush	5 cents a quart
Boiled Hominy	5 ” ” ”
Oatmeal Mush	5 ” ” ”
Cracked Wheat	5 ” ” ”
Indian Pudding	16 cents a quart

The menu grew with experience. But the base fare was scientifically formulated bread, beef broth, and milk, evaporated without the use of sugar. Not only were these among the first scientifically devised foods in America (some were developed at the MIT laboratory), the kitchen also innovated "Community Taste Panels." "Each dish is . . . perfected by the cooperation of the whole neighborhood . . . tasting and commenting to obtain a cosmopolitan flavor," a technique industry would later use.

The evaporated milk developed by the Kitchen Laboratory, so important in the unrefrigerated summers, at 7½ cents a pint, may have been the best buy in town. To find the largest pure milk supply, Ellen went to Orange and Montgomery Counties in New York where her patronage helped develop the New York Health Food Company. Testing the milk in Boston's hospitals alone affirmed her stand that the Kitchen was not the failure some would have others believe.

"The fact that every child put on a diet of this milk during this summer has been saved, would alone justify the existence of the Kitchen," she wrote. Still, there were those who criticized the experiments in the Kitchen as a social plot. Atkinson, too, rose to its defense. "If nothing else had been accomplished but the mere example . . . this wide education [for] the whole world justifies the outlay." He was not exaggerating. The many off-shoots of the New England Kitchen firmly established nutrition in America, not just in science but in the public sector as well. It was soon to become an international attraction.

As agreed, after six months, Mary Abel left the Kitchen to join her husband, who was teaching at the University of Michigan. Sarah Wentworth, Ellen's friend, student, and live-in from the old Women's Laboratory days, replaced her. Before the trio broke up, however, Mary Abel, Edward Atkinson, and Ellen Swallow went together to the "A₃S." There, food science was winning ever more support.

Within a year, a second kitchen was opened in Boston. Next came Providence, Rhode Island. Then:

"I was in New York four days hunting a place for the Kitchen," Ellen Swallow wrote Anne Mineah in 1892. Shortly after, ". . . I go to New York once a month at least to look after [the] kitchen." She also lectured at colleges and clubs in towns along the way. She visited Pratt Institute, a new school, to set up a "Domestic Science" course.

Letters came in from other towns and cities—from Buffalo and Chicago. The Kitchen's rising reputation was such that the state asked the MIT scientist to build an exhibit representing them at the World's Columbian Exposition in Chicago planned for the next year. It was this kind of success that gave Ellen Swallow the confidence to think she could take Oekology to the public in December 1892.

Even while she looked at food from this higher plain, as part of environmental science, however, the practical Yankee kept a hard eye on its day-to-day applications. A staff member of the Kitchen complained "the Indian Pudding is not well received. . . ." Ellen's solution was to "turn them over." Upside down Indian pudding became a top seller. (In the restaurants of Boston, Indian pudding still is upside down.)

With all her high-level plans, the daily attention to nagging details, Ellen Swallow was always ready for the unplanned, the unexpected.

"Miss Talbot is laid up with multiple abscesses on the eyebrow and nose. She was seriously ill last week . . . I [took] her classes at Wellesley. This means cutting up my time pretty fine . . . you see it is not a favorable time to ask me to do anything," she wrote to a group that wanted her help on a "women's project" at the exposition. She declined that connection. Other events, however, were leading her west.

Jane Addams Hull House in Chicago was interested in the New England Kitchen. There also was a rumor that Alice Freeman Palmer would leave Wellesley with her Harvard husband for the University of Chicago. Marion Talbot might go, too. Anne Mineah was already living in Chicago. She had helped organize a Western Association of Collegiate Alumnae, modeled after Ellen's eastern organization. Then Ellen, Anne, and a few others had worked to merge the groups, and they succeeded finally in 1889. Now the Chicago women, with such as Mrs. Potter Palmer and Mrs. Charles Henrotin, joined parts of Ellen's multidimensional crusade. She traveled frequently to Chicago on these matters and was eager to represent the State Bureau of Hygiene and Sanitation with her Nutrition Kitchen exhibit at the exposition. Then a "minor complication" arose. There was no money, the state said.

In March 1893, the entire burden of this project fell on her shoulders. Mary Abel was downed by scarlet fever. Atkinson, too, was ill. Both had promised to help her.

"My Dear Mr. Atkinson: I am sorry to hear that you are not

well. I hope you have quite recovered. It will not do for you to be an invalid now—people will say the science of nutrition is humbug . . ." Sick or not, she asked him for "8 or 10 used" Aladdin Ovens that "are not being used." Of course he agreed.

By May, Atkinson was healthy again. "I am glad you are back —I miss you when I know you are beyond reach. . . . I have about half the money I need—the remaining $2,500 I shall borrow if I can't beg it. . . ." Her plan for the kitchen was taking shape, but a national economic crisis was starting to form, too. Once again she turned to Atkinson.

> You must put on your thinking cap for me and help again. I must have a bank account of $5,000 to draw on for expenses. Most of it —I hope all—will come back in the fall—but I can not do this hampered for a dollar. Shall I get my life insured and offer it as security or will some of our friends loan it for the purpose, do you think? I will come tomorrow—Sat.—if you will telephone to me that you will be at liberty for 1/4 hr. either at 10 or 12:45. You can always send a message thus—"Tell Mrs. Richards thus and so"— but do not try to call me to the telephone to answer, please. . . .

Of course, the chivalrous Atkinson would not hear of her life insurance plan. Her begging and borrowing paid off. The money was raised and Ellen was on her way to the fair, ". . . the most wonderful exhibition of American brag, courage and persistence . . . a grand scene [of] everything good and bad at the same time . . ." she wrote. In the summer of 1893, in a small frame building at the south end of the World's Columbian Exposition in Chicago, hundreds of thousands of people saw the Rumford Kitchen. Those who went inside read a menu with food values computed to price. They saw a "scientific and educational exhibit" of glass walls to show the visitor every kitchen procedure, an innovation to encourage laws requiring restaurants to be open for public inspection. The doors and walls of nineteenth century eating places hid a host of sanitary evils, Ellen knew.

The Rumford Kitchen was an enormous success. Signs with pithy sayings attracted crowds flocking to sample the healthful food, and nutrition became a national movement. But the exhibit drew praise from more than its visitors. America's medical schools and universities recognized and praised the effort, especially Johns Hopkins, where Mary Abel's husband was teaching and where Ellen Swallow's Baltimore followers had secured the admission of women to the medical school as a condition to raising the money needed to open it.

The Rumford Kitchen was cited for "the first public use of such food terms as proteids [sic], carbohydrates, and calories, et al."

"The event that made nutrition a matter of public education" demanded only part of Ellen's time at the exposition, however. She also set up an exhibit to promote The Society for Study at Home. She was delighted by the extra enrollment she signed up. Unofficially, she advised on at least one other educational exhibit there. "The trouble is, the humbug is the one who has the most money to spend . . . the good work must take a back place," she said.

Always one to use her time and situation to best advantage, during the fair Ellen also introduced nutrition to Hull House in Chicago. Working through a new staff member there, Julia Lathrop, she indoctrinated the kitchen staff and gave them an operating plan. "Call me if you need anything else," she told them. Then, as the fair drew to a close, she went to see Alice Palmer, dean of women, and Marion Talbot, helping her at the University of Chicago. Rather than take the Rumford Kitchen back to Boston, she sold it to the university, confident her protégées would see to it that Oekology was included in the school's kitchen, as well as the classroom.

Returning to Boston, tired but pleased, she learned the true impact of her success in the Midwest. Everyone, it seemed, had seen the value of nutrition. Doors were opened to her she hadn't known existed. People who had criticized the New England Kitchen praised the Rumford Kitchen at the Columbian Exposition.

A publisher approached her. Would she lend the kitchen's name to a new magazine venture? The Rumford name belongs to the state, she told him. It is not for commercial exploitation. But she would agree to name the publication *The New England Kitchen Magazine,* providing she had some say in its editorial and advertising policies. She despised the exploitation of public ignorance she saw in most mass media. It would not happen to this one, she promised herself.

The New England Kitchen Magazine started with a flourish. It gave Ellen Swallow a regular channel into the homes and minds of the American consumer. She excerpted her books, rewrote and reprinted her articles, and kept up a steady barrage of information not always complimentary to manufacturers and advertisers. Other food scientists around the country and abroad found editorial space in the magazine that seemed to be on its way to becoming one of the most successful "shelter" publications in America.

There was one event that gave her more encouragement to "christen" Oekology than any other, however—an invitation, when she returned from the exposition, to address the annual meeting of the Massachusetts Medical Society. For an applied scientist, this was the ultimate recognition.

Her hair was snow white now, in stark contrast to the jet black eyebrows and fiercely intent eyes. Her stern voice reached out to that august body.

The best form of provender and the right quantity of nutriment have been carefully determined for horses, cows and pigs. Whatever we know about food for human animals is, in large part, derived by analogy. . . . Heretofore, civilized man has proclaimed, as his God-like privilege, and as a proof of his superiority to animals, the right to eat what he liked, whether it was suitable or not, and as a result, he has been compelled to employ a band of skilled magicians to exorcise the devils . . . invited to enter his body. But man is . . . only an upright animal, amenable to the same laws of growth and decay as other[s]. . . . The science of human nutrition is to play a larger part in therapeutics than heretofore and it will be of great advantage to the physician to be able to prescribe certain food requirements with as much confidence as he now prescribes medicine. At present, he has less confidence in the cook than in the druggist, hence the latter has often to make good the deficiencies of the former. The various "extracts" and "prepared foods" have come into use because of this need, but they are too often made with little regard for truth or for science.

In spite of her reference to doctors as "skilled magicians" and bad diet as a stimulant for the use of medicines, which would graduate to abuse in the twentieth century, the speech was well received by the doctors.

"I am writing an outline of some lessons on food for the sick to be given to the medical students. . . ." she wrote soon after.

Now, she thought, is the time to take maximum advantage of the movement's popularity. Now is the time to take nutrition to where it will do the most good. The magazine was already putting translated digests of the world's nutritional studies into. the home, so in 1894, Ellen Swallow approached the Boston School Committee to introduce nutritional lunches into the public schools.

With the prestige of medicine's acceptance of nutrition, the success of the fair, and the availability of the Kitchen supporting her, the school committee thought her suggestion "a good idea." Go ahead, they said, with a pilot program. The pilot soon flew into unexpected resistance.

School lunches in Boston, as in most cities at that time, were prepared and served to children by school janitors. The janitors did not think her proposal a good idea, for obvious reasons. They weren't eager to give up the duty or the revenue it brought. The oekologist explained she had nothing against the men themselves who emptied garbage, swept floors, and cleaned toilets in the same clothes they wore to handle food and serve children. But the school board politicians were worried. The janitors, they knew, could vote. Women couldn't.

Before they could reverse their decision, however, Ellen rushed the kitchen into operation over the protest and without the cooperation of the rebellious janitors.

Then, in a scenario resembling some of today's educational confrontations, the janitors pressured the school committee. Intimidated, the committee ordered the Laboratory Kitchen to serve all school students at the same time or the program would be scrapped. Apparently they thought they had hit on a solution. "All or none," they said, sure the project would collapse under the impossible demand. Hardly begun, the school nutrition lunch program faced extinction. Even Ellen was pessimistic.

Then, "smelling a good fight," the crusty Atkinson threw his weight into the battle.

Neither janitors nor politicians were quite ready for this lion. Quickly raising money for more equipment and personnel, he cowed the opposition long enough for the cooks to cook. The students ate and the janitors stewed. But the school nutrition program—the first of its kind—went on.

Next a new group tried to undermine the program. Restaurant and store owners in school neighborhoods—egged on by their janitor customers—also felt threatened. Signs began to appear in store windows aimed at impressionable minds. "Don't Let Anyone Tell You What You Should Eat," and, "I'd Rather Eat What I Want Than What Someone Says I Should" were typical.

Unknowing parents, convinced their children were guinea pigs in some dark scientific scheme, joined the opposition. It was a campaign based on ignorance and weak will, not unlike some television advertising today.

Thanks to its leadership, the lunch program survived the assault. Soon 4,000 school children a day were fed from the food laboratory. The program was established. It continued for at least thirty years into the next century, transferred to the Women's Educational and Industrial Union after Ellen Swallow's death. More important, it was adopted gradually by public school systems throughout the country. She would lead this movement, too, through the Association of Collegiate Alumnae and by creating a new food science and a new profession for women.

Ellen related food value to the potential value of human life. With Atkinson's help, she took the same nutrition lunch program into America's factories. Atkinson could see the advantages of a healthier work force, even if some labor leaders couldn't. The "Shin Bone Diet," they said, was a scheme to reduce living costs so that management could pay lower wages. Nevertheless, Massachusett's textile mills first, then more and more factories operated by enlightened industrialists around the country called on Ellen Swallow to improve the diet and the condition of the American working man.

From Boston's public schools and Massachusetts's factories, she pushed nutrition kitchens into the center of life of other American institutions. In 1894, she returned to Chicago. There, with Julia Lathrop, she put the final touches on the Hull House kitchen and set in motion nutritional studies that would have national precedence and impact. She stopped off at the University of Chicago to tabulate the results of a test program she had set up with Marion Talbot. When results were published that year, "Food in Relation to Student Diet," the scientific paper opened still other doors to better food in American colleges. As these new opportunities presented themselves, Ellen Swallow was there waiting.

"I believe it will be held a crime in the twentieth century to lure young bodies and minds to college under the pretense of education only to poison them slowly with bad . . . food," she said.

She believed nutritional food, properly balanced and scientifically prepared, was a vital element in the environment affecting human health. But she advocated such an improved subsistence for more than just the average child, worker, and housewife. Ellen Swallow believed food had therapeutic value as well. Now, added to the growing number of schools, colleges, factories, and settlement houses, she introduced therapeutic nutrition into hospitals, asylums, jails, and other institutions. If she couldn't prove better diet actually heals ailing bodies and minds (like she suspected that sunlight or air gave it added value), certainly it aided the healing process.

She expanded the hospital dietary studies she had begun at Massachusetts General Hospital in Boston. Published in *The Journal of Insanity* and other media, including consumer publications in the mid-1890s, her reports of these studies built a nationwide interest in the work and a demand for her scientific services. She won permission to study the foods and physical conditions of the inmates of "The Nine Institutions of Boston" for a special commission formed to study the facilities.

What she had intended as a subdiscipline of Oekology became —after Oekology's rejection—the new field of dietetics: the efficient and scientific feeding of institutionalized persons in schools, colleges, factories, hospitals, jails, and asylums. She became a national consultant on the subject, not just for the improved quality, but for the economic savings she built into her programs. Her students and protégées became the first dieticians. In some cases, she took over an entire operation herself to get it started, bringing in trained staff to operate the kitchen along the lines of her plan. Other times she just recommended. But she always insisted that whoever ran the operation have full control of food, from purchasing to serving to waste disposal and the supervision of every related procedure. At educational institutions, she fought to have these experts posted to the faculty to teach what they knew about foods.

All this activity added immensely to Ellen Swallow's hope for the future of her interdisciplinary environmental science. How could they accept its major parts without accepting the total? she thought. But if she was optimistic before, her hopes soared in 1893 when she was given the opportunity to make nutritional science a part of United States government policy.

Abraham Lincoln had created the Department of Agriculture in 1862, envisioning it as "the people's department" rather than the servant of agribusiness it would become. Thirty years later, Ellen Swallow added her own democratic scope to Lincoln's vision.

Congress had enacted legislation for agricultural experiment stations in each state and territory. W. O. Atwater, a well-connected food chemist whose career had been stimulated by Ellen Swallow's extensive work and following, was appointed first director of this new government office.

Work in the experiment stations should cover more than just soil, sunshine, and rainfall studies; produce and its preparation also should be subjected to science, she believed. But how to penetrate the Washington maze to make her point? The answer was very close to her. Edward Atkinson had been a prominent Washington figure since President Lincoln's time. He was especially well connected with the Department of Agriculture through his work on the economics of cotton and the introduction of new seeds and grains in America. While Atkinson worked on his friend J. Sterling Morton, Secretary of Agriculture, Ellen prepared the materials and collected the I.O.U.'s of Atwater. As much as Washington was a man's world then, the views of a woman nutritionist married to a mineralogist were seen in her collaborators' economic theory that:

Land itself may be exhausted when treated as a mine; it may be maintained when worked as a laboratory . . .

It was Ellen Swallow who personally drew up the ground rules for government nutrition tests. In 1892, she had written with Atkinson listed as co-author, "Suggestions Regarding the Cooking of Food Materials." Her "Nutritive Value of Common Food Materials" was "one of the first public bulletins ever put out by the Department of Agriculture." An "important factor in public education," it meant a lot to Ellen that she had not only won investigation of nutritional factors by government, she had secured public access to the results.

She initiated the very first technical bulletin issued by the Department of Agriculture as a result of these investigations. "Methods and Results of Investigating the Chemistry and Economy of Food" was hers also. It outlined ". . . the essentials for cooking apparatus, cookery of meats, composition of beef, beef tea, pea soups and the keeping qualities of food." The New England Kitchen's legacy loomed larger; a very "interesting failure."

Now she turned back to the original purpose of her kitchen laboratory: the diet of the poor. Her Philadelphia and Chicago studies, "Food Consumption and Dietary Habits of Families Living in Thickly Congested Districts," were very probably America's first scientific analyses of the diet of ghetto dwellers. These studies she saw incorporated into government documents, too. "Dietaries for Wage Earners and Their Families" was another effort to understand and improve the conditions of poverty, this time for the New Jersey Board of Health.

The food laboratory became an even busier place. In "The Distribution of Phosphorus and Nitrogen in Products of Modern Milling," she examined the quality of flours for the home. "The Effect of Heat on the Digestibility of Gluten" added to the findings of German scientists on the compatability of vegetable aluminoids. Her own and Mary Hinman Abel's accounts of the New England Kitchen were published, reprinted, and merchandised to an expanding public consciousness through an expanding media and consumer interest in nutrition.

All this was enough to occupy the energies of the thousands who now followed this wing of the movement. But it was, incredibly, hardly half of Swallow's work during this period. While the early Oekologists grew more and more enamored of these more attractive aspects of environmental science, still there was much work to be done on the less interesting but equally important matters of air, water, and sewage. There was not the public appeal in these elements that there was in food and consumerism. Nevertheless, there was work to be done.

FOURTEEN

Environment-Education

Nature has done much for our country and man is rivaling Nature . . . perhaps natural in a country where Nature defied man. A new race is springing up to whom the labors of Hercules will not seem impossible. An enthusiastic Yankee, I am afraid I am of the present age which tears away the veil to see what is behind. . . .

Ellen Swallow made that statement in 1872 when she first put her mind to the matter she found in Massachusetts water. By 1884, twelve years later, she had seen behind the veil. What she saw was frighteningly grim. Her words became more urgent, sadly similar, if dated by style, to what is said about the environment crisis today. The basic difference was that the crisis was just beginning then.

This is the urban age, the age of cities . . . most of the ills science is called to cure arise from [its] crowded life.

But even then her analogy of the house environment had a modern, McLuhanesque ring.

"The house is sort of an outer garment . . ." she said. People are offended if you criticize their environment, "as if you told them their boots need blacking."

[But] science has to apply its knowledge to [improve] that unit of the community, the home; for upon the welfare of the home depends the welfare of the commonwealth. Upon this common

141

factor should be lavished whatever knowledge and science this century has.

This was her theme as she made her way along the popular lecture circuit in the days before film, radio, and television entertainment. But she was not always so entertaining.

"We need missionaries who will go among the people and show the dense darkness in which they are living," she preached. And she became chief of that mission.

Using statistics from England, she told her audiences how 16,600 people scattered over 100 miles were likely to lose 282 people to environmental conditions each year. When people were drawn together within fourteen square miles, deaths increased to 415 persons. Concentrated in a one-quarter mile area, 647 or one twenty-fifth of the population would die.

She spoke of the mythological city of Hygeia where environment would be improved by science to halt disease. She quoted estimates that during each year for the five years since 1880, 102,000 lives had been saved in England alone by just rudimentary environmental improvements. To attain Hygeia, a Herculean task awaited. Back in Boston, she got on with it.

In MIT's Sanitary Laboratory, behind the small glassed-in office at one end, was the place where she proved the growing proportions of the crisis.

Her awareness of the problem grew with "her journeys often," as Caroline Hunt poetically phrased this woman's perpetual motion. Always she returned to study what she collected and gleaned on these trips. As her inventory grew, so did her concern. Environmental quality became her paramount objective, the desire to wake others to the crisis, her obsession.

The concern spilled over into her private life. She became a feminine version of the legendary Johnny Appleseed in the cause for pure water. When friends announced plans to move or to build a new house, the Richards's "housewarming gift" came before the fact—an analysis of the water supply of the site, complete with equipment, installation, and maintenance suggestions. Considering the high rate of typhoid and other water-connected diseases at the time, theirs was a gift of lifelong value.

She performed similar services, usually without charge, for schools, hospitals, and churches. "She was the first to recognize the importance of pure private drinking water supplies," said Dr. Bryant. "The half of what she did to save human life will never be known," said others. Simultaneously, she studied water supply from the public point of view—local and regional water supplies and their handling and treatment. Her concern for both —private and public—she planted wherever she went, irrigating her ideas and hoping for a human harvest of government awareness. She waited impatiently for approval to make a thorough examination of Massachusetts's water resources.

The seeds of her labor sprouted in other places. The Summer Seaside Laboratory was now so successful it threatened to close. Paleontologist Hyatt had done his work well. In 1884, the student lab attracted no less than "a distinguished assistant to Dr. A. S. Packard. Another is Harlan Ballard, president and projector of the Agassiz Society . . . now exercising a marked influence upon some 8,000 persons of all ages and in all parts of America."

But the Woman's Education Association could no longer support the venture. Tuition did not begin to cover costs, now approaching the astronomical sum of $5,000 a year. The winter of 1885, Ellen spoke with MIT's young biologist, William Sedgwick. On January 3, 1886, she wrote,

". . . We have been deep in plans for a summer laboratory on the coast . . . and had yesterday a meeting of some 20 biology teachers to consider the matter. . . ." More participation was needed, perhaps more space. Ellen and Bea Capen planned a trip to Cape Cod the following summer.

Then suddenly everything seemed to come to a halt. All Ellen Swallow's plans had to be put aside. Word from Europe said William Ripley Nichols was gravely ill. Surgery was scheduled there. She waited for Robert's return from the West to give him the bad news. He arrived, pale, damp, and feverish. She knew the symptoms too well. The word that passed her lips so often now seemed unutterable: typhoid! Robert's case was complicated with pneumonia. In those days, either took the lives of most victims. He had both.

She drew up a strict schedule of diet and duties when the staff volunteered to stay with her through the siege. "We managed to plan [his] work so the students have not suffered," she wrote. "Of course, my outside work has all been put aside."

Later she referred to the period as "our very great trial. . . . He was out of his head for four weeks and many days we despaired of saving him." The crisis passed in three months. But it was almost two years before Robert Richards completely regained his health. Meanwhile, his wife took over some of his mining engineering classes. At home, in her quiet evening vigil, she busied herself by expanding her *First Lessons in Minerals* pamphlets into a full-length book published by the Boston Society of Natural History.

As the germ raged in Richards's body, Nichols died in Europe. This pioneer sanitarian left one last posthumous contribution to his school, to science, and to Ellen Swallow. Among his effects was found a bacteria culture from Robert Koch's laboratory in Germany. Its gelatin mold had liquified by the time it arrived in America. But always the expert chemist, Ellen managed to salvage some of the specimen. With Sedgwick, she spent hours studying the rare organism.

In the days when gentlemen gave their seats to women but not their chairs in science, a newcomer, Dr. Thomas Messinger Drown, was appointed to fill Nichols's vacancy at MIT's Sanitary Laboratory. There was no apparent rancor on Swallow's part. ". . . still the number two man," she quipped. In 1887, when the legislature finally appropriated funds for a statewide survey of Massachusetts water and sewerage, the oddly named duo of Drown and Swallow were in charge.

It was history's most thorough analysis of water resources— "unprecedented in scale . . . a classic in its field. . . ." Already partially planned by Nichols and Swallow, it was executed almost wholly by Swallow and the corps of personnel she had personally trained, selected, and supervised.

For nearly two years she analyzed the water and sewerage of 83 percent of the state's population—twice each month—adhering to strict clinical controls. In what must have been a delivery organization to rival the pony express, samples from every source—streams to seashore to the green Berkshire mountains— were rushed immediately to her laboratory.

Her system required that each sample be analyzed "within two hours." If they arrived too late or were mishandled in extraction or enroute, the work lagged and the load doubled. Worse, "gaps" were left in the meticulously detailed profile she was composing of the state's most valuable resource and refuse.

It was hard work. Setting the pace, it was especially hard on her. Although on a "formal schedule" from 8 AM to 6 PM, she worked much longer. At home, Robert was still recuperating.

"I have been under water since June 1 of last year. . . ." she wrote in the spring of 1888. ". . . it will be the same for another year."

Before it was over, she would personally analyze, in whole or in part, each of more than 40,000 individual samples of water. More than 100,000 analyses were made in the study.

"I worked fourteen hours a day on five and sometimes seven days of the week," she said. But not just analyzing water and sewerage. This was the first sanitary chemistry laboratory, its work the model for other states, nations, and universities. She perfected the laboratory, constantly modifying the procedures and equipment as the survey progressed. In her persistence for accuracy, speed, and efficiency, she discarded some, refined others, and designed new methods and equipment. But unknown even to her, a new discovery was about to be made; it would be a fundamental contribution to the world's undeclared war on water pollution, one of the first tools to fight that battle.

At the end of each day, Swallow personally tabulated the results of analyses, marking them on a large map of the state of Massachusetts she had hung on the laboratory wall. As the Great Sanitary Survey neared completion, she studied the map and its markings.

To visualize the data, she drew lines to connect those areas in the state where water chemistry was alike. Gradually these lines began to look like today's TV weatherman's map that shows pressures and flows of temperatures and moisture. She meant to illustrate for uneducated eyes a dramatic profile of the state's water pollution. But the map was about to expand her education, too.

Carefully she drew her lines—isochors—over the map. Stepping back, she noticed a new form taking shape. There on the map on the wall, staring out at this woman so concerned with inland water quality, new "coastlines" for the state were taking shape. The lines she had drawn to connect almost identical pollution points were astonishingly similar to the actual shape of the craggy Massachusetts coastline, which she knew so well.

Chlorine, Swallow knew, is the one permanent resident of water. Once there, always there. All other impurities are transients. The oceans are "the great natural repository" of chlorine. Coastal waters naturally contain more chlorine than those further inland. But over the ages, winds, rain, and snow carried the "salt" spray inland, too. Hence the "coastlines" across the state appeared on her map.

This "one new important fact" gave civilization a way, if it would take it, to "photograph" the normal chlorine content of water. From this "picture" man could tell scientifically in the future how much of the pollution in water was natural and how much was caused by human, municipal, and industrial waste.

An early warning system for inland water pollution was born. But it also seemed to sound another alarm. There was higher chlorine content in ocean water closest to the coastline. Was this natural or man made? Was man polluting the ocean, too? How long these facts of progressive pollution would have eluded a society concerned more with productivity and "progress" than with environmental sanctity is hard to say. It is not impossible to say, however, that the Normal Chlorine Map gave man an opportunity to make a choice between progress and environmental sanctity based on scientific fact. Nor is it impossible to see today which he chose.

It was never revealed who actually named the Normal Chlorine Map, nor has Ellen Swallow ever been singled out for the credit due her environmental work. Perhaps the abstraction that is the environment was too far beyond the comprehension of either science or government then. If so, credit withheld—like wages, titles, and degrees—has built interest over the years.

The survey intensified her concern for the Seaside Laboratory. The w.e.a., in 1887, said it had done all it could. Probably with Swallow's guidance a letter went out "to prominent naturalists, seeking advice."

On March 5, 1887, a meeting was held in the library of the

Boston Society of Natural History, Bouve's successor, Samuel Scudder, presiding. "Twenty-one persons" from Harvard, Wesleyan, Williams, Tufts, Smith, Wellesley, the Shaw School of Botany at St. Louis, and MIT appointed a committee to form a corporation. The W.E.A. voted to transfer the laboratory at Annisquam to the corporation, thereafter known as the Marine Biological Laboratory. Three W.E.A. women, two of them former students of Swallow, were appointed to the board. Another, Florence Cushing, was made a trustee along with Hyatt and Sedgwick "to receive funds." Through these people, her presence assured, Ellen Swallow contented herself with her usual anonymous back seat, as a member, contributor, and unofficial advisor.

In 1888, the laboratory was moved from Annisquam to Cape Cod. It was located at a quaintly named area of Hyannis known for its rich flora and fauna, Woods Holl at Buzzards Bay. Botany was added to the field of study, and a Dr. C. O. Whitman, a morphologist of Clark University in Worcester, was appointed director. By 1891, the facility had 189 students, teachers, and researchers from all points of the United States and Canada. Seventy-eight colleges and lower schools across North America affiliated to support the work.

No less than two other water sciences were nurtured at this facility: oceanography and limnology, the latter being a kind of fresh water version of the former. Ellen Swallow had a leading role in the founding or development of each, especially limnology, although the history of it credits more her work than her name. Ironically, as the Marine Biological Laboratory developed its botanical and zoological functions, she contributed in a way to the defeat of her Oekology as the public environmental science.

Back at MIT, there were more direct results of the Great Sanitary Survey. Her work produced the world's first Water Purity Tables and established the first state water quality standards in the United States. America took the undisputed leadership in this basic phase of environmental knowledge. Because of the survey, the State Board of Health was also persuaded to look after sewage in the state.

The sanitary survey resulted in the world's first modern sewage treatment, as well. Some ground work had been done in

Europe. But the Lawrence Experimental Station, opened by the state in Lowell, began to test newer, better methods to manage and treat sewage. The contribution of that lab to modern sewage treatment was greater than all other such facilities combined, the experts said.

Here again, everyone got due professional credit, and then some, for his part in this revolutionary work. Everyone, that is, save Ellen Swallow. Hiriam Mills, the board of health politician who dared put the survey's recommendations into effect, was called "The Father of Modern Sanitation." William Sedgwick, the young biologist Ellen Swallow helped become a bacteriologist in the sanitary lab, was named "The Father of Public Health" by those who chose to overlook Stephen Smith's contribution in founding the American Public Health Association in 1871.

Swallow's students, Edwin O. Jordan, Allen Hazen, and C.-E. A. Winslow went to work early at the sewage station and on to international acclaim for the great sanitary scientists and engineers they became. Ellen Swallow, who taught them all more than they knew or admitted, had personally executed the survey that brought the laboratory into existence. Dr. Thomas Messinger Drown got official credit for that.

In the chauvinist record of this unique series of events, Swallow gets a footnote as "assistant to Edwin O. Jordan," her student a year or so before, if not after he took on the assignment that she very possibly arranged for him.

In the official history of the Massachusetts Board of Health, Mills is credited with the vision of bringing together "the various scientific . . . and engineering" capacities that gave America supremacy in treating sewage, as well as producing it. But whose vision really was this concept?

"It is clear [Mills] had to begin from 'scratch'," the record says. But whose "scratch" was it? "Lacking the background of other people's findings," the record goes on, "Mills was nevertheless able to combine the talents of an amazingly productive group of engineers and chemists and biologists and to lead them in an attack upon a single goal: the safe disposal of sewage."

There is a political scent, as well as the taint of chauvinism, to that publicity. Politicians have always been eager to take credit from science. As long as the politicians pay for the posture, science is always ready to cooperate. Yet if the men got fame and fortune, the missionary got what she wanted, too.

Mills said he "discovered" Allen Hazen. But who recommended this outstanding chemistry student to the Lawrence lab? Jordan is credited as being the "first in America to study the process of nitrification . . ." of sewage. From whom he studied is seen in what appears to be Jordan's first professional paper, published in 1890: "Investigations Upon Nitrification and the Nitrifying Organism," by Edwin O. Jordan and Ellen H. Richards. Winslow, who followed later, likewise, learned from Ellen Swallow. But if the teacher was the proud promoter of her students, they seem less able to recognize her common role in their success.

It was a man's world then, in spite of Swallow's trail blazing, especially in science. She was well aware of the situation, content to accept it as long as she could still contribute to its correction. But if these were the "fathers" of their individual fields, she was the "mother" of them all.

A clearer picture emerges at MIT. In 1889, the Department of Biology was fully formed, offering MIT's first course in bacteriology. That it was made at least partially possible by the sanitary laboratory work seems a moot point, even at this distance in time. Then, in 1890, another new course was added: the first of its kind in any college in the world: sanitary engineering. Ellen Swallow taught this amalgam of chemistry, bacteriology, and engineering, according to Caroline Hunt, educating the men who went on to design and operate the world's first modern municipal sanitation facilities. "Missionaries for a better world," she lectured them.

The Sanitary Survey, an unparalleled success, inaugurated a new era in environmental improvement. Recognizing the need for continuing scientific analysis, the board of health underwrote yet another environmental facility, the State Water Laboratory. Not coincidentally, it was located in Ellen Swallow's cubicle at MIT. This was her reward, and she was happy for it.

While in 1891 the males won bright feathers for their caps, the white haired woman at the center and source of their knowledge was looking forward to yet another new field. The next year she would unveil her new science of Oekology.

There was more to Ellen Swallow's view of environment than water, however. In 1887, she had directed student Marion Talbot on a thesis, "The Determination of the Organic Matter in Air." In spite of an accident that left Ellen to get around on crutches or with a cane, she began teaching the treatment of air: ventilation, humidification, and heating. In 1892, she took on a new course, air analysis, to go with her water analysis and sanitary chemistry classes. In 1893, the year after Oekology's debut, she stepped up the pace.

In her published study, "Carbon Dioxide as a Measure of the Efficiency of Ventilation," delivered to the World Congress of Chemists, she urged cities now spending millions for water and sewerage treatment not to lag behind on the matter of air.

"The reason for this apathy is not far to seek. Chemists and sanitarians have disagreed . . . as to what constituted 'bad air'." She proceeded to clarify that not air, nor even the odors it carries, "but . . . the dust particles bearing living germs and spores is to be attributed the cause of disease; therefore filtered air like filtered water had become a necessity. . . . The resistance [of] healthy blood and tissue . . . to disease . . . is, we believe, due to the perfect nutrition of the blood . . . and this is largely dependent on inhalation of air containing sufficient oxygen." The individual inhaling "bad air, then, is poisoned from within rather than from without." Air is food, she said, like water.

She urged chemists and sanitarians to combine and "urge on the community the importance of a sufficient supply of air . . . especially in school rooms [where] these views will command more respect . . . than heretofore.

"The Laboratory of Sanitary Chemistry at the Massachusetts Institute of Technology has had, for the past nine years, exceptional opportunities for the study of air. During these years, some 5,000 determinations of the amount of carbon dioxide have been made," she reported. (They were "the findings of some 200 students" she had supervised in those studies, many of whom would come to her aid in a vicious battle forming over the issues of air, water, and sanitation.)

She proposed during this period a study of "the distance bacteria travel like airplanes from the force of a cough," a doctor recalled.

Her work with water continued, too. "The Coloring Matter of Natural Waters, Its Source, Composition and Quantitative Measurement," completed in 1895, is a landmark study, quoted in college textbooks as late as 1950. Here she exposed myths about colored surface waters not all as poetically named as Thoreau's "Meadow Tea." The work identified the sources, processes, and analyses of naturally colored water.

In 1896, her "Laboratory Notes on Water Analysis," a comprehensive survey course of the composite water science she helped found, was published by MIT.

> The examination of water . . . to determine its fitness for domestic use . . . comprises the determination of three points: first, the amount, if any, of organic matter in a living or dead condition suspended or dissolved in the water; second, the amount and character of the products of decomposition or organic matter and their relative proportions to each other; and third, the amount of certain mineral substances dissolved in the water. From these . . . we draw conclusions as to the present condition and past history of the water.
>
> To facilitate this examination, waters may be divided into three classes: first, brook, pond and river water—so-called surface water; second, spring and deep well water; third, shallow wells and sewage effluents.

She seemed to be succeeding with this wing of Oekology, too. More students—at least hers—showed an interest in the careers being offered in these new fields. But, as she put it, the scientist "will drown in his own work if no one takes it up." It is not enough to use this knowledge in classrooms. It must be used in the community. That point came home to her sharply in an 1894 incident when Ellen Swallow was elected a trustee of Vassar College and went to Poughkeepsie for her first meeting.

The trustees took up the matter of sewage disposal at the school. Vassar had been dumping its wastes into nearby Caspar-kill Creek. The practice had not yet killed anyone named Caspar, but it made for an unhealthy environment downstream and along the Hudson River, six miles away.

The townspeople were complaining about the problem. The trustees were asked to approve a pipeline that would by-pass the

Casparkill and dump raw sewage directly into the Hudson. Careful to observe propriety at her first meeting, the alumna restrained herself. She sat in respectful silence until asked to speak.

"What are your thoughts, Mrs. Richards?"

"It seems to me," she replied softly, "that an educational institution should lead rather than follow." To discharge raw waste into public waters, she thought, was "medieval," be it the Casparkill, the Hudson, or a local reservoir.

"Well, then," asked a pipeline proponent, "what would Madame suggest?"

More than suggest, Ellen drew them a picture. It was a sketch of a new and reliable method of treating waste, "a sewage disposal plant that will neither pollute the water nor sicken the population." More, it might be used to fertilize crops.

"Ah, yes, but the cost?" they asked.

"Much less," the oekologist assured them, "than six miles of ditch and pipe." And it was. Installed, the unit she designed from her experience at the Lawrence Experiment Station cost $7,500, compared to the $50,000 the administration was prepared to pay for a far worse method. The real savings, she knew, however, were not in dollars.

This 1894 incident may have warned Ellen Swallow what would happen to her first environmental science. If trustees of a major college were so unconscious of environment, what could she expect from the rest of the world?

As the nineteenth century went into its last five years, Ellen Swallow was grappling with the strings of the sub-sciences she had woven together. But each string seemed to pull away because of its own weight. Still, that wasn't her worst problem with Oekology. There were destructive forces at work as early as 1893. Each year, each project, each step forward in each individual phase of Oekology seemed only to make those forces more ominous. With every advance that should have enhanced the total, a reverse pressure seemed to set in.

There were three major problems confronting Ellen Swallow's Oekology. It was, in spite of the validity of its parts, seen as an unpedigreed, mixed breed by the specialized science aristocracy. Less and less support for its interdisciplinary knowledge was growing toward total rejection of the concept.

There were other problems in the times and in the temper of the times. Scapegoats, if not witches, were being hunted out for the changes that were complicating society as the nineteenth and twentieth centuries came together.

The third problem was the oldest, and perhaps the most insurmountable. Swallow and most of her Oekology followers were women, and too few were scientists.

Ellen Swallow suffered great professional and personal disappointment in the years from 1895 to 1900. She also won some of the most important battles of her "pugnacious" and "interloping" lifetime. But each "victory" was a defeat for Oekology. By 1898, its interdisciplinary body was not yet quite dead. But bleeding badly from dismemberment, the torso was claimed for "higher" undertakings. Ellen Swallow was left with the pieces.

FIFTEEN

Backlash

The demise of Ellen Swallow's Oekology began even as she was christening the public science at the Vendome Hotel that November night in 1893. In Europe, life scientists were staking out a narrower, purer scope for Haeckel's word. America has always followed Europe's lead, especially England's, and particularly in science. There was support, if not always advancement, in looking back for the way to proceed.

Ellen's ideal of humanism in Oekology was doomed when the September 16, 1893, *British Medical Journal* went to press with its definition: "Oekology uses all the knowledge it can obtain from [morphology and physiology] but chiefly rests on the *exploitation* of the endless phenomena of animal and plant life as they manifest themselves under natural conditions." (Author's italics.)

Eventually, circulation of this view in the hierarchy of science spelled the end for an environmental science that included the human factor, especially an applied science and more so for a public application of science applied to man's environment. Humanity's "natural conditions" would be exploited by science and technology without concern for human and environmental consequences. Swallow's purpose—improving the environment for people—was rejected. If these omissions weren't enough to arrest the development of her subversive science, the fact that a woman dared usurp man's christening powers was the final death knell.

Let your women keep silence in the churches: for it is not permitted unto them to speak; but they are commanded to be under obedience, as also saith the law. (I Corinthians, 14:34)

In a similar man-made judgment, the high priests of science in the 1890s condemned an environmental science founded by a woman. "Everyman's House" was repossessed and exorcised of all the humanity save that which filled the circle of life science. Plants and animals were responsive to environment. But not man. Heredity predestined the human species, not environment, they said.

Not until fifteen years later would Oekology—respelled Oecology and then Ecology—dare to touch the common man as Ellen Swallow had proposed. Even then, the flirtation would be brief and suppressed. Environment is more than plants and animals in the technological twentieth century. Ellen Swallow knew that long before science would admit it.

She realized the important role life science must play. She had tried to interface morphology and physiology, paleontology and bacteriology, even botany and zoology. When Whitman, Hyatt, and Sedgwick et al. absented themselves from the Vendome ceremonies, perhaps they told her of the heresy of her proposal. But Oekology was more than a proposal to the woman who had worked since 1873 to develop it.

Slowly, as the decade progressed, the trunk of life science pulled away from the branches of physics and chemistry in Ellen Swallow's Oekology. As it pulled away, however, Ellen Swallow never did concede complete defeat.

There were other complications. To understand what happened to Oekology and our environment, one must understand that decade of misnomers. The Gay Nineties were gay only when they were very young and very old. In between was one of the most turbulent periods in American history.

Monetary instability over gold vs. silver vs. greenbacks vs. tariffs, as well as imports and exports, brought the Panic of 1893 and the greatest industrial depression in the nation's history. Trade was unbalanced. America's gold flowed out at a rate unequalled until 1972. The United States Treasury verged on collapse. Depression flowed down through every fiber of society. Angry reaction boiled up through the same channels.

United States population growth was at its highest. Immigration ports were flooded with foreign born. Farmers with large families flocked to cities for factory jobs. Chicago doubled its population to one million in ten years. New York had that many people in slums alone. Crime, violence, drugs, alcoholism, prostitution became epidemic. Corrupt political machines formed on these social sores. "Reform!" the nation demanded in the midst of depression.

The labor movement was organized. Bloody strikes broke out. Higher wages, shorter hours, and better working conditions were demanded and refused. Industry "couldn't afford it." Organizers were beaten and killed in the street; executives were shot in their offices. Fortunes were lost; others were hoarded to buy later at depressed prices. Mortgages were called. Banks closed. Stocks fell. Profits collapsed and factories closed. Unemployment soared.

The second half of the Gay Nineties brought another apocalypse. In a Cuban harbor, the United States battleship Maine exploded. In New York, Hearst's *Journal* and Pulitzer's *World* hired artists to dramatize in color on the front pages events that never happened. Yellow journalism was born. And an American legend was launched when New York's police commissioner formed an equestrian elite to charge up San Juan Hill. America's war with Spain brought Teddy Roosevelt to the White House, his Great White Fleet to the Pacific, and Big Stick Imperialism to the United States.

Edward Atkinson exploded, too, soon after the Maine. This foremost expert on fires said his studies showed the ship exploded from spontaneous combustion, not Spanish sabotage. The war was a farce, he said.

> . . . The Maine carried a large quantity of bituminous coal of a type highly liable to spontaneous combustion . . . located next to the ammunition chambers, on the outer skin of the ship . . .

Skirting the center of the depression-reform-war cataclysm was another provocation: social feminism. The women's movement was at its greatest strength since Abolition. Women fought for freedom from economic and political enslavement; for better pay for themselves; for release for their children from factories and mines; for better hours and better working conditions.

Some women attacked industry as a heartless criminal, government as an accessory before and after the fact. Others broke up bars and saloons, perhaps encouraging Samuel Gompers to make the labor movement a "closed shop" as far as females were concerned. So women formed their own unions.

Consumer leagues were very real pressure groups. They organized factory workers, sales clerks, and the customers, too. But underlying nearly all the social feminist factions was suffrage, the *Common Cause* as one group named its house organ.

Ellen Swallow and Oekology were caught up in the maelstrom. Among the feminists' "pronounced manhaters" who attacked all things male, she found justification for her long stand against sexual separatism.

"I prefer to give my time and influence to work in which men and women are in accord. . . ." she said. When asked to serve on the women's board at the World's Columbian Exposition in Chicago and to exhibit in the women's building there, she declined.

> . . . I have racked my brains in vain to find anything which as a woman I have done . . . which could be shown as woman's work. The only thing I can think of is a little course on minerals . . . for the public schools . . . my work in the main is so interwoven with that of men that it is impossible to separate and it would be an injustice to do so. The 200 young men and 100 young women, my pupils, are my best exhibit and they are not available.

The exposition managers insisted. Certainly there was something this distinguished woman could show. She wrote back:

> From the start I have declined every appointment on the women's branch . . . and I do not know how it happens that my name is still on your council. . . . I do not wish to be identified with a body, the very existence of which seems to be out of keeping with the spirit of the times. Twenty years ago I was glad to work on women's boards for the education of women. *The time is now some years past when it seemed to me wise to work that way.* (Author's italics.) Women have now more rights and duties than they are fitted to perform. They need to measure themselves with men on the same terms and in the same work in order to learn their own needs. . . . [Separatism] seemed always a mistake to me and one which I prefer not to be connected with in any way. . . .

Her stand was all the more vigorous because of the tenor of the times and Oekology's precarious position. Support from men in science was imperative. But Ellen Swallow—and Oekology—were trapped by her sex, as well as her work.

As thousands of people across the country seized on the scientist's words to fight their battles for better health and environment, Swallow was in no small way guilty of the brand put on her as a reformer. Since most reformers were women, the trap was unavoidable.

She had criticized medicine. "The essential principles of health are not understood by the people . . . and, alas! not by all our physicians, who as a rule have been educated to cure disease, not to prevent it. Too many have been taught to fight Nature's Laws, not to stand by . . . as her adjutant."

She offended city planners, real estate people, professionals, and artisans. A population concentrated in a small space allows swollen rentals for small, sunless, and smoke-filled houses. People, she said, must challenge labor, industry, and government to secure better conditions.

"Find out . . . the rules [in your city] and report to the Health Department if they are not obeyed. . . ." Insist, she urged, on better sewers, water, and refuse handling. Make cities clean up their air. Food, too, must be improved.

Scientific skepticism has not yet touched the purchasers. . . . Manufacturers are not slow to perceive this and to take advantage . . . To meet the craving for variety it is only necessary to make slight changes in the outward appearance of common substances, and then to advertise widely the discovery of some new process by which the food value is [supposedly] increased tenfold.

The modern "pure food" manufacturer is a sophist who, with great skill and by the aid of the well-paid expert, persuades the general public that he is their benefactor in that his chemists have penetrated Nature's secrets, hidden from the ordinary man, and therefore he is able to offer them long life and prosperity at so many cents a pound.

She exposed that offer and showed how to respond to it.

Production is limited by choice; manufacture ceases when demand ceases; hence . . . to influence production, choice must be wisely directed.

She helped direct that choice, much to the chagrin of powerful people. She identified poor goods in the marketplace. She exposed the practice of adding "annatto, caramel and carrot extract" to color watered milk. She refuted by chemical analysis the butterman's myths and his lobbying on the dangers of oleomargarine. Oleo was safe, she showed chemically, but "it has become a not infrequent practice to add as much as one-third of curd or other nitrogeneous materials to fresh butter. If eaten at once, [this] is not dangerous." But few families ate a pound of butter "at once."

She also put the finger on grocers. "Learn what markets are clean . . . pay attention and they will become cleaner . . ."

By the emotional measure that was often the feminists mode, Ellen Swallow was not a reformer. Acting within the quiet discipline of science, she was. To an economic and political establishment beseiged with criticism, her scientific exposés were the most difficult testimony to refute. There was, of course, one way to dismiss her: as a woman dissatisfied with man's world.

Her letters during the depression show her sensitivity to this danger as she saw anti-feminism on the rise.

"It was perfectly clear the majority of the men were with me," she wrote of her speech to New York's Nineteenth Century Club.

A lower profile might have been a wiser, if less noble, course during this inflammable time. But Ellen Swallow had never achieved anything through inaction. Then, in 1894, her experiences in the school nutrition lunch project drew her slowly, inextricably into a national confrontation that put the brand of "radical" on Ellen Swallow and brought the final rejection of her ideal of Oekology.

At the Vendome, she had made her most important point on the environment-human relationship when she said: *the environment that people live in is the environment that they learn to live in, respond to, and perpetuate.* If that environment is good, so be it. But if it is poor, so is the quality of life within it. Whichever it is will influence the quality of living and learning in the future.

What she saw in the learning environment called the public school seared her senses. Not even in factories or jails had she seen such "disgusting, degrading filth," she reported to the authorities. When they said they doubted it was all that bad, it made her angry. When they said there are no laws that say we have to do anything about it, the fifty-two-year-old scientist turned organizer. She would see that there *were* laws.

In the Boston branch of the Association of Collegiate Alumnae, the Woman's Education Association, and the Boston School and Home Society, Ellen Swallow formed school sanitation committees. She assumed the direction of each and brought them together to pressure the politicians. Still they resisted. She realized, a co-worker said, "such arguments have little effect unless supplemented by many other types of pressure by forces of which [the politicians] stood in awe." If that was the game, Ellen Swallow would play it for keeps.

In 1896, the nation's foremost physicians and hygienists gathered for the annual meeting of the distinguished American Public Health Association. With the press in attendance, they sat back in their chairs as a woman approached the podium. In front of the world, Ellen Swallow delivered a paper that charged politicians, parents, and "the great tax paying public of Boston with the murder of some 200 school children a year."

"The chivalry and justice of man can not be depended on in cases where self interest in the acquisition of power or money is concerned," she began.

"Fully one half of [Boston's] school houses [are] deleterious to health . . . 5,053 cases . . ." of disease among students are caused by poor, illegal conditions: no ventilation, open sewer pipes, filthy toilets, and buildings where "41 percent of the floors went unscrubbed since laid." Out of 186 school houses, only twenty-seven had fire escapes that worked, she said. These conditions killed more than students, her data showed. Boston teachers had the highest death rate in the nation.

Ellen Swallow's brazen paper rudely awakened a nation to the evils of disease, corruption, and indolence in America's public schools. The city of Boston—"The New Athens"—was shamed in front of the world. When Ellen Swallow asked the American Public Health Association to assist in reforming the schools of Boston, the city so proud of its academic heritage was humiliated. Instead of changing the schools, however, they challenged the reformer. The politicians refused to budge. Ellen Swallow, on her part, refused to give up. She scheduled more speeches.

Children die by the hundreds, back alleys remain foul . . . the
streets unswept; school houses . . . unwashed, danger lurks in the
drinking cups and among the towels. Dirt is stirred up each morning with a feather duster to greet the warm, moist noses and
throats of children. . . . it seems like [politicians] dancing in the
streets and making merry on the eve of catastrophe.

She wrote articles for national publications. "Health and
Schools" she published herself to mail across the nation. The text
of a speech she called "Municipal Responsibility for School
Houses" was printed and circulated.

It was, according to one who studied the incident, "a dark
chapter" in the history of Boston's education.

Ellen Swallow realized, however, the problem was not confined to the City of Boston. She appealed for help to the National
Education Association. When the city still refused to act, she
organized a citizens committee to go over the politicians heads to
the state legislature. She appealed to educators and opinion
leaders in other states and organized a showdown in 1897 between them and Massachusetts state legislators.

Cornered and outnumbered, the legislators agreed to consider
the citizens' grievances. A committee was appointed to draft
them.

In five succinct points, the committee proposed to reduce the
size of the political school committee; take educational policy
from the politicians and give it to school superintendents; give
teachers a voice in course and text selection; create volunteer
committees of parents in each ward of the city to meet with
teachers on education matters; take finance from politicians and
hire professional "business agents."

James Phinney Munroe, an internationally known educator
and officer of the MIT corporation thirty years later, reviewed the
campaign.

For four years this committee of hers fought the powers of reaction in extended hearings before the Legislature. In this uphill
contest, [she] took a leading part, though with her usual modesty
she kept herself scrupulously in the background. In . . . conducting
the campaigns [she showed] in a superlative degree her special
qualities: pugnacity, tempered by extraordinary tact; thorough-

ness, leaving nothing to chance but making certain every witness
should be present, and that the testimony of all the witnesses
should be both impressive and cumulative; and wisdom. . . ."

In four "masterly campaigns," only one point passed the legislators: the removal of money from the control of politicians to a
business agent. "At the time, it seemed like failure," but "within
two or three years . . . bills passed under which the schools of
Boston were greatly changed for the better. Her experience enabled her to assist many other cities in similar fights . . . and the
infinitely better school conditions of 1928 are due, in unreckoned
measure, to the initiative and hard work of this versatile woman."

The school fight had grown from a sanitary reform issue to
include curricula, administration, finance, personnel, and community responsibility for education. She had led a ward-by-ward,
city-by-city, state-wide overhaul that eventually reached out to
the nation's public school system. Interestingly, the two points of
her plan that were not made law left a vacuum from which a
national parent-teachers association and teacher unions would
evolve in the twentieth century.

Ellen Swallow had won an enormous victory. But the bitter,
highly publicized battle did irreparable damage to her standing as
a scientist. She made many powerful enemies.

"She has deserted science," they said. So science, it seemed in
the late 1890s, deserted her.

Reform had reached its peak. Reaction set in to expand the
search for scapegoats. The heel of repression came down on
women nationally. At least one college—in Connecticut—re-
versed its policy and closed its doors to women. Others, on the
verge of admitting them, reconsidered. Fewer than 5,000 women
had graduated from American colleges at this point, but nearly
50,000—almost half the total enrollment—were in colleges. There
were less than a million activists in the woman's movement, but
they had the sympathies of 3 million more. And the leaders were
educated women. It was proved that women's higher education
didn't damage their reproductive organs. What it had done to the
men in industry and government was another question.

When the backlash came, Ellen Swallow felt the sting more
than most. In social reform, the reaction of power is a force

the rebel can exploit. To the scientist, who looks to the establishment for support, disfavor weakens. And Ellen Swallow had earned a lot of disfavor.

"Keep the feathers well oiled," she wrote, "and the waters of criticism will roll away." As they did, however, stains were left on Ellen Swallow's good standing with the establishment.

Strange things began to happen in her work. First, the *New England Kitchen Magazine* publisher withdrew his support, just when the publication had achieved success.

In 1896, when Thomas Drown left MIT for the presidency of Lehigh University, rather than appoint Swallow to head the state water lab, it was pulled out of MIT and put in the statehouse.

Boston was building America's most modern water supply system, connecting water resources, building reservoirs, dams, and other facilities throughout the state. Although city authorities may have made use of her work, Ellen Swallow herself seems to have been overlooked in this monumental undertaking in which she would have been a leading authority.

Sedgwick, she learned, was forming a national society of bacteriologists. She was not invited to join.

Also in 1896, Florence Cushing and seven trustees, including three women and Ellen's old friend Samuel Scudder, president, were ousted in a coup d'etat at Woods Holl Laboratory.

"All the enterprises in which I am involved seem . . . to be in an uncertain condition. . . . There have been many perplexing things during the summer," Ellen wrote.

Even her work with Atkinson seemed to taper off. Atkinson and MIT President Walker had "fallen out" earlier. But Atkinson was now helping the Institute solicit needed funds from the state. Perhaps the legislature cautioned President Walker about a certain faculty member so much in the news and in their hair. In any event, with Atkinson and MIT back on good footing, Ellen's hope revived in the Underwriter's Lab they had discussed over the years. Then she learned that Professor James Norton, another newcomer, had the inside track on that project.

Her association with Atkinson outside the Institute was hardly an asset anymore. He had become an ardent environmentalist, even buying the Brookline Reservoir to save it from speculators. He also published a book in 1896, *The Science of Nutrition*. Ellen wrote the foreword and Andrew Carnegie bought it for American libraries. But Atkinson was deeply involved in America's monetary controversies. He had printed $50,000 worth of phoney money and spent it enroute to Washington to convince the Secretary of the Treasury that merchants would accept any substitute. "The old curmudgeon," was more volatile than ever, attacking political parties, candidates, the postal department, the cabinet and the president alike. He was about to come tooth to tooth with Teddy Roosevelt over the Imperialism issue.

In 1896, Ellen resigned as a Vassar trustee after only two years. She said it was to make room for a western woman on the board of the eastern college. She nominated Julia Lathrop from Chicago and was bitterly disappointed when the seat went to another easterner instead.

The incident paralleled a problem in the Association of Collegiate Alumnae. The group had become quite conservative. In 1889, she had engineered a merger with the Western Association of Collegiate Alumnae through Anne Mineah in Chicago. But to her mind the group needed more and fresher blood from the far West and South, where more than 150 colleges were considered "inferior." Critics of the A.C.A. said the organization had become an elitist "trade association for teachers."

There were personal losses, too. Fanny Swallow passed away. So did "a woman who meant so much to our early work with the W.E.A." Minnie Glover died in childbirth. Robert was laid up again, "blindsided" by a bicycle. Ellen was back using her cane because of a resprain of the ankle she had injured earlier.

Slowly, the nation shrugged off its many hurts.

"I wish you could see the signs of prosperity. . . . We are all delighted over the [Boston] subway . . . [and] the rearrangement of Copley Square. The Institute is rejoicing in the prospect of a goodly sum . . . $500,000," she wrote.

Ellen Swallow paused to appraise her situation. It could be worse. Even if Cushing was out at Woods Holl, Ellen's original influence was present in other ways. Women outnumbered men there.

There was other evidence of her work: better municipal water and sewer systems, cleaner streets, and better schools across the nation. There were tables and standards for air and water. The first pure food laws had been enacted. The federal government was involved in nutrition, and it was preparing its first water pollution bill, which became the Refuse Act of 1899. Thanks to her legions, better health, environment, and education were spreading across the country.

Her state water lab was gone, but MIT's Institute for Water Analysis under her took its place. Atkinson and Norton included her in their plans for the Insurance Engineering Laboratory. Perhaps she could be useful there.

Still, Ellen Swallow was very aware that she had incurred the wrath of the scientific and academic communities, to say nothing of government and large parts of industry.

"I am moving out of my labs and one of my offices to condense my work in one room . . ." she wrote. "Miss Wentworth is to be my private secretary this Winter and I shall feel safe."

She had been forced almost completely to the women's sphere of anything she might do outside the school, a position she had painfully tried to avoid. But she hadn't yet given up her primary goal. There were thousands of people—men and women—in her national audience if she dared speak to them. She made one more effort to apply science to the roots of civilization: the home and school.

Reorganizing the *New England Kitchen Magazine* as the *American Kitchen Magazine,* she kept its editorial staff and began again to work at Oekology's public theme. But now, more cautious, she referred to domestic science.

Then in the spring of 1897, she wrote an article for *The Outlook,* a national opinion magazine.

Domestic Science may be defined as the application of all modern scientific knowledge. . . . It is eminently an applied science, and, because it is practical and comprehensive, educators in general have looked very much askance at it, and have put aside those who have advocated its adoption as one of the topics in the curriculum, with the assertion that it was too crude and too indefinite to be given a place as a mentally nutritive subject. It is, however, not by keeping an acorn on a shelf, but by planting and watering it, that a strong tree is produced.

Since this topic was first suggested, both bacteriology and sociology have sprung up and have become accepted university studies, and oecology is still held at arms' length . . .

Among other things, the piece shed some light on the repression
she and other women experienced.

> Woman was originally the inventor, the manufacturer, the pro-
> vider. She has allowed one office after another gradually to slip
> from her hand until she retains, with loose grasp, only the so-
> called housekeeping. . . .
> Having thus given up one by one the occupations which require
> knowledge of materials and processes, and skill in using them . . .
> she rightly feels that what is left is mere deadening drudgery, and
> that escape from this condition is essential to her well being as an
> individual.

The article then listed a curriculum for study to prepare woman
to prepare others to improve man's basic environment. If she was
to be relegated to women, so be it. Woman, she knew, is man's
first environment. If woman could comprehend and teach environmental knowledge, people would learn it in childhood.

Apparently the article or some other statement was not well
received at MIT.

"I am . . . vowed not to talk or write on Domestic Science for a
year," she confided to Anne Mineah.

Swallow kept that vow, but no more. If biology would not
accept her subversive science, she would create an interdisciplinary profession.

On a crisp fall day in 1898, Ellen Swallow boarded a train at
Boston's Back Bay station for Lake Placid, New York. There she
would meet with the man who had reorganized knowledge into a
modern library system: Melvil Dewey. Oekology would become
home economics.

SIXTEEN

Phoenix

When pure life science repossessed and respelled the Greek word for the Science of House—Oecology—the applied scientist fell back on the Saxon word for a house with life in it: Home

Home economics, before it was given that name, was home ecology to Ellen Swallow. When she was relegated to women and "their proper place," she set out to establish her interdisciplines. If science wouldn't accept the public, this was a way to get the public to accept science.

"The primary meaning of the Saxon word home," she wrote, "seems to convey the idea of a place of safety as well as a place of shelter, and seems to have been applied to the castle or fortified dwellings where the wife and children were left . . . while the warrior went out to battle. . . . This thought seems carried out in the expression, 'Everyman's house is his castle'."

But civilization, she believed, had passed that barbarian stage. Or it should have. The house was something more than just a place for man to leave his woman and offspring.

"Correlated with this idea of home is that of the family, as the father, mother, and children, distinct from the tribe of the early savage," she said.

"The essentials for life in a home [are those which] can attain the best physical, mental and moral development," (the three environmental factors seen in the preamble of the resolution creating America's first board of health). "Everything within the home is done for the good of the family, not for the individual. Each must, to a degree, subordinate his own wishes for the good

of the rest. It is the *family,* not the *individual,* that is the unit of
. . . Civilization." (Author's italics.)

Ergo, the home, not the house, is the unit of community. Men,
women, and children are all cultured first in that environment. If
science and technology looked down on the home as a menial
place, if industry saw it as a place to profit and government to
control, Ellen Swallow saw the home as the physical and social
root of something much deeper.

"Modern life makes many demands on us," she had said in
1890. "But no demand can supersede the home." Eighteen years
later she told a meeting in Washington, D.C., "So long as the
nurture of the human mind is best accomplished in the home, so
long will the word Home stand first in our title."

But that was 1908, ten years after she met at Lake Placid with
Melvil Dewey. During those years, the new profession she was
organizing went by the nondescript title of the Lake Placid Conference; named for ". . . a fit place for the organization of those
seeking to learn from Nature through science how to live. . . ."
For most of these ten years Ellen Swallow still held some hope
that the work around which she was cross-fertilizing this association would become home oecology.

There is an interesting background to the conception, birth,
and christening of this latest, but not last, child of Ellen Swallow—a background that tells something of the problems she
faced, the dreams she dreamed, and the direction of her crusade.
It also tells something important about the environment crisis
today.

Home Economics then was not the "lowly" academic subject
so many consider it today. Then it was a major reform in American education that eventually spread around the globe. In ways
that can't be measured or appreciated today—the improvements it
made possible across and through the physical and social fabric
of society—it was one of the most significant reforms in public
education.

The two broad wings of Ellen Swallow's crusade were joined
only in her. Understandably, but unfortunately, their followings
were separate. The human environment part of the movement was
absorbed more by the men of science called sanitary scientists and

engineers, and by municipalities. Biology's ecology, except for bacteriology, excluded human life from its environmental study and went on to plants and lower animals.

The Consumer-Nutrition wing split from the water-air-sewage wing to focus on more appetizing and appealing aspects of the everyday environment. While some men involved themselves in this movement—men like Edward Atkinson and W. O. Atwater— it was a movement that drew primary support and patronage from women.

By the mid-1890s, a noticeable distance separated the two interests. As advances were made on each side, the separation widened. Ellen Swallow was torn between them. The difference became impossible to reconcile. Professionally and personally she could straddle the gap no longer. She had to make a decision.

Maybe she would have chosen the environmental dimension first. It was, after all, the way she started her career. But a million and more people were climbing on the consumer-nutrition bandwagon she had mobilized, while men in water-air-sewage science weren't exactly begging for her participation, and the life sciences were ignoring her completely. While men naturally assumed leadership in the environmental sciences she pioneered, the leaderless consumer-nutrition cause was weak with confusion. On the masculine side, science and progression were assured. On the feminine side, the reverse was true: there were too few scientists, less discipline, little agreement, and no direction.

It was clear where Ellen Swallow was needed more. Yet she hesitated. There were her needs to consider, too. To join the army she'd recruited—rather than just provide them with arms and ammunition from science—would only make true much of the criticism already aimed at her. Yet she must have seen that without cohesion and direction the consumer-nutrition movement was likely to wear itself out. It wouldn't be easy to pull it together. The decision to commit herself to do it was also difficult.

By her research, books, articles, lectures, and projects of the past thirty years, she was more responsible than anyone for introducing applications of science into the home. Likewise, she was a major figure in putting these applied sciences into the few schools that taught them. But in spite of the spread of the subject matter, there was little agreement on what that subject was or should be, let alone how to teach it or practice it. It went by a growing variety of names—Household Science, Housekeeping, Domestic Economics, Home Science, Household Economics in high school. More courses were being taught in colleges, thanks to her. There were isolated courses in normal and elementary schools, mostly under the manual training classes she had worked for. But each seemed competitive, often contradictory to the other, open to individual interpretations by teachers. There was greater confusion among the rank and file. The discipline of science was in short supply, and the scientist knew it.

Ellen Swallow was responsible for starting the movement. She felt responsible for what she had created. It was quite a change from those early days of food investigation and product testing at MIT and the Home Lab. Since *The Chemistry of Cooking and Cleaning, The Adulteration of Food,* the New England Kitchen, the World's Columbian Exposition, the founding of dietetics, and her other work, hundreds of writers, teachers, and lecturers had taken up the cause. Now dozens of popular magazines, hundreds of newspapers put parts of the broad theme into millions of homes. But there was too little agreement all along the line.

When the publishers of the *New England Kitchen Magazine* dropped out, Ellen Swallow tipped her hand on which way she would go. She brought herself more involvement and responsibility when she reorganized and renamed the magazine (the *American Kitchen Magazine*) rather than let it lapse. Early in 1895, an issue carried the following announcement:

> The present owners and editors of the *American Kitchen Magazine* are the same women who have been its editors from the first and who, since June 1894, have been its managers.

She also indicated her option, if not her preference, for a name to embody the new knowledge she had once called Oekology when she set up a firm to put out the magazine: The Home Science Publishing Company.

The *American Kitchen Magazine* came on the scene a bit later than some of the other "shelter" publications Swallow stimulated. But with it there came to the American home each month a much more professional information medium; ". . . the first periodical that represented the teacher's point of view . . . exerted an educative and unifying influence that did much to prepare the way for organization . . ."

". . . a repository of first rate papers. . . ." said one newspaper review. ". . . the best journal of its kind," said another. "Every issue is well worth reading. . . ."; "The current number . . . contains more than one article worth many times the price of the monthly for the whole year"; ". . . cannot help but benefit . . ." said others. Papers and critics in Binghamton, Bangor, and Buffalo, Dayton, Dallas, and Detroit, and Worcester, Pittsburgh, Salt Lake City, Los Angeles, Cincinnati, and Sioux City—even the *Journal of Education*—agreed.

The magazine opened its pages wide to such groups as Mary Green's American Household Economics Association. It helped make public figures of writers, lecturers, and teachers such as Helen Campbell, Emma Ewing, Marty Chittenden, Julia Lathrop, Jane Addams, and more. The legend of Edward Atkinson and the stature of W. O. Atwater were enhanced in it. Meetings and proceedings were promoted and printed for such as the National Education Association and the American Public Health Association. The magazine sponsored such events as the Home Congress and the Pure Food Fair. Scientific papers from other countries were translated and digested. Each month, home science in another nation was featured by the *American Kitchen Magazine*. Articles such as "Home Science Among the North Dakota Indians" looked at the previously overlooked ideas of America's native environmental management.

The magazine that covered the Sunday school classes on nutrition and hygiene taught by Mrs. Booker T. Washington also carried the esoterica—more than half a century before Timothy Leary—of Harvard's Hollis Webster's report on a mushroom feast in ". . . edible fungi collected and eaten by members of the Boston Mycological Club in 1896 . . ."

Physical exercise and fitness of women, coming events and courses on health and homemaking, government documents available on nutrition and hygiene—all were brought to the home and hearth through the *American Kitchen Magazine*. It even covered experiments such as the Chicago Board of Education's plan to equip twenty schools with apparatus to boil drinking water and 280 other schools with "germ proof filters. A comparative study to follow." When the office was not busy—not often—Swallow and her staff organized special home science classes for readers, teachers, and anyone else who could help spread professionalism in an amateur field.

As far back as 1879, Ellen Swallow had proposed a national citizens association in each city "with one of their number a chemist" to test foods and products coming into the home. Over the years she had expanded that theme. She had seen her home science put into colleges and some lower schools. Added to the number of chemists she educated, she was also seeing educators educated. Now here they were, waiting. The one person who could lead them, however, still held back.

In 1897, she made her vow "not to speak or write" on the subject for a year. She broke this vow long enough to discuss the situation over breakfast at the Vendome Hotel with two people she respected more than most: Julia Ward Howe and Alice Freeman Palmer. She probably discussed it with others during that year; with Atkinson and certainly with Robert. In the end, however, it was the counsel of still another man that appears to have been the deciding factor in Ellen's decision to throw her time, energy, and bruised reputation back into the public arena she had learned about the hard way in the school reform fight.

> The science of household economics is in what chemists call a state of supersaturated solution; it needs only the insertion of a needle point to start a crystalization.

After her meeting with Melvil Dewey in September 1898, Ellen Swallow decided to become that needle point.

Dewey and Swallow had met before her "social visit" to his Lake Placid resort home: first in the 1880s at an A.C.A. conference when he spoke of library science as a career for educated women; more recently, in 1896, he had helped her get home science—they called it domestic science—into the New York Regents exams. Director of the State Library and a member of the regents that governed higher education in the state in 1898, the man who devised the Dewey Decimal System invited Swallow to Lake Placid to discuss domestic science questions for the Regents exams.

Her last reservations about home oecology were settled in discussion with this man who had created the library classification of knowledge. The logic went something like this:

Given the hierarchy of science, it is futile to dispute life scientists' claim to oecology. Accept it. You've come too far to give new knowledge a home where it isn't wanted, Dewey argued. More important, she had created a demand for that knowledge, arousing the interest and energy of thousands of people. The man who perhaps understood better than anyone else what happens to knowledge once it is recorded and stored for public consumption, pointed out to this perceptive woman the value of putting the knowledge she now called home oecology where it would get maximum exposure and use.

Ellen Swallow's oecology, sometimes known as home science, sometimes as domestic science, was converted to a social science of production and consumption: economics. Men may control science, as they do the world of finance. But in America, woman in the daily pursuit of her "place," controls the lion's share of consumer spending. America is built on economics. And if American women were not franchised politically, their economic franchise was real and could be improved.

Ellen Swallow also knew both sciences had the same origin. Oekonomics was everyman's system of production and consumption, just as Oekology was everyman's house in which production and consumption took place. By classifying this new knowledge as a social science, more people would have greater access to it than they would to a life science reserved as a private domain.

Letting them have their limited view of the environment as plants and animals—for the moment—Swallow agreed with Dewey. "The time has come," she said, "when the same kind of care must be given to the family as the stock raiser gives his animals," the farmer gives his crops.

In 1898, her year's sentence served, she officially broke her silence with an address to the National Education Association.

Production has been stimulated by combination and competition; many thoughts of many minds have gone into the perfection of a machine . . . the design of a building. Whatever may be said from the artistic standpoint . . . the economic, collective industry alone has made possible the rapid advance of the 19th Century.

The home is still an individualistic industry, protected from competition, hedged about by tradition, and nearly smothered by dust from the wheel of progress now far ahead [of us]; it [is] no longer the center of enjoyment for the products of wealth because the woman has lost her grip and the cable travels only the faster without her; because in her struggle to become an active producer she has lost sight of the science of consumption—that destruction of wealth which gives the highest satisfaction. It is her privilege to stand on a higher level and say what shall be produced and in what combination . . . It is for her to transform the crude products of the factory and workshop. . . .

Ellen Swallow served notice that she meant to make collective the homes that industry had collectively exploited, to organize them by educating their occupants for intellectual self-defense. She had made her decision. Committed to improve the home environment by economic means, she would use science to do it.

In 1899, only months before a new century of greater change would replace the century where change already had become the dominant characteristic, Ellen Swallow returned to Dewey's Adirondack mountain retreat. There, with nine women and one man in a large room above a boathouse overlooking Lake Placid, Ellen Swallow agreed to take the reins of the newly formed Lake Placid Conference.

It is the spirit of the age which rebels against the dictates of an individual but submits freely to the despotism of an organization. There is one [thing] the spirit of the age reveres more than an organization . . . in fact, the organization holds its place because it is supposed to have this one desirable thing: Knowledge. Listen to the common sayings of the street: "He knows what he is talking about." "He knows the inside track." "The crowd follows the man who knows!" Knowing brings confidence and obedience to truth and fact. . . . Ignorance is tyrannical. . . .

Ellen Swallow's knowledge became the core of the organization known as the Lake Placid Conference, which nine years later became the American Home Economics Association. Once more she began to build, this time out in the open. For the first time in her life she allowed herself the full prominence of leadership. It was a long overdue casting, and she excelled in the role.

With her co-founders, she culled from every organization, every connection, and every source all the intelligence she could bring to her plan. She saw each member—the originals and those selectively brought in at different stages—as block and pillar in a foundation on which to construct an interdisciplinary profession that would touch every primary institution in the land through the home, the institution that reached them all. Each member was given specific duties, wide responsibility, and general direction for the first year's work. When they came back, she meshed their results into an expanded plan for the next year. Carefully and boldly, methodically and with vision, she saw each block put in place, always planning the next.

As the Lake Placid Conference showed the way, other groups voted to join it for more definitive direction and progressive leadership. Its chairman, "the inspiring genius and leader of it all, [gave] quickened thought and a vision of 'how all things work together'."

> Never was there such a leader . . . before she came to a meeting . . . she had all her plans fully laid. . . . She had provided . . . reports to newspapers and periodicals and decided how she . . . would use every hour, almost every minute . . .
>
> She could cut off fruitless debate without injuring anyone's feelings . . . bring out all of value . . . members had to contribute and at the same time suppress all that was irrelevant.

Each year "a certain prosperous businessman" was seen listening and watching just outside the doors of the Lake Placid meeting room. Finally someone asked him what he was doing there.

"I always like to see that little woman conduct a meeting. It is an education in itself," he said.

Still the zealot for woman's physical fitness, Swallow organized members for early morning climbs up an Adirondack mountain trail. At the top, when everyone stopped to catch their breath, their leader would throw out her thoughts on the issues for the day's meeting. Then as the heavy breathing died down and they were about to speak, down the mountain she would take them to breakfast and the day's work.

She held a tight rein at first, each year delegating more responsibility, always watching the transplants perpetuate the work she started as she went on to begin a new phase. She started a professional journal to communicate with those in the field. Since the group was concerned with "fundamental needs of human life—food, clothing, and shelter—and these needs are at the foundation of great commercial enterprises, keen after profits, [she] . . . steer[ed] the new publication around many danger points." She installed dependable Mary Hinman Abel as the *Journal's* first editor, along with some staff from the *American Kitchen Magazine.*

The Ellen Swallow road show was rolling again—not that it had ever really stopped. At New York Teacher's College she developed a major source of supply of educators to expand the trickle coming into the field. At Knoxville, Tennessee, and up and down the coast of California, she was successful in getting courses into universities. At Boston's Women's Educational and Industrial Union, she organized a division that became the home economics department at Simmons College. She saw that Smith, Vassar, Wellesley, and others, naturally, had courses. Then more, larger colleges fell in step. She visited towns and cities to promote public interest in this new education. Weekends, summers, and holidays were best for this work. (She still had MIT classes along with other work.) March 31, Easter Sunday, she wrote Anne Mineah from Pittsburgh:

> I hope you are escaping the epidemic which is really bad here and which is reported from Chicago—the papers always make the most of such things, but here it is really serious.
>
> I am off now to a food talk at Altoona, Pa., to the working men, and ran up here for Easter to get a little rest to be ready for the Spring pull.

She served as her own "advance man" to make sure these engagements were effective.

Altoona, April 2—Evening
We had a very successful time. The foundation I laid last week
told now . . . I send you the little circular we had printed up to
distribute at the door.

Walking out of Logan House, she boarded the train to take
her out of the valley and over the Allegheny Mountains by the
Horseshoe Curve to always more lectures and demonstrations.

As the public responded, industry felt the pressure. So did
government. In 1908, the Lake Placid Conference was held in
Washington, D.C., and voted to become the American Home
Economics Association, the national organization towards which
Ellen had been working. In 1909, W. O. Atwater's graduate
school at Wesleyan University, Middletown, Connecticut, voted
to join. This was an important milestone, as it not only brought
in new academic specialties—agriculture, dairying, animal and
plant physiology, landscape architecture, and other postgraduate
disciplines—it also was the keystone that attracted the large state
universities in Illinois, Ohio, and Iowa, and private schools such
as Cornell and Yale. Also important, these developments brought
a major increase in the male membership of the AHEA and some
international following.

Ellen Swallow was always conscious of the danger of home
economics becoming a woman's movement.

I think [the home environment] needs all the wisdom available . . .
and I prefer to give my time and influence to work in which men
and women are in accord.

By 1910, home economics as a subject was incorporated into
the annual meetings of the National Education Association, and
the AHEA was working with the American Public Health Association through her. The United States Congress responded to
the AHEA's petition for more money for additional nutrition investigations by the Department of Agriculture. The mixed bag
of knowledge Ellen Swallow had crystalized was taught in
correspondence and extension courses, rural schools, trade
schools, professional schools, as well as elementary and high
schools.

Farmer's institutes were set up within the large Grange organizations; members of the General Federation of Women's Clubs (more than a million) were given special education in the improvement of America's homes—food, clothing, and shelter and the use of science and economics by the families in those homes.

The professions, too, came under instruction: medicine, nursing, dentistry, architecture, even theology. Seeds sown in Canada, England, and Australia made home economics, nee home ecology, an international undertaking.

As this interdisciplinary profession spread, Ellen Swallow worked to perfect a syllabus of instruction for the thousands of schools, the millions of students, the homes, and the families it would touch—art, history, anthropology, sociology, esthetics, economics, physiology, hygiene, mathematics, chemistry, physics, and finally the "impertinent interloper," biology, was proudly added.

"To Leibig belongs the credit more than anyone else for bringing together isolated facts and for so adding to them as to produce the new subject of Agricultural Chemistry, which is almost the same as saying Agriculture," stated Dr. C. F. Langworthy, Atwater's successor in the United States Department of Agriculture. "In the same way, [Ellen Swallow] did more than anyone else to bring together a great many known facts and to add a new . . . member to the group of subjects which a man or woman may select for serious study or for practical application."

Langworthy's respect was shown in another way. He became an officer of the AHEA, and soon home economics became part of the United States government through the Department of Agriculture. It would expand into other levels of the federal system in the future.

In 1910, Ellen Swallow arrived at the annual meeting of the AHEA with two documents: a detailed, visionary ten-year master plan for the association and her letter of resignation. Another new work was calling her.

The AHEA voted to make the only chief executive it had ever had "President for Life." No one knew it would be a one-year term.

SEVENTEEN

A Second Science

The years of fighting took time from Ellen Swallow's life. Her hair was a coarse silver mane now above the bushy, still black brows. The flesh was still firm—taut on the bones of a face dominated by a strong, set jaw. But the creases of time were apparent, especially in the fine lines pinched together at the corners of her eyes. Yet there was a beauty to that face that was missing in younger years; a strange mix of peace, strength, and mirth governed by the mood of those flint-blue eyes.

Less visible, there was another indication of the cost of the years of struggle.

... my store of energy gets exhausted now ... quicker than it did. I am more careful to draw upon it.

"Careful," however, meant something less than slowing down. In the 1880s, she had found time to preserve that strong face for posterity.

"Miss Ellen Hale, the daughter of Edward Everett Hale, painted my picture last Spring. . . . It is called a very good one." Now that portrait hung in the Margaret Cheney Room at MIT. There, young women preparing for careers in science could look on the one who had made it possible.

Time was passing, and there was still work to do. Tired or not, Ellen Swallow exercised to keep up her strength.

"I am learning to wheel," she wrote, ". . . but the toes get cold" on the bicycles she and Robert pedaled over the streets of Jamaica Plain.

179

Her mind was more active, but the blood moved more slowly through the sixty-year-old body. She was no longer the woman who wrote twenty years before from a Virginia mining camp: "I went up a rope some twenty feet, hand over hand."

She still took her morning walk with Robert around Jamaica Pond, keeping up with his long strides, but keeping her fatigue to herself. Robert had fully recovered; he was lean, strong again, and tanned from his jaunts to mining camps across the country. He, too, was working on a new level, writing "that everlasting book"—she called it—on ore dressing and inventing new equipment and machinery. Robert Richards was deeply preoccupied by the work that would win him an honorary doctorate from the University of Missouri.

If the husband was unaware of his wife's weakening condition, it was because she always seemed to be doing more instead of less. Like so many others who looked on her stamina with awe, Robert had come to take it for granted.

There was something almost unnatural about the energy of this offspring of a demanding father and a helpless mother. Consumed by the passion "to pioneer . . . to be useful to mankind," she already had accomplished enough for several careers. Still something drove her on. She reached down deeper for the strength to carry her through the last years of her life. Unbelievably, they would be the most productive.

A new century arrived. Change accelerated. Old faces passed from the scene. The sudden death of Alice Freeman Palmer in Paris deeply depressed her old friend and advisor. Alice Palmer had come back to help fight the war for school reform. Ellen had returned the compliment, working with Alice Palmer to help make the Harvard annex Radcliffe College. She would miss the doctor's daughter from Coleville, New York, who opened the University of Michigan to women, revitalized Wellesley, and influenced the University of Chicago.

An even greater blow struck on a sunny September morning in 1905. The larger-than-life Edward Atkinson was stilled forever. The end came quickly, "almost painlessly," in his carriage on the way to his Milk Street office.

The Brooklyn Eagle, one of Atkinson's most severe critics, summed him up in an editorial:

By the death of Edward Atkinson, Boston loses a venerable citizen, Massachusetts an aggressive reformer, the United States a business magnate of integrity and wisdom, and the world a statistician and a moralist who deserved the confidence which he inspired and the attention which he commanded.

The Eagle totally differed from Mr. Atkinson in his views touching expansion, but his objection to that policy was absolutely sincere and his statements . . . the most difficult to meet of any . . . advanced from any quarter.

Aside from all that and far more than all that, this wise, learned, earnest and intellectually tolerant American stood for the best type of thought and action which has honored Massachusetts in the past, and which honors Massachusetts in the present. There was no gathering of great Bostonians that was complete without him. Every such gathering was richer while he lived and for a long time will be poorer because he is dead.

There was no service to any worthy cause that he could render which he withheld. There was no appeal in his judgment or to his knowledge which he did not gratefully answer. There was no kindness and there was no courtesy which he did not more than requite. He was among the chief delights of one of the most delightful cities and states in the world.

In his last years, Atkinson had not been the asset he once was to Ellen Swallow's work. In fact, some said their association had kept her off of Theodore Roosevelt's Presidential Commission on National Health. Atkinson, the most outspoken critic of Big Stick foreign policy, had founded the Anti-Imperialist League to publish his *Broadside,* a propaganda sheet that he sent to American troops in the Philippines provoking an incident that pulled the United States Post Office Department and Roosevelt's cabinet into public debate. "A graduate school for imbeciles," he had called the cabinet. Now the biting tongue was silent.

Ellen Swallow dismissed from her mind the presidential appointment that would have been another first in her distinguished career. Instead, she paid a tribute particularly her own to the memory of her friend and ally.

A Boston newspaper asked the distinguished, if controversial, scientist to join in a symposium on how to spend Boston's share of the money that would be saved should Roosevelt cancel plans to build the Great White Fleet.

In her paper, Ellen Swallow proposed a comprehensive system of modern sewage handling: from a Great White Fleet of modern sanitary trucks and wagons to a new municipal facility—a "Sanitary Crematorium." She submitted Robert Richard's engineering design for this "incinerator" device. She proposed the training of sanitation inspectors, but not just to supervise and police collection and disposal of waste. In Swallow's plan, these men and women, "Instructive Inspectors," would also teach in public schools, motivate civic groups, and give neighborhood lectures to improve the worsening urban environment.

It was Swallow's practical testament to the friend who had shared her advocacy of the use of the environment as a laboratory to improve, not as a mine to be exhausted. As usual, in a negative situation, she found constructive potential.

At MIT, too, names and faces were changing. Gone were Ordway and Nichols. Sedgwick, the young plebe she had helped, became a national figure with the founding of the American Bacteriological Society. Rogers, Runkle, and Walker were gone. James Crafts, her professor during the old Blowpipe Conspiracy, was president. Another colleague in that chemistry lab, Arthur Amos Noyes, following Runkle's path as acting president, would succeed Crafts. But unlike 1871, when she vowed to "roil no waters," Swallow would be critical of Noyes's performance.

The instructor who saw her co-workers and even her students rise above her, also watched the flow of students speed up to meet and help make the twentieth century. New faces—young, bright, and eager—quickly became familiar in class and at the family-style dinners at Jamaica Plain. But she noticed how suddenly it seemed that they were gone. She was proud of their progress—the Winslows, the Jordans, the Munroes, and even Arthur Little, a dropout before graduation. But Little remembered a lot from the lessons of early wood pulp and the soap studies in the MIT chemistry lab. He became chemist and superintendent of America's first sulphite paper mill. Later, in partnership with others, he built the first great commercial science laboratory with his chemical methods of making artificial soaps and cleansers. This successful student and his teacher would meet again.

There were new women's faces too, expanding the original cadre of Capen, Cushing, Talbot, and Palmer. Thousands became members of the Association of Collegiate Alumnae and the American Home Economics Association. Still more educated women met the distinguished scientist in her visits to colleges around the country. She recruited the cream of the crop to her many causes. But those in science she brought together in still another new organization: the Naples Table Association.

Interestingly, Swallow co-founded this body to support scientific research by American women at the Zoological Station on the Gulf of Naples in 1897, the same year as the Woods Holl fiasco. Whether or not there was a connection, she had chaffed for years at the poor opportunities in science education for American women. For proof, she pointed to the very few American women qualified to enter European science schools. Mary Hinman Abel was an early exception. Ida Hyde, with a doctor's degree from Heidelberg in 1896, was a more recent exception.

Ida Hyde also had studied at the Naples laboratory founded in 1872 by Dr. Anton Dohrn. Dohrn—another Jena zoologist and a colleague of Ernst Haeckel—and his unique "university" were well known to Swallow, who may have visited there on her whirlwind 1876 tour.

When Ida Hyde returned to the United States in 1897, she contacted America's first lady of science. Hyde had an idea for sponsoring a "Table" at Naples for American women scientists. She knew Swallow's interest and realized only someone of her prestige and influence could make the idea a reality. Swallow did make it a reality, and then some.

Calling together fourteen of America's top women scientists, she organized "The Association for Maintaining the American Women's Table at the Zoological Station at Naples." Among that original group were familiar names—Cushing, Talbot, and Palmer—along with younger women.

The group raised enough money that year to finance research by two American women at the Naples Station in 1898. By 1900 —the year that under a Swedish munitions maker's will the Nobel Prize was initiated—other women and now educational institutions had come to support the Naples group. Suddenly the association found itself with more money than it needed.

Rather than increase the number of women going to Naples (space was limited) and rather than bank the money for interest, Swallow advised investing it another way—by establishing an annual science competition to stimulate and reward original research by women.

The association agreed, announcing that the first international science prize—$1,000—would be given in 1903. But to whom? For what? Who would judge? The chairman of the prize committee pulled it all together.

Ellen Swallow enlisted eminent doctors—four each from the biological sciences, chemical sciences, and physical sciences, representing Yale, Harvard, Johns Hopkins, Columbia, Clark, Brown, Washington, Western Reserve, and Chicago—into an unimpeachable board of examiners. This feat accomplished, the chairman of the prize committee turned over eleven original scientific theses for judgment. The science community waited doubtfully to see what American women could do.

In 1903, the examiners judged "The Origin of the Lymphatic System," by Florence Sabin, as the winning work. It was, they said, and the scientific world agreed, "the most valuable contribution yet made to the morphology of the lymphatic system."

It was a great moment, overshadowed only by the Nobel Committee's decision to award its prize to another woman, Physicist Marie Sklodowska Curie, for her work with her husband and Henri Becquerel in the discovery of radioactivity.

Without questioning the coincidence, it was a poignant moment for Ellen Swallow. Denied her doctorate exactly thirty years before, she had never stopped encouraging women to take up careers in science. Now she could point not just to the example of a Curie, but to the simultaneous achievement of an American woman, too. But that wasn't all.

Florence Sabin's success was even more personally satisfying to Ellen Swallow. Sabin was a Smith student whose class had been lectured by and about the first lady of science in a science department that itself was traceable to Swallow's influence. After Smith, the inspired Sabin had gone on to study at Johns Hopkins, where there was another Swallow legacy. And now she became the first woman faculty member of any American medical school—an achievement not unlike Ellen Swallow's at MIT. Ellen

Swallow had entered MIT the year Florence Sabin was born. Ellen could appreciate the situation. So could Florence Sabin, who wrote:

> It gives me great pleasure to accept and to acknowledge your generous encouragement of research work. Your Association is one of the influences that is clothing research work with new dignity in American universities and one [who works] with students who have to choose between the scientific and practical life can appreciate the importance of this.
> The piece of my work which you have been so kindly interested in is, I hope, only a beginning.

The Naples Association grew—it became the Association to Advance Scientific Research by Women—and so did the number of American women who became doctors of science. In a few years, women in other countries competed for its recognition. In 1910, a year before she died, an ever weary, ever pioneering Ellen Swallow wrote to still another MIT president:

> My Dear Dr. Maclaurin: Shall I continue to represent the Institute on the Naples Table Board for another year? The money for membership ($50) is contributed by outside friends. The last prize was awarded to Miss Florence Buchanen of the Oxford Museum and several English women competed.

Very probably the Institute's fee was paid by its representative, Ellen Swallow. In any case, Maclaurin replied:

> I shall be much grateful if you can continue. . . . This is an important field . . . that you have made specially your own, and we could not possibly find anyone else to represent us so appropriately or so effectively. . . .

In the first years of the twentieth century, the house at 32 Eliot Street changed, too. It was not so much a laboratory anymore as it was an ongoing exhibit of the knowledge its mistress had accumulated. It was also a clearing house and command post for the always newer knowledge of a new crusade.

Tulip bulbs from Holland were still stored in the cellar, but Dutchess was gone from the stable and the dining room was enlarged to accommodate a larger number of new people who came there.

> You come in at the new South Station . . . exchange baggage checks and take a train for Jamaica Plain, in the same station. At Jamaica Plain, you take a carriage to the house, giving the man your checks. Our trains come every 15 minutes. Most of the time [it takes] 15 minutes to get out here.

By virtue of new transportation technology, they came more often from ever farther away—staff and line officers in the individual causes of this multifaceted leader—coming to consult and to carry out her work.

> Come again when you are not in such a hurry. . . .

> I think you are very bad to think you could do Boston in so short a time. . . .

> You fitted in like an old belonging. . . .

Always the hostess, always the leader, always the medium: "I heard from Flora Hughes. . . . She is very well, for her. . . ."

The new faces were those of Julia Lathrop; Margaret Maltby; M. Carey Thomas; Cornelia Clapp; Alice Blood; Amy Pope; Alice Norton; "the two Isabels," Bevier and Hyams; and "the three Marias," Parloa, Daniel, and Elliott; Anna Barrows from Teacher's College (later Columbia); and Alice Ravenhill from England's Royal Sanitary Institute, joining with the old guard of Howe, Talbot, Cushing, and Abel. There were men, too, in this laboratory for ideas: Chittenden of Yale, Remson and Howell of Johns Hopkins, Le Bosquet, Langworthy, Prudden, Munroe, and many, many more of both sexes from the A_3S, APHA, NEA, AHEA, A.C.A., and the Naples group—men and women from education and science, the arts, and agriculture.

In each field in which Ellen cut new ground, she cultivated a line of executive succession. But who would replace her as supervisor of it all?

More and more, Ellen Swallow enjoyed the rare quiet hours at home in the evening. If Robert was there, they read, talked, or planned together—things like a cottage in the New Hampshire mountains. If he was out of town, she wrote, read, or planned the days, weeks, or even the years ahead. Before bed, she pulled out the full set of weather maps and charts she used to forecast the weather, a pastime since the days at Vassar when she was picked to keep the Smithsonian's meteorological records. If the newspaper forecast disagreed with hers, "she was as often right," it was said.

One evening an earthquake shook the Boston area. She was home, alone. Grabbing a pen and tablet, she sat calmly recording the upheaval—how far the picture flew from the wall, which direction the lamp fell, and into how many pieces they broke. The next day she mailed her notes to "a leading authority on seismic disturbances."

The range of her interests, like the amount of her work, never diminished. It only grew. "A busy life but not an idle one." At MIT she taught sanitary chemistry, sanitary engineering, and air analysis. In 1900, she added classes in the chemistry of water and sewage; in 1902, classes in air, water, and food analysis. In 1903, these subjects were reorganized and became "Chemistry of Air Supply," "Chemistry of Water Supply and Waste Disposal," "Industrial Water Analysis," and "Air, Water, and Food Analysis." Her instruction continued to evolve as more knowledge became available.

A younger professor, James Norton, had taken over in 1902 where she left off with the Insurance Engineering Experiment Station Edward Atkinson had set up at MIT, continuing experiments into "factory ribbed glass" for indirect lighting, new fuels, fireproof and even sound-proof materials. Swallow was sad when Atkinson died that he had seen this bold forerunner of the Underwriters' Laboratories close for lack of support by those it was meant to help: industry. Andrew Carnegie had finally responded to "My Dear Irrepressible Atkinson" only after U. S. Steel had declined. John D. Rockefeller, Sr., did not support it ". . . because of his many commitments. . . . My father must ask you to excuse him from contributing . . ." wrote John D. Rockefeller, Jr.

But Ellen had organized every minute of "new time" given to her. From the walk around Jamaica Pond, where for years she collected samples for ". . . A Prolonged Study of the Oscillaria"

—a basic paper in the yet unnamed science of limnology—to her classes, meetings, and suppers during the week, and to her lectures to teachers, clubs, factory workers, church goers, and other groups on weekends, she was always busy. Somehow, she also found time to quadruple her literary output.

There was only one escape from the exhausting schedule: "We start for California in a month. . . ."

Travel was the tonic for confinement in laboratories, classrooms.

"I have always wanted to run away in the Spring," she wrote the May she did just that, visiting the Talbots' cottage in the mountains. She was back with wildflowers in time for exams.

But whenever, wherever she traveled—even pleasure trips— she planned to advance her work.

"Both Robert and I have been a little used up, and I hope we can have a restful and profitable summer [in the west]," she wrote. There were speeches to make at universities in San Francisco and Los Angeles. A tour of mines and smelteries were "his"; a tour of fruit farms and laboratories were "hers." And, of course, there was water to sample, and she had interviews to hold and appointments to keep. And speeches. There were always more speeches.

Whether to California, to the North or to the South, or to Europe, her travel constantly brought her new knowledge. She noted "the blight" of clouds over England's industrial towns, "the odors of Leipzig," water tables, sanitary systems, soil fertility, vegetation, and menus in countries, states, and cities, in homes, schools, factories, and hospitals. Few people registered new, varied experience to the extent that Ellen Swallow did.

"It is so strange," she wrote from Europe, "to be where everything is the same since earliest time. . . . the same homes and streets that have been the same for one thousand years." Yet she admired the "enterprise and bold adventure" of the American pioneer. "When I emigrate from New England, I shall go West where there is a little 'go' in the air."

She retained her "uncommon devotion to Nature": A "sunrise on the Jungfrau," "Trees with a capital T" in the Northwest, Cape Cod sand dunes, wild pear and cranberry bogs, the "sandstone strata and great rifts" of the Grand Canyon. When she traveled she stopped to see, speak, or study and then move on. She wrote of "thirty miles of wheat" on the Great Plains, of "cactus and shrubs" in the desert, and of watching "curing codfish . . . in this queer old town . . ." on the seacoast. She loved the mountains. She wrote of "the trail [that] runs through a meadow across [a] river on stepping stones . . . [to climb] over felled trees, wading several bogs, then every step is up, 4,000 feet in four miles. . . . [She stopped] to admire the trees and moss . . . to exclaim over the view below or test the clear cold spring water."

No matter where she traveled or for what, Ellen Swallow saw the environment from her total, inclusive perspective. It wasn't just seeing sunrises, clouds, rainfall, vegetation, geological formations; seeing industry, shelter, sustenance, and institutions. All these things were to Ellen Swallow only the bits and pieces; they were fragments in a majestic, sometimes sad, and always fascinating interlocking organic whole—a gigantic chemical, biological, and physical jigsaw puzzle, which millions of people took apart to find a piece of their own. But no one saw the environment overall quite the way she did. No one saw as she did the need to keep it intact.

Water came first in that total environment. Water was the first environment for life. If it covers two-thirds of the earth, she also knew it was the largest component of the human body. At a time when few people thought much about water except when they were thirsty, when cities built public bath houses to get people to wash, when only a minority of people had ever seen the sea, Ellen Swallow saw and sampled this vital fluid in nearly every major body of water used to float, clean, and quench the western world and its people.

Always she returned to Room 32 in MIT, her Laboratory for Water Analysis—to know water better.

She reported her findings to the state on "The Hardness of Massachusetts Water." For science, she published "The Significance of Carbon Dioxide in Potable Waters" and "The Reduction of Nitrates by Bacteria and the Consequent Loss of Nitrogen." For the world, she provided "Permanent Standards of Water Analysis."

Every year of her professional life she grew more alarmed

by what she saw happening to the waters of the industrialized world. She wanted to stimulate use of the Normal Chlorine Map and use "the one important new fact" it made possible; that was, how much pollution in a given body of water was natural and how much was man's.

Toward this end, which she hoped would begin the improvement of the world's water, and with the same ingenuity that they had developed portable mining laboratories years before, Robert and Ellen—the synergistic engineer and scientist—designed a movable water analysis laboratory. Then one day at the turn of the century, Robert took it and his wife down to the Boston waterfront, and Robert waved from the dock as Ellen and her lab sailed out of view south on the deck of a banana boat.

In Jamaica, with two mules furnished by the Boston Fruit Company, she slowly circled the island, studying its topography, winds, rainfall, and climate, tasting the native foods while testing the water. The Normal Chlorine Map of Jamaica and her report comprised the most compact and comprehensive environmental profile for any integral land mass of that time.

A year or so later, husband and wife packed the laboratory along to Mexico for a meeting of the American Institute of Mining Engineers. Between professional papers and a bullfight in their honor ("they needn't have bothered—horrid"), Ellen tested the water from Ajusco on the Divide, from Cuernavaca on the Pacific, and from Pachuca to the east.

"Tired," she wrote again. But she rode a burro to a village that she found steeped in filth and infection. "Worse than the Bullfight!"

The next year, "believing that a record of the condition of the available waters in this early stage of development" had immediate and "future value," she headed north and west from Boston. In the unindustrialized Black Hills of South Dakota, she tested water supplies at Lead and Deadwood—with time out to study the American Indian culture. Then she proceeded north-northwest with Robert to the Territory of Alaska.

In 1903, she wrote: *"It is hard to find anyplace in the world where the water does not show the effect of human agencies."* (Author's italics.) That was seventy years ago.

If human agencies were polluting the world then, they were

also changing time and distance in another assault on the environment. The fact of a smaller world was brought home to Ellen Swallow in a lighter but significant way in an incident that began on their Alaskan trip. Standing at the rail of the ship in order to see the icebergs close up off the coast of Alaska, Robert waved across the frigid water to a ship passing nearby.

The next winter, the Richards were invited, along with an old friend and classmate of Robert named Swain, to see a demonstration of the new "moving photographs" at Boston Symphony Hall. Fascinated by this new medium, Ellen and Robert watched other times and places come alive in images projected on a screen. As the scenes flickered by, a familiar looking ship on icy waters came into view.

Robert and Ellen thought they saw something familiar in a scene of a ship with a group of people at the rail. As the scene came into focus, a large man bundled up in fur coat and hat grew larger on the screen. Then, to that very proper audience in Symphony Hall, Robert Richards waved from the waters off Alaska. "Swain fairly screamed with delight."

This seemingly trivial experience played a symbolic, if not significant part, in the remaining years of Ellen Swallow's life. It was around this time that she made a new discovery, one that she believed to be the most important of her career.

EIGHTEEN

The Third Environment

Few, if any, scientists of her hime had a greater range of experiences than Ellen Swallow in her life time. They were experiences that grew in dimension and diversity. But at a time when science and the industrialized world were specializing, in a way, so was she. If other scientists saw the world through their individual frames of reference, so did she. The difference was that Ellen Swallow's frame of reference held more. It was the total environment.

There is an Eastern legend that helps illustrate this often forgotten woman's work. An Indian mystic, fable has it, chose to understand the world from the perspective of a single object: a stone. In the lifetime that he sat silently studying one stone, it is said he came to know the whole world from its relationship to that single bit of matter.

Ellen Swallow's stone was the environment. In her perspective, everything was organized and channeled through this single frame. Perhaps more than anyone living then—or now—she understood the integrity of the human-environment relationship.

She isolated the physical environment in her work: nature's water, air, soil, food, and sunlight; man's houses, cities, streets, sanitation, and other structures, and the interaction of all. She understood that people living in these physical environments react physically to them. She believed people respond socially, too, whether they realize it or not.

Ellen Swallow saw in the response of people to their surroundings a second environment. Like people react to physical things, they react to one another: social environment. It was a term she often used to describe the human behavior occurring in physical space. But if she allowed herself to distinguish between these two environmental forces, she knew the environments themselves were inseparable. They were interactive, interrelative to one another.

Over the years she had observed the relationship between the condition of one environment and the condition of the other. And vice versa. In slum houses, schools, and streets, she noticed how the poor quality of physical environment seemed to accompany an often poor social environment—higher rates of crime and poverty to match higher rates of physical disease and mental illness. On the other hand, in "better" neighborhoods, except when epidemic disease ran indiscriminately through the populace, she noted how crime, violence, child abuse, alcoholism, mental illness, and other pathologies were lower, matching a lower poverty incidence. She herself said that the connection between poverty and poor health was so great that any assessment of the cause of poverty "immediately finds itself involved in the public health movement."

Moreover, she often spoke of how technology was giving greater definition to these phenomena, particularly in cities. As more people gravitated to the cities for jobs, as the tide of immigration flooded in from abroad, crowding people together in economic and ethnic groups, social and physical environmental characteristics became clearer to those who would notice.

For most of her life, Ellen Swallow had accepted these facts at face value, dedicating herself to improve them when and where she could. But as time went on, she became more involved with that mission, examining the actual relationship between people and their environments ever more closely. It was an interest that often brought her into disfavor with science. "She has deserted true science," said her peers. "Sociologist," others called her.

Sociology was then an imperfect science, too: less popular than even today among the better established disciplines. Rather than deny the comparison, Ellen Swallow enigmatically explained that her desire to reduce human suffering had drawn her to science in the first place; she wanted to help, to be useful. If that made a chemist a sociologist, so be it. She was many things, an educator included; she was deeply involved "in nearly every major educational reform" of her time. She saw no contradiction, no conflict between her interests in these fields. To the contrary, Ellen Swallow saw the need for their unity.

So she ignored still another disdain of her peers, continuing to focus on the vague, illusive, even disputed bridge that she believed exists between environment, health, and behavior, a bridge across which she believed intelligent life and environment interact.

That such a relationship exists was not the popular knowledge then that it is today, especially in science. Heredity was king, the all-determining factor in the human condition. Life science said so. If a man or woman was poor, ignorant, or had "criminal tendencies," it was because they were born that way. (The shape of forehead, lips, and earlobes were then believed to be dead giveaways.) If a person was sickly or diseased, many, if not most, medical men chalked it up to "inborn weakness."

There was a man-made truth to this myth. "Predestined" socially, as well as physically, poor, ignorant, criminal, and diseased men, women, and children continued to breed new generations of the same in environments that supported the hereditists' view, setting up many of the physical and social problems "inherited" today.

In a science hierarchy dominated by life science, the way to improve human development—like plants and animals—was to breed it: eugenics, in other words. Swallow only increased her alienation when she proposed, as early as the 1890s, an improved environment to produce "better people now."

Her scientific training made her certain that human health was as much or more dependent on environment—air, water, food, and soil; its houses and factories—as it was on heredity and breeding. More and more, she became convinced similar basic principles were involved in social environment and human health and development. But how? The answer was hidden in the invisible link between environment and intelligent life.

As with the Normal Chlorine Map, the new fact had been there all the time, like the chlorine in water, a tell-all link between water of that day and its history. Ellen Swallow had worked with this third environment all her life without fully conceptualizing it. The more she worked with environment and with education, the more clearly this elusive environmental form materialized in her perception.

Just as modern man was making a greater imprint on his physical world, he was impacting a greater mark on his social world. By 1900, Ellen Swallow seems to have seen how modern man was mocking up this third environment—the increasing amount of information and knowledge in which he lives and responds. And within this emerging force, she concluded, the shape of tomorrow's total environment will be decided.

Ellen Swallow foresaw environmental crisis. A student of civilization, she knew that crisis had been building for some time. Population's natural environment was giving way to a new one; "artificial" she called it; man-made. Human use of the old environment was being abused in the Industrial Age. In the 10,000 years since the discovery of agriculture had begun "civilization," population had been unlearning its environmental relationship as hunters, and then relearning it as farmers. In the future, man would have to unlearn and learn and relearn once again to live in a new environment.

Science and technology were bringing wealth and comfort. But they were also plowing under basic and traditional concepts of life, society, and environment. Human perception was as much a victim of progress as nature. The steam engine had turned the wheel into a device that reduced distance and time as it increased production and consumption. Electric power made the wheel do more, go faster in every direction, bearing down on nature, tradition, and perception, while the hammer, mechanized, pounded out a new shape and form for society.

Within this new physical form, social environment was changing and the human faculty for bringing environment under control—communication—was altering dramatically. Only a few years earlier it would have taken Ellen Swallow three years to get a message around the world. Now she could do it in minutes by cable and telegram. Before, she could communicate quickly with another person only if he was within sight or sound. Then came the telephone, the camera, and the recorder. Environment had shrunk.

Knowledge doubled for the first time since anyone bothered

to check. The individual's environment—and all its attendant information—expanded to wherever electricity, cable, camera, and recorder could go. Instantly. And more new technology to alter human perception was on the boards.

If an environment that shrank and expanded instantly at the same time disoriented human perception, much of its new information disputed the old; human perception was innundated. Life was changing. Environment was changing. Life, environment, and human perception were on a course of collision. What Swallow had hoped for was a cooperative meeting of the minds.

If there is one truism about the environment crisis today, it is the oversight or underestimation of the impact of these fundamental and radical alterations of information, perception, and environment that occurred in such a short space of time.

Yet somehow, Ellen Swallow grasped these dynamics of her lifetime. She saw them "happen." She saw the collision coming, in spite of all the new knowledge, or because of it.

The scientist, technologist, and educator saw the need for people, perception, and environment to stay in balance. She wrote:

A few enlightened souls recognize the tendency of environment to kick the man that is down; to be subservient to the man of bodily and mental vigor, of keen understanding and human insight; but the majority must be led to believe [and understand] these . . . principles.

Indefatigable, she tried again to make a case for human environment partnership. Science admitted that plants and lower animals respond to their environments. Ellen Swallow believed man does too. But man—the most intelligent organism—was relating to his environment with all the authority of ignorance. The danger was compounded because it was a new environment man had not yet learned. Now the provider as well as the product of his environment, intelligent man had become his own nemesis. But science, seeing human intelligence as God-given, therefore placed man above and beyond the laws governing other life.

Ellen Swallow conceded that human intelligence is fundamentally the product of heredity. But its development, she maintained, is the product of environment:

We have certain inherent capacities as to bodily strength, length of life, etc., but it lies largely within ourselves to adopt a mode of life which may make an actual difference in height, weight, physical strength and intellectual capacity.

And:

There are two recognized ways of improving the quality of human [development]; one by giving them a better heredity—starting them in life with a stronger heart, better digestion, steadier nerves; the other by so combining the factors of daily life that even a weak heart may grow strong, a poor digestion may become good, and frayed nerves gain steadiness.

And:

The relation of environment to man's efficiency is a vital consideration; how far it is responsible for his character, his views, and his health [we do not know].

She seems to have held the view that intelligence is an inherited potential for environment to develop or deny; that genes are basically not much more than yesterday's environment, processed by the species; that the body's still-evolving design is yesterday's environment incorporated for today's development. And finally that today's environment is a major determinant for our development tomorrow.

The work of the last ten years of Ellen Swallow's life indicates that she felt human intelligence had better start looking for ways to bring environment and population and perception into line— into today and into the twentieth century. To find a way, this humanistic scientist took the mathematician's course of reducing physical and social environments to their lowest common denominator: the information they contain. Ellen Swallow could see enough entropy in the information process between man and his environment at the end of the nineteenth century to cause her concern.

There was more than the problem of physical pollution. There were new social pathologies. Traditions were being subverted and must have substitutes. The information and learning functions of the home—the traditional seat of civilized culture, where "pass it on" was a family game for life—had shifted. It had gone out the door of the home when labor, skills, and crafts passed to industry.

The female scientist focused on one other place where women were allowed: the school. If science reserved oecology for plants and animals, withholding it from human application, then another environmental science must be applied publicly to pull people, perception, and environment into alignment. Otherwise, she warned, there are bad days ahead.

At this late point in her life, Ellen Swallow seems to have envisioned a nation, if not a world, so beset by spiraling environmental problems that democracy itself might be threatened by a dictatorship to manage environmental problems, capitalism subverted by another ism for the social mass.

The sum total of her broad experience through the years led Ellen Swallow to conclude that the single most pressing need of the day was an education that would produce a population tomorrow that could live in harmony with its environment.

There was a word in the lexicon then describing such a population: *mentaculture*. Not coincidentally, it was a word that later became defunct in a society that lost sight of its environmental partnership.

To give meaning to mentaculture, Ellen Swallow coined another word. Unlike the time she borrowed a name from Ernst Haeckel, this time she went to classical Greek herself for the name for a science that could educate a population to live in harmony with its environment: Euthenics.

If scientists had thought Ellen Swallow's Oekology was subversive, Euthenics was downright promiscuous. But if people are the source of pollution, they must be the source of its cure—if one is to be found. She knew the industry that produces pollution, the public ignorance that produces pathology, and the government that permits it all to happen are all made up of people.

She reasoned that if those who rose to manage the government, the public, and industry, and the people who put them there and patronized them, if they were all educated toward an *Environmentaculture,* democracy, the profit system, environment, and human development could survive. People were the active ingredient in the environment, the intelligent organism to improve or exploit it.

Ellen Swallow wrote:

Not through chance, but through increase of scientific knowledge; not through [economic] compulsion but through democratic idealism consciously working through common interest will be brought about the creation of right conditions [for] the control of environment.

The betterment of living conditions through conscious endeavor for the purpose of securing better [human development] is what the author means by *Euthenics*.

Ellen Swallow was off and riding again. And try as they might to continue in their old set ways, not all the windmills could ignore her second environmental science for the third environment: the first environmental education.

NINETEEN

The Education of Ellen Swallow

Ellen Swallow was not an unrecognized woman in her time, in spite of her anonymity today. Only in a more illuminated, if not enlightened age, an age dominated by the technological devices she saw creating a new environment are the name and works of Ellen Swallow unknown.

Her career did not begin until she was nearly thirty. Yet she became, almost overnight, a prominent figure of the time, only to vanish in the explosive environmental exploitations since her death. Only by rejecting, revising, or ignoring her work have the people of today been able to lose sight of her—the woman who founded environmental science a century ago. The oversight, not coincidentally, allowed people to proceed undisturbed with exploitation of environment.

Nor was Ellen Henrietta Swallow recognized only for her work in environmental, consumer, and food sciences. In fact, from the time she ran the male MIT gauntlet, she was more and more renowned in education. And if her ideas for science were heresy to the high priests, her educational concepts were only slightly less revolutionary. Somehow, the country managed to ignore the best of them, too.

Ellen Swallow discovered a basic flaw in America's educational system early in her career. She noticed it first in the late 1870s in her classes on minerals for young children and for school teachers at Boston's Museum of Natural History.

Parts of those lessons were the same for both groups. But the children, it seemed, grasped certain things better than the adults. She decided to make a controlled experiment.

Giving the same lessons on minerals to a class of Harvard undergraduates and to a group of elementary school children, "the results were surprising, though probably not so much to her," Caroline Hunt says. "The children trusted to their own observations . . . and were able much sooner than the older pupils to identify and classify minerals." It worried the young scientist. If that's what education does, it's wrong; something is missing or mistaken in an education that makes nature less perceptible as learning goes on.

If educated people can't see the nature of their world, what can be expected in the future? Schools should be "readily adapting" to the new environment, Ellen said, "but they aren't." The family was "foregoing its educational responsibility" and "schools are usurping it." But if the home is "retrograding as an education center," she said, "schools are not advancing fast enough."

"Where will tomorrow's leaders come from? Where will they lead us?" Education, Swallow said, must teach environment.

To find "a new epoch in education [to meet] the twentieth century demands," she began to study the learning systems of the world. In Japan, Belgium, Sweden, England, Russia and other countries she found desirable characteristics in each system for teaching the human-environmental relationship. She noticed how a nation's culture was reflected by its education and how its education returned the complement.

America's culture was only now beginning to emerge. It was a composite of many. But overall, America's education and culture were energized by the most highly powered industrial engine of all time, hooked up to the most dynamic fuel ever: the profits of free enterprise. Ellen saw inherent danger in a system with an engine so powerful it could outrun its environment and had a built-in incentive to do so. Educating the operator of that vehicle became the obsession of her life.

"She had a steadfast belief that education should make man the right kind of master of his environment," Caroline Hunt said, an observation made by many. But it would seem that Ellen Swallow felt even more deeply; she believed education must bind population to environment by knowledge, not unlike religion binds population by faith.

This student of civilization seemed to sense how the western world's education reflected the institutions that had created and developed it. The church began schools. And in the classroom there was still dogmatic rote and unquestioned information. Industry had become a vast and pervasive force in education in the eighteenth century. Now, that influence was visible seat by seat, row by row, class by class, and grade by grade in the subject-by-subject instruction manufactured year after year in non-distractive environments. The pattern of fragmented specialization was made to order for industrial productivity. But the human mind, Ellen Swallow said, learns by putting things together, not taking them apart.

Ellen had made a first-hand acquaintance with the most recent institution to make its mark on the public school. State by state, then town by town, government had come into education in the nineteenth century. The advantage of mandatory schooling aside, the influence of government had its disadvantages, too. School boards and committees were made up of people elected for their favors or appointed for their talents in managing the status quo. Some members were corrupt; some didn't care; others meant well. But almost all were devoted to resist change that threatened procedures, efficiency, patronage, and costs. In essence, Ellen Swallow saw these bodies as obstacles to innovation and spontaneity that struck at the heart and soul of the learning process.

All told, a great deal of the school system veered away from the human process. Sometimes it seemed to exist more for parents and politicians, teachers and administrators. If the student wasn't completely lost in the picture, at least the student's picture of environment seemed to grow dimmer the more he was taught.

"I envy a child who rides a bicycle without learning," Ellen once told an audience of educators; "he just jumps on and rides. We should give children a chance to do more. They do not require much teaching. . . . We teach too much. The child is far quicker than the adult to grasp what is suited to him. We present to him something he cannot grasp—the large end—and he wisely refuses it. We call him stubborn when he is only wise. We forget that the abstract is arrived at only after much experience with the concrete."

By concrete, however, she didn't mean the man-made environment; she meant the one it was replacing. In student minds she saw nature's concreteness becoming more obtuse, if not abstract.

> What we do to kill learning! We put young children on hard seats, in cramped positions, force into their heads a dead book which must not be crumpled or torn, and exclaim: 'Study! Study! Recite!' And this when human instinct demands objects to be handled and put together . . .

People began to pay attention to Ellen Swallow's ideas on education. In 1881, she agreed to an Associated Charities interview on "Manual Training," one public school version of "The Natural Method" of teaching. She was an advocate of both. Each had an environmental learning potential. But more and more, she was becoming convinced of the necessity for teaching the human-environment partnership in the early grades.

"When should this education begin?" they asked.

"As soon as anything is taught. . . . Nature seems to have pointed the way in this. . . ." Ellen replied.

It made sense. People began to respond. In 1887, Ellen wrote to Anne Mineah:

> I have been a little worried by an attempt to make me think it is my duty to accept a nomination to fill the vacancy made by Miss Crocker's death on the Board of Supervisors of the Boston Schools.

But she was wise to that age-old power tactic—absorbing critics by drawing them into the system.

> I could not see [the argument] in that light, however. A political place with no [sic] power and influence are not to my taste.

The twentieth century grew closer. Environment was changing faster. Her theories on education grew more definite. After joining the National Education Association, Ellen Swallow became a familiar figure on its podium.

> Place the child in an environment rich in suggestion . . . furnish the [natural] materials for discovery. . . . [he] needs pleasant sur-

roundings—color, form, flowers, music—to express his ideas and to stimulate imaginative thoughts . . . to become master of his environment. . . .

It is contrary to all the laws of [human] development to allow the child to pull to pieces [in learning] without putting together. [Yet] Botany and Zoology are . . . taught by dissection . . . the destruction of life which has built up the delicate structure. . . . Not until the cycle so evident in all nature can be understood in its entirety should [the] analytical habit be formed.

In one of the most succinct summaries of environmental education, she said, "Schools should not teach how to make a living before they teach how to live."

She kept up the lectures on learning:

It behooves us all to search for the ideals which lifted the [human] race highest and not to waste time on mere survivals. The modern child does not need to search for subsistence . . . shelter . . . or invent a language. . . . His environment offers these. . . . He needs only to correlate himself with it. . . ."

Now her objective was clear.

Our experience has convinced us that early and consistent progressive training of human beings, whether men or women, by means of a knowledge of the objects in and [the] laws of Nature is the best means of developing the powers of the human mind to grasp the meaning of the facts of history . . . to appreciate the best [art] and finally, [for men and women] to take their place as makers of the history [and art] of the future. . . .

Hers was the environmental education "that never ends." It begins in the home, the preschool, the kindergarten, and in the day care centers she called "Nursery Trusts," but it goes on through elementary and high schools and on into college.

"If only the college, the university, the school will give the right direction . . . and not remain so hypnotized by the past as to neglect the present opportunity . . ." to make the future better, she pleaded. "I believe one year out of four could be saved" with the right reorganization, she said.

Nor for her did environmental education stop with schools

and universities. "There is no connection with knowledge in our daily lives," she said. In the after-school years she saw another pressing need. Knowledge was just beginning its rapid increase; more was being created daily. Calling for America's mass media to cooperate on one level, she urged the conversion of the public schools in each city into "community centers," to utilize them evenings and weekends for adult and family education. Since the school had become a "foster home," "we might as well use it to a nicety," she thought. She tried, but could not find, however, a way to utilize "the knowledge lying idle on the shelves," the wealth of original information produced in graduate theses and then filed away.

At this point in time, Ellen Swallow hoped to see her environmental education become an integral part of her environmental science, Oekology. But as the 1890s passed, her public "house" was shut down by indignant authorities. When she agreed in 1898 to incorporate parts of Oekology into the interdisciplinary profession of home economics, nee home oecology, she did so because it would be accessible at least in the public schools. But environmental science per se was not visible enough in home economics. One recurring reality that nagged her was how people tend to see environment only through their own limited perception of it. To have a true environmental education, education had to have that specific identity and objective.

With all their disagreements, Ellen Swallow concurred with the life scientists in one important respect: She believed man is something more than a predatory animal; at least he can be if he can expand and elevate his perception of his environment. In 1899 she wrote:

It is the attitude of mind toward the objects with which we surround ourselves, not the objects themselves, which makes or mars our welfare. For this reason, the teaching in the public schools should include right ideals of life from a material point of view and right notions as to values.

If we read the history of the rocks and seas right, each animal has risen to a culmination when the food supply and general environment became such as to permit . . . it, and then has declined or passed away. . . . The conditions under which the human race are [sic] at present living, lead us to ask most seriously if such is to be [mankind's] fate. There is, however, one difference between animals and man. Men have the power of choice. Looking into the future there is a possibility man may rise to a greater height and persist for a longer time.

Intelligence and choice are the only hope that man will escape the fate that has so far befallen each dominant species which has left footprints in the sands of time. [Intelligence and choice] . . . to enable us to resist the appetites and inclinations which, though raising us in the animal scale, tend to bring us to the brink from which we shall fall.

It wasn't just the environment Ellen Swallow saw being exploited. The exploitation of human appetites and inclinations that consume and abuse the environment unnecessarily and incorrectly will only speed up catastrophe by catering to our animalism. On the other hand, she believed, mankind can truly graduate above the animal and his fate by "the right education."

"People know all this," she wrote. "But there is a danger that the incentive to effort will be withdrawn." Ellen Swallow was not one to lose sight of reality in her idealism. She knew the tendency to declining effort and responsibility in the span of an individual lifetime. "If there is one fact that stands clear through the organic evolution, it is that through effort alone has progress been made."

The difficulty is to arouse an appreciation . . . to educate the taste of the people so they will use aright the environment provided them. . . . Judged by the money spent, the mass of people have far more of what stands to them for comfort than ever before . . . but it is questionable if health, peace or [real] comfort have correspondingly increased.

Only by effort alone has any species risen above the limitations of his environment. Be it 100 years or 1,000, mankind would need every minute of time, every molecule of gray matter to make and adapt to a new environmental life style.

The time has come for a new [human] development.

"The school is the *agent* of the first consequence in exerting a profound influence upon the environment in the next generation," she said. The first consequence, in her mind, was the home.

But even as she wrote these words, over two-thirds of a century ago, this woman, worn from the battles of her nearly sixty years, felt a sharp pain in her chest. A scientist was not dumb to that message. Yet many years before she had recited a principle of science that she now drew on to make an intelligent choice for the remainder of her life.

She knew that a solution to environmental problems in the future, like those of the past, would require the participation of all population. She had preached the need "to cultivate a sense of personal responsibility" for the environment. Angina pectoris or not, she could hardly excuse herself from that task:

> In blaming people for their indifference, we forget that a body
> of men obeys the same law as a body of matter, i.e., a body in
> motion will continue in motion and a body at rest will remain at
> rest unless acted upon by some external force. . . .

Ellen Henrietta Swallow, "small, compactly built and absolutely unafraid," moved to create the "external force" to bring about a new era in human development and environmental improvement. In making that decision, she was fully aware that her own failing "internal force" gave her very little time in which to do it.

It was 1900.

TWENTY

Death's Cause

Fourteen books in eleven years, dozens of scientific papers, magazine articles, and hundreds of speeches and lectures; back and forth across the continent to speak, meet, and recruit, living on trains, out of suitcases, in hotel rooms, in dormitories, and in guest houses; visiting schools and auditoria; dedicating buildings; starting new curricula; organizing and teaching, experimenting and proving, proposing and predicting, Ellen Swallow ended her life in a titanic wave of creative labor.

Increasing her experience and her knowledge and getting others to apply it and carry on her work all required an outlay of energy out of proportion to what the small body, for all its discipline, could support. But the focus on environment had become sharper, better defined. It was a movement now—legitimate. A growing number of scientists, educators, and writers came aboard the vehicle this woman had made credible.

She who saw air, water, food, and soil interacting to produce and sustain and evolve life, saw people, too, in that light. But the most intelligent organism seemed the least conscious of its environmental interdependency. Ellen Swallow saw civilization as a highly advanced colony of organisms, evolved from a natural environment to structure a new one. Along the way, she thought, they had lost contact with the nature that was partner on the journey. Worse, they did not understand the new arrangement.

Animals do not ignore environmental law. They obey it. If they don't, they're gone. Man, the most adaptable of all animals, could ignore these laws more than others. But what would be created in his ignorance? Swallow studied this problem, dedicating her last years, her last energies to resolve certain crises, or at least to ease the collision.

To some she was merely a cyclonic worker, a mercurial dynamo scattering her many interests in every direction. But as definitely as mercury separates, it reforms. And in the mind of Ellen Swallow, the diversity of her work was a very precise whole. As a moth is drawn to the flame that destroys it, she flew ever closer to the light of her idea to avert what she saw darkening the future.

The crux of the environment problem, she knew then—as many are beginning to see today—is the economics of production and consumption. She believed mankind's ability to consume his environment—especially as population grows—is unlimited; she believed that the ability to produce from that environment is limited. Thus, the dilemma that confronts every evolving organism will one day confront people. She knew that the higher organisms that can solve environmental dilemmas, evolve higher forms; she knew they also degenerate, even become extinct, by ignoring the dilemmas. Human intelligence can and should rise above that fate; human ignorance and greed will only hasten it. She knew, too, that intelligence, ignorance, and greed are not always separate forces.

Industry, for example, was just then finding profit in the principle of enforced obsolescence. She saw this technique as a shameful waste of natural resources at a time when industry should be conserving them. "The present only is considered." At the other end of the horn of plenty, she saw the relative problems of increased consumption called "better living." "Nothing is used as if it were to be needed again," from coal and lumber down to air and water and food, increasing garbage and refuse cluttering the home and community, straining facilities. Instead of "better living," better they should learn "right living."

> It is customary to lay the blame on economic conditions alone. . . . [But] . . . the reason the cost of living has increased thirty times in ten years is the absence of standards of living. . . . It depends upon the ideals and standards of the person spending the money. . . . [The cost of living] is a mental rather than a material limitation; a

result of education. . . . Man is a practical being . . . whose mind
is given to aid him in adapting to his environment. . . .

But it wasn't happening the "right way." In the end, she said,
in urging a "study of the forces of nature" to determine the
limitations of the environment, only our mental potential can
overcome the material limitations of the environment.

If industry was becoming more proficient in exploiting environmental resources by increasing production, advertising—"the
science of creating needs and wants"—was becoming more proficient at exploiting people and expanding consumption. Ellen
deplored this manipulation of knowledge, but she was fascinated
by its effectiveness. Frustrated, she asked, why can't advertising
be used for euthenic purposes?

> In a civilized country, those who cater to the wants of its own
> citizens should be forced by public opinion to use their capital and
> . . . skill in ways which will elevate and not degrade the ideals of
> the people. . . .

She quoted the French economist who said:

> The human race could increase its welfare almost as much by a
> better ordering of its consumption as by an increased production,
> without any real retrenchment in consumption.

Ellen Swallow believed it was the falsest kind of economy to
exploit environment merely for money.

> It may seem more economical to discharge all wastes into the
> stream running through the town and to take the water supply
> from the same stream, but it is . . . economy [of a higher kind] to
> spend thousands on sewer and reservoir.

By the same logic, she held there is a need to spend millions on
educating people toward environmentally compatible standards
of producing and consuming their environment.

> This would go far in cutting off the arms of the octopus which
> threatens to squeeze the life out of the American Republic. . . .

In the age of great trusts, such as that of the Rockefellers, this
was dangerous stuff, in spite of the popular trust-busting of an-

other New Yorker, President Teddy Roosevelt. But even in 1900, this woman foresaw the need of a "service economy" to balance the exploitation of environment and people with their improvement. We can buy and sell, build and make, produce and consume ourselves into oblivion at worst, environmental crisis at best. Or we can develop a population of efficient, economic animals able to live in optimum, intelligent balance with environment, she said.

> It is not the material portion of the daily living that we are to look for improvement [of our lives or our environment] but . . . in the ideals, standards and aspirations by which the uses of the materials are governed. . . . The only criterion of true economic value [is not] in dollars and cents, but in the character of the men and women we produce.

What Ellen Swallow was getting at became clearer in the last ten years of her life: to link the incomparable force of the profit system to environmental improvement and human development. "The affairs of the purse must be considered," she said. But ". . . in this age of money worship" if it hadn't been proved that a capitalist would shoot his grandmother for a dollar, she saw evidence that he wasn't above poisoning the old woman's air, water, or food for far less than a dollar—on a per capita basis, of course.

Typically, she didn't waste time asking if this link could be made. Rather, she labored over how to go about it. The woman who had already been slapped down by the hierarchy of science now took aim at the economic establishment. It was, to say the least, ambitious. "There is no pain like the pain of a new idea," she quoted Bagehot. But someone had to start, and the sooner the better.

> It is because I believe in the possibility of control of [the environment] and even economic conditions that I urge so strongly the dissemination of what knowledge we have. . . . [Otherwise] . . . a cry for state interference will come in that day when it is clear that the carelessness of men threatens to extinguish the race.

A capitalist, the last thing she wanted was state interference. To avoid it:

Let the dictum go forth that for every dollar spent in the material
wants . . . there shall be a dollar put into the hands of a manager
for higher purposes. . . .

The key to educating a population toward environmentaculture "is with the plastic middle layer, the fermentable mass of
humanity out of which rises the cream of society or from which
sinks the dregs." Then, quoting a contemporary, Mark Twain:
"You cannot throw habit out of the window; it must be coaxed
down the stairs one step at a time," the aging, indefatigable
woman sat down to write step-by-step, day-by-day instructions
for the consumer, the educator, the legislator, and any one else
who would read and heed it.

The *Cost of Living*, published in 1899, was the first in a series
of four "Cost" books to help the consumer grapple with the everyday economics of environmental consumption. Next came *The
Cost of Food*, in 1901; *The Cost of Shelter*, in 1905; and *The Cost
of Cleanness*, in 1908. Each gave specific standards, suggestions,
and budgets for daily and annual consumption for the individual
home and family. Everything—food, fashion, laundry, rent,
building—was tied together in the series, including how, why,
and how much.

But food, three times a day for each person, 1,095 times a year
for 85 million people was the greatest environmental variable.
To nurture a better human intelligence in the purchase, preparation, and protection of food supplies, she wrote another series of
books known as *The Rumford Leaflets: Plain Words About Food*,
in 1900; *The Dietary Computer*, in 1902; and *First Lessons in
Food and Diet*, in 1904.

The "plain words" in *The Rumford Leaflets* came from a symposium of leading scientific essays on the body's relationship to
food. *The Dietary Computer*, long before the computer age, gave
interchangeable tables on the per person cost, weight, measure,
and nutrition for some 200 different foods and included 100
recipes for a balanced family diet. *First Lessons on Food and Diet*
was just that, an international survey of the world's scientific
knowledge of food and diet for use as a text in schools.

In environment, as seen by Ellen Swallow, all things were

connected. Each book in these two series related to all the others. In a third series of six books, all the parts were tied together in an environmental overview. She knew now how prone people are to see only the parts of the whole. In this third series, she put them all into a single environmental perspective.

Air, Water and Food came first, in 1900. A summary of scientific knowledge on how air, water, and food interact and depend on one another in human health, she discussed in the book the normality and abnormality of these elements and their function or disfunction in the human body.

Air: In the neighborhood of factories, smelting works, or [in] cities burning soft coal there is a noticeable amount of sulpherous and sulphuric acids, sometimes so considerable as to destroy vegetation. . . . where gas is burned, oxides of nitrogen are formed, the effect of which is known to be harmful. . . . Minute quantities of hydrogen sulphide and compounds of carbon and hydrogen and other gases . . . may reach dangerous proportions. . . .

There exists, suspended matter in the air: fine dust, pollen spores, algae, dried bacteria, diatoms, small seeds of plants, soot and finely pulverized earth from roads. . . . streets are macadamized allowing finely ground particles to fill the air with every puff of wind. [In the country] a cubic inch of air may carry 2000 particles. . . . 3,000,000 and more in the city, and 30,000,000 in inhabited rooms [unventilated or unhumidified].

Water: Pure water is no longer possible. . . . Safe water is the 20th Century's goal. [We need] a serious study of water [and] laws [as] the daily quantity required for each person has increased from two to four gallons drawn by bucket from the well, to thirty or forty taken from the town supply by . . . faucet, and in cities where much more is used for manufacturing, running elevators and motors, the daily amount may reach 100 gallons per inhabitant. . . . It is quite probable that double treatment [of water] may be more frequently required as unpolluted water becomes more scarce.

Oxygen in the air, she showed, is required to release food energy; water, "the coin of the world," is needed to take the value of foods to body tissues and to carry off waste.

> Of little use it is [however] to provide pure air and clean water
> if the [foods] are not capable of combining with the oxygen of the
> air or of being dissolved in the water . . . [especially] the so-called
> pre-digested (prepared) foods . . . countless proprietary packages,
> which, designed to meet the demand for quick results, prove traps
> for the unwary . . . [adding to the amount of garbage and refuse we
> have to deal with].

She also singled out at the turn of the century, in words so
familiar today, special criticism for "proliferating preservatives
. . . and unduly light bread which has not sufficient food value."

She saved a very special vehemence for those unethical, if legal,
chemists, "employed by manufacturing concerns in making
adulterated and fraudulent food stuffs . . ."

For disbelievers who boast, "I can eat anything," she added:

> It is true, like a tree bending with the wind, the [human] organism
> adapts itself to its [environment]. But like the exposed tree, the
> living being is never quite as vigorous and symmetrical as it should
> have been. . . .

She called for an extensive scientific study of air, water, and
food for the public. And more. Much more.

Her next three books took a more definite tack. In *The Art of
Right Living,* published in 1904, she made an urgent plea for
environmental education to resist the trends she saw emerging.

> From the study of plant and animal life we have come to a glimmer
> of understanding of what life means. . . . If by study and experi-
> ment man has discovered the laws of life to an extent shown by
> every agricultural experiment station in the country, should we
> not expect [man could learn] to develop himself? [Yet] in spite of
> all these lessons we go on, careless [of them], neglectful of con-
> ditions. . . .
>
> We seem to have assimilated so deeply the idea that man is lord
> of all the earth that . . . we do not grasp the thought that man
> must be lord of himself, also, if he is not to succumb to nature's
> rule in the end. . . .
>
> It would appear that the higher civilization rises, the less common
> sense it shows, the less science it applies to daily affairs. . . . The
> child at school should become accustomed to the best conditions

known to science, and science knows far more than is yet applied.
. . . The public school is the natural medium for the spread of
better ideas . . . if the teachers would cooperate and use all the
material [now] available. . . .

She was specific:

There is no better way to begin a child's [education] than to give
him a garden, indoors or out. The care of a garden combines exercise, amusement, and work to a degree not attained by anything
else. It adds indirect instruction into the mysteries of living. . . .

America must teach a few facts about rocks and soil . . . with
reference to the disposal of waste . . . the principles of polluted
water . . . refuse [and] sanitation generally. . . . [Such] would tie
in mineralogy, geology, municipal structures [and more] . . .
practical knowledge of their environment, natural and man-made,
and how the two interact to help or hinder one another. . . .

We react to our environment, therefore we must act upon it to
make it satisfactory. Since the future depends upon the children, it
behooves us to see to it they have a fair chance [and] . . . bring up
their children in a better way . . . so that when they become tax-
payers, they will see the value of this sort of instruction sufficiently
clear to sustain it. . . .

Adaptation to our environment is the great need . . . today. Shall
we who boast that we outdo the world with our mechanical devices, stop short of at least a long step toward the production of
a better human race?

In 1907, came the third of the series, *Sanitation in Daily Life.*
It was fifteen years since that hopeful night at the Vendome Hotel.
Now Ellen Swallow reasserted her claim on Oekology, once more
respelled, as ecology.

To secure and maintain a safe environment . . . to promote and not
diminish human development . . . It is important that everyone
should acquire habits of belief in the importance of environment.
One of the most difficult lessons to learn is that our tolerance of
evil conditions is not proof that the conditions are not evil.

Human Ecology is the study of the surroundings of human beings
in the effects they produce on [other] lives. . . . The features of the

environment are natural, as climate; and artificial, produced by human activity such as noise, [dirt], poisonous vapors, vitiated air, dirty water and unclean food.

The woman who had christened Oekology as a public science had been rejected for that "crime." Now she tried again to insert the human dimension. Doing so, she laid the ground for the formal introduction of her second environmental science—one to use the results of the ecological study of the human-environment relationship by teaching it. No dinner would christen this one. Publish or perish the thought. In 1910, the Boston firm of Whitcomb & Barrows brought out Ellen Swallow's eleventh book in less than ten years, her fourth in this series titled *Euthenics: The Science of Controllable Environment, A Plea for Better Living Conditions as a First Step Toward Higher Human Development.*

Euthenics was the sum total of her remarkable life. All she had learned, all she knew, she brought to bear on an analysis of the problem and a plea for action: Give America an Environmental Education! But euthenics was more than a plea; it was a plan. Fundamental to that plan was the attempt in the book to link environmental improvement and human development to the profit motive. She began in terms the capitalist could understand.

She computed the estimated economic value of a human being in the United States at $2,900 each. There were 85 million or about $250 billion worth of human resources then living. "This exceeds the value of all other wealth," she pointed out. "The minimum savings to government and industry in preventing death, illness, and other nonproductivity due to environmental conditions is certainly far greater than $1,500,000,000 and may be three or four times as great." We must invest in this resource, she argued; we must improve the asset rather than liquidate it prematurely.

Where responsibility for environmental quality had been taken over by the state, she showed that science had achieved enormous decreases in deaths and illnesses and their costs. Since 1882, tuberculosis had dropped 49 percent; typhoid 39 percent. They were still going down. But where environment and health were still personal responsibilities—with no science available to the public—there were monstrous increases: kidney disease up 130 percent; apoplexy up 84 percent; heart disease up 57 percent, on its way to the top of the class of killers.

These increases, Ellen said, are at least partly due to changing environmental conditions in air, water, food, speed, stress.

Today the dangers are unseen and insidious . . . the microscope must be used to detect them.

Even then, for some of modern maladies, the microscope was insufficient.

Because retribution does not instantly follow infraction of Nature's laws, [we] become callous and unbelieving . . . [But] the relation to environment . . . is a vital consideration . . . it is responsible for [man's] character, his views and his health.

It is possible to improve environment, character, and health and make a profit doing it, she said. For example, the Committee of 100 for Public Health (she was a leading member) had conducted a study showing how, for $200,000 annually, an insurance company could educate its policyholders for its own "net savings of one and a half million dollars a year. . . ." True, other industries were growing up by treating man's miseries, but she argued, as much, if not more, profit could be made in the long run by preventing human suffering and improving environment.

Motives of both economy and humanity . . . dictate immediate and generous expenditures of public moneys for improving the air we breathe, the water we drink and the food we eat.

In the incalculable social gain inherent in improving physical conditions, none, she said, was as ready as the overripe urban rot, "the rapid, irresponsible growth of cities, so often beyond anticipation." Housing is a disgrace, a void from which both industry and society can profit by improving, Ellen Swallow said. Using such terms as "city planning" and "rapid transit," she proposed a company:

Instead of investing millions in some uncertain gold mine . . . invest in a plot of land whether an open field or a slum district . . . and thereon cause to be erected . . . a model city. . . . There is virgin field for the capitalist who wishes to use millions for the prosperity of the country, to build a short trolley line to a district of sanitary houses . . . with garden and playgrounds, entertainment halls, etc. . . . Such a village to contain not long blocks of [tenements] but both separate and [apartment] houses, from two rooms up, where [residents] may have light and air . . . more grass and trees, even if the buildings tower fifteen [stories] high.

In her experimental city, aged and young people had special roles. The young were to be an environmental improvement corps, learning as they went; the aged were to help the young, as mothers and fathers had less and less time to devote to their children. There would be central heating, sanitary bakeries and laundries, and a particular view of government and politics in her city. Using H. G. Wells's term, "a sense of community," Ellen urged the old town meeting kind of participatory city management.

The common man is likely to be possessed of one idea at a time. If such a one be a leader, there is danger that equally vital factors will be overlooked. Safety is found in a combination of leaders . . . the man who caters to the public need does not look far ahead to consequences, and if unrestrained may prove more of a menace than a convenience. . . . The steps need to be carefully measured, for if the [citizenry] begins to rely on the state for the backbone it should have, it will not stand up and its fall will be lower than the stage it rose from.

In Ellen Swallow's view, responsibility for environmental quality was a three-way street shared by public, industry and government institutions.

America today is wasting its human possibilities even more prodigiously than its material wealth. . . . In the confusion of ideas resulting from the rapid, almost cancerous growth . . . made possible by mechanized invention, the people have lost sight of their own conception of right and wrong.

If Industry have no sense of their humanity, if they do not use the human power of looking ahead, that power which differentiates man from animals, what better are they than animals?

If factories are incorporated under State Laws, they must also be governed by state regulations for [environmental] health. The control of man's environment for his own good as a function of government is a comparatively new idea in republican democracy.

She saw rising crime rates rooted in these same environmental conditions, passage of more laws as the last resort—a poor cure—instead of the prevention she believed in. She traced this law and order dilemma back to Anglo-Saxon heritage.

Personal conduct was free . . . the home [a] castle inviolate. Laws interfering with personal liberty—a man's right to drink tea, punish his children, beat his wife or keep his own muck heap [are] deeply resented by the American citizen. Each step in the protection of his neighbor has been taken only by struggle extending the common law of nuisance to a [greater] variety of conditions. [Yet] the protection of man against himself is one of the 20th Century tasks hardly begun.

Still, Ellen Swallow believed it far more efficient all around to educate, rather than legislate.

Evolution from within, not a dragging from outside, even if it is in the right direction, is the right method of human development. . . . Authority is exactly that; it is coercian from without. If the result is simply obedience to authority and not the underlying principles, it will not be a force in [the individual's] life.

Principles. Physical principles. Social principles. These were the great needs of the physical and social environments this scientist analyzed in the first decade of this century. If principles are not "inculcated" by population, she saw disaster. So another principle, that of human perception, must be developed.

"The whole question is one of ethics." Ellen Swallow sought the environmental ethic.

Here in America we are always locking the barn door after the horse has been stolen. . . . Time presses! A whole generation has been lost because the machine ran wild without guidance. . . . Persons fail to realize that the 20th Century is practically a new world. . . . Speed is the watchword. No one can stop to see what injury he has caused. Get There! seem[s] to be the motto. In this scramble for [money] and power, the purpose for which life is lived has been lost. . . .

The change in point of view has been growing like a root underground. It seems to have suddenly sent up shoots in every direction. In no line of thought has this change come more generally than in relation to the things youth should be taught. Himself and his relationship to environment [must be brought] to the front. Instead of extolling man as lord of all created things . . . youth must see that man unaided by scientific knowledge is at the mercy of Nature's forces. . . . [Instead] the senses [of children] are blunted at an age when they should be keenly sensitive.

This was euthenics. If Ellen Swallow's human ecology was the study of mankind's supramultidimensional surroundings, euthenics was her supramultidimensional science to improve those surroundings, physically and socially. It seemed simple: Improve man's perception of his physical and social environment. But it was not that simple, she knew.

Again and again the scientist and the humanitarian must return the attack . . . they must present their knowledge in language that will attract and hold the attention.

Not just schools—from kindergarten through college—but people at home, in industry, and in government, in neighborhoods and in organizations; all had a role—and a stake—in her new science. Especially media.

Magazines: There is no concern of human life that cannot be made interesting, and the magazine writers of today understand that art.

Newspapers: In the past, newspaper science was largely discounted as sensation and only one tenth fact . . . the popularizing of knowledge, [however], is now proceeding on somewhat better lines. Intermediaries between laboratory and people are springing up to interpret one to the other.

Among science writers and other "intermediaries," she cited an advertising firm organized to use "the psychology of influence" to promote public health. On the horizon, she saw an even greater promise.

Of all, that product of man's ingenuity, the motion picture, is destined to play the greatest part in quick education. It is the essence of democracy.

No one is right all the time. What if she had lived to hear radio?

The printed word can never reach the untrained as can the voice and personality of an earnest speaker with a compelling personality. . . .

Or television?

It is well that . . . there is stimulus in hearing or seeing the person. . . . The forceful person . . . seen . . . is ten times more valuable than even the most attractively illustrated article. . . .

All media have important roles in improving human perception of environment, she believed. What would her critique be of that role today?

Our leaders must show how . . . [but] the individual himself must adopt it. . . . He will [Adopt a better environmental perception] . . . when he has been saturated with knowledge. Every known method must be used . . . to develop [the] belief wide enough to reach all members of every section of the community and deep enough to become a vital working principle . . . each must understand that [environment] does affect him, that it is his concern, that he must give heed to his environment, then he will have the will to make the effort.

Environment begins in the home, she knew, but today:

Conditions change so rapidly that grown people may not . . . keep up with them. . . . [Parents'] ways are superceded before the children are grown. . . . The school, if it is to be maintained as a defense against predatory ideas, is the people's safeguard from being crushed by the irresistable car of progress.

In 1910, however, she noted:

The school is hurried with a curriculum . . . wasteful of time and money, [and] lacking correlation in studies . . . has little time to relate its work. . . . There must come an intermediate step . . .

to bring to millions of receptive minds the best knowledge in daily living . . . [for population to achieve environmental harmony].

Ellen Swallow had a plan for that "intermediate step." What it was is not known. But she had scheduled its public unveiling for 1915. She planned that far ahead—a five-year plan to begin to bring human perception into balance with environment. There are hints that in 1910 she saw a way to put private enterprise into the public schools; to profit from environmental education. Her proposal for "Instructive Inspection" of cities and towns seems to have been a way to take children and teachers out of the schools, to learn in a larger, more relevant environment. Whatever it was, whatever combination of innovations she envisioned, whether or not the plan would have worked, she felt it could change the education system, which today, sixty snowballing years later, is essentially the same as it was then. Meanwhile, the environment has changed a great deal—in the direction she predicted.

However the applied scientist planned to develop euthenics, its underlying premise still has value today. Ellen Swallow believed there is an organic whole to knowledge. Like Bacon, like Rumford, she sought to develop an ethic that would realize that integrity to bring the most intelligent organism into harmony with its environment.

Ellen Swallow's thirteenth and fourteenth books in this period aimed at another worsening part of the pollution problem. In 1908, a New York and London publisher brought out her *Industrial Water Analysis—A Survey Course for Engineers.* Another text was published posthumously. *Conservation by Sanitation* was a masterful book tracing the world's water, air, and waste systems since Rome, citing the best features of the past and present, recommending for the future. It included "A Laboratory Guide for Sanitary Engineers." She was working on a now lost manuscript, Industrial Hygiene, at her death.

Productivity alone was not enough. She was nothing if not economically efficient with the time and energy left to her. To add to the impact of these books, she revised and updated her earlier volumes, *The Chemistry of Cooking and Cleaning, Home Sanitation,* and *The Adulteration of Food.* Nor was this all. Many of her last books were published and reissued through the early

1900s by Whitcomb & Barrows, Boston. A specialty publishing house, Whitcomb & Barrows gave circulation to other writers on health and environment. The firm readily admitted it was Ellen Swallow who put them into the business of putting euthenic information in print. Whitcomb & Barrows had actually evolved out of the old Home Science Publishing Company that Swallow had helped organize to save the old *New England Kitchen Magazine*. Her books were Whitcomb & Barrows's first.

Environment was becoming a major international movement by 1910, slowly overcoming the hereditists' objections to its role in human development and behavior. Swallow was a major force in that temporary victory. Her books were vital to the movement, as were her speeches, articles, and scientific work over the years. But she had still other influences.

In 1907, she attended the Zoological Congress to lobby for "human ecology," as she did at the A₃S "Darwin Day" that year. It was an old idea to her, but it would not be taken up by the science establishment for another thirteen years—and then only fleetingly. By then, Ellen Swallow would be gone from the scene. But, she said just before she died, "real happiness had come [to her] only when she learned to put seed into the ground and wait twenty years for it to spring up."

The books and thoughts of Ellen Swallow were, however, only words. And she knew well what the eminent anthropologist Ashley Montagu stresses in his lectures today: the meaning of a word is the action it produces. Even as she formed her words on paper, Ellen Swallow gave them action.

Many of her books—especially the "Cost" series—were biblical material for the home economics movement she was organizing at this time; they were tablets handed down to improve environment through its "first agencies," home and school. Millions of minds were exposed to her knowledge in these and in hundreds of books that were modeled after hers in the years ahead.

Now she took over as chairman of the Health Education League, a nonprofit public information agency that disseminated information on health and environment. She never missed a meeting in seven years. "All that we are we owe to her," they remembered. For good reason. Swallow wrote more than a fourth of the agency's materials, was its chief lecturer, and turned over her fees to finance the league or to pay for the tracts she wrote to hand out on her tours.

She had a habit of "early morning meditation," according to her friends; it was a period in the day when "ideas came to her" that she jotted down to "see to." The Louisa May Alcott Club was born this way, the name she gave to an experimental environmental education course for children "4 to 15 years of age." At the Fifth International Congress on Tuberculosis in 1905, this early environmental education model, "Laws of Hygiene Taught Through Domestic Science and Nature Study," won a Silver Medal.

It helped that she was an organizational genius along with all her other talents. Whenever there was a free moment, she found a way to use it. Whenever there was a group available, or needed, she found a way to it. And whomever she met looking for something to do, she found something for them. "Keep thinking," she signed her letters, while she did the same.

She was a natural leader, officially and otherwise. "I will give you the substance of the report," she wrote a follower, "and you can make an informed statement to your association. I would rather you not make it as an official statement, as I have no authority to do so. As chairman of the committee, I do not write this. As one [advocate] to another, I do."

Robert and Ellen finally built their little cottage, The Balsams, in the crisp, clear air of the New Hampshire mountains. But they seldom got a chance to enjoy The Balsams; even there, she found little rest or solitude. Friends, seekers, and co-workers found their way up the steep slope of the tree-covered hill to visit, ask, and plan. There was always something new or unfinished. There was never enough time, but somehow Ellen Swallow found the time, if only at the expense of the little left to her.

"I wish I were triplets," she told Caroline Hunt, who observed; "she then trebled her energies" to compensate.

In her lifetime, she advanced the sciences of air, water, and food enormously; combined, she advanced them more than anyone else. In later years, she turned her attention more and more to air. In the American Public Health Association, she served on the Committee on Standard Methods for the Examination of Air. She urged ventilation and air purification systems in factories, better air and humidification for homes, schools, and other public buildings.

At MIT, too, she stepped up her campaign, and not just academically. Times had changed. Far from the practiced caution of an earlier time, she now engaged no less than the MIT president's office in a running battle on the matter of air. The agitation seems to have begun around 1906 when she wrote:

> My dear Dr. Noyes:
> The next serious problem of civilization after clean water [is] clean air, not only for ourselves but for the world. . . . We seem to have not [the] impetus to make investigations and our own system is breaking down . . . we hushed up the little outbreak last year but we really need to do something and do it this year. . . .

Noyes, a practical man, replied that a course in heating and ventilating would "certainly be desirable." Two years later, she was still fighting. Teaching heating and ventilation was one thing. What about the foul air in our own classrooms? The environment we teach in is the environment the students learn. And she, along with others, suspected new impurities in the air of MIT's halls and classes.

> My dear Dr. Noyes:
> May I again call your attention to the condition of our buildings. They show great deterioration as to the air in them, which must have an effect upon the quality of the students' work. . . . It is a disgrace to our educational institutions to allow such conditions.

Again Noyes replied. He thanked her, suggesting the problem would be good material for a student thesis. Swallow was disturbed. Something was happening to the ideals of Rumford and Rogers in the growth of "Tech."

> The Institute is fast losing its prestige in sanitary matters and its students are put under great disadvantage. [The purpose of their education should be] not sordid money-getting . . . but the education of TODAY that the people demand . . . that which enables the youth to grapple with today's problems. . . . [Technology's] torrent has burst forth [and] nothing can stop it; guiding it is the only

possibility and NOW is the Institute's opportunity. It was the most potent factor in starting the flow. . . . Its early ideals were those of this great [environment] movement. Is it to stand aside and disavow its work? [We] no longer lead in these councils. . . . If the Institute will, it can again lead in thought and example. . . . If [it] is too timid . . . too ignorant of the pulse of the time to step forward, other leaders will be found. . . .

Another leader was found, for MIT at least. Whether Dr. Richard Maclaurin was able to put applied science back on the human track, he seems at least to have sanctioned a greater emphasis on air examinations.

My dear Dr. Maclaurin:
You may be interested to know of the Ozone machine which Mr. Gilbert has got into working order now. The laboratory is now fully equipped . . . handling about 60 students this term. It is like a ship's kitchen in compactness.

The woman who wrote that note had created, if not the first, certainly the most comprehensive environmental science laboratory in the world. But she was far from pleased with its status alone. She wrote a proposal, "University Laboratories," urging other colleges to connect with their communities to study environmental matters. She also made "valuable contributions to the Reports of the Commission on Country Life," wrote a major section on "Domestic Waste" for the Massachusetts Commission on the Cost of Living, contributed various papers on "Sanitary and Social Progress" to L. H. Bailey's *Cyclopedia of American Agriculture,* and wrote others on "The Cost of Cooked and Purchased Foods," "Vocational Subjects in High Schools" for the National Society for Science Education. "Good Lunches for Rural Schools," and, with Lily Kendall, a protégée, "Permanent Standards of Water Analysis."

The range of her work amazes. She was as much at home reporting on "Ten Years of Broad Irrigation" in an engineering journal as she was in asking "Who Is to Blame for the High Prices?" in the *Ladies Home Journal.* She helped found what is called the first sanitary commercial laundry, The Sunshine Laundry in Brookline, and agreed finally to write for various women's suffrage magazines.

At the time of her death, she was consulting "some 200 institutions" on scientific feeding and "some two score corporations" on industrial water treatment. There were, as she said, ". . . many irons in the fire . . . too many for an old woman."

Age and irons aside, the scientist-educator stayed loyal to her sex in the quest for knowledge and function in a changing world. Still active in the Woman's Educational Association, she was a senior counsel for it, as she was for The School and Home Association, the forerunner of the National Congress of Parents and Teachers. She prepared for the transition of the school and factory lunch programs to the Woman's Industrial and Educational Union and guided this organization's milestone labor studies on women. Progress in the Association to Advance Scientific Research by Women was an annual delight in her life. She also established in her last years the Household Aid Company and the Intermunicipal Research League to collect data and devise methods to adjust inequities in the "outstripped" home environment. As she put it, these were meant to bring "efficient engineering principles" into the home.

"The world cannot far progress if one half its population is a drag," she said in referring to a world run by men only. The environmentaculture she worked for "cannot be accomplished without the efforts of both men and women. The two counter currents neutralize one another." If there was a sexual balance to environmental management, there was also a balance to the point of view that criticized sexual separatism—by men or women—on the one hand and chastized complaining females for their "vain kicking against the pricks" in life.

Do something; seek knowledge; apply it, Swallow urged. Facts are the equipment needed in the struggle. To women demanding their rights but not prepared, "she never forgot to remind them of the absence of pockets in their skirts." Nor was woman's mind alone required. "Nowadays the last card they can trump against us is that we are not physically able to do what we try. . . . The more prominent we become, the more closely we are watched."

She was frank. "The great majority of marriages are getting to be unhappy. . . . The artificial life . . . [and] . . . struggles for position . . . are ruining many a home. . . ." She worried about what those homes would contribute to the future. Still, she was hopeful. "It is becoming true that woman has a personality that is not in her husband's control, that the mere fact of marrying him does not make her [his] slave." She believed developing woman's personality and talents would open up a better future for all. "All the drags hung on the wheels of the evolution of the ideal society will only delay its progress." Give women an equal education, she said, and they can be equal. Her dedication to this cause prompted the "most impassioned speech" of her life.

The incident was unplanned and unexpected, by both her and her all-male audience. She was testifying in front of an educational policy board to plead for equal education for women. They told her curtly there would be no need for women's "industrial training" if women would stay home where they belong! Slapped, blood rushing to ignite the steel flecks in her eyes, Ellen Swallow exploded in the gentlemen's collectively shocked faces:

> Industrial Training may make matters worse! That is why I make this plea, for it may take more and more of the interest [out of] home life, which, I must reiterate, has [already] been robbed by removal of creative work. You cannot make women content with [just] cooking and cleaning, and you need not try! All industrial education is doomed to fail unless you take account of the girls. You cannot put them where their great grandmothers were, while you take to yourselves the spinning, the weaving, and the soap-making! The time was when there was always something to do in the home. Now there is only something to be *done!*
>
> We are not quite idiots, although we have been dumb because you did not understand our language! We demand a hearing and the help of wise leaders to reorder our lives to the advantage of the country!

Ellen Swallow was the wisest of the leaders who tried. She "had need of every ounce of pugnacity so characteristic of her," said James Phinney Munroe many years later. "When a woman dared to challenge not merely the relations of her sex to the existing order, but that very order itself, she aroused shocked protest, not only among the men, but among her fellow women, too." In her last years, Swallow confronted some of that resistance within her own creation, the Association of Collegiate Alumnae.

The A.C.A. had growing pains. More than a few of its members felt rather larger than their bustleless skirts. Elitely, they still refused membership to southern college alumnae. In 1904, Ellen had helped organize a Southern Association of College Women when she was the featured attraction at summer session at Knoxville, Tennessee. In 1907, when the A.C.A celebrated its twenty-fifth anniversary, she made her point sharply. The A.C.A.'s founder showed up representing the Southern Association.

There were other A.C.A. imbroglios. A group of midwestern women opposed the entry of the University of Illinois to the A.C.A. Using questionable tactics, they managed to disqualify the school year after year. Finally, in angry frustration, Illinois President Richard Draper called them out. "Ask Mrs. Richards . . . she has been here . . . she is our friend." The fighting Illini came in. Home economics did not.

It was a major disappointment to Swallow when the elitist A.C.A. agreed with the validity of the home economics home ecology curricula but refused to recognize it "under its present name." These career women could not see the interdisciplinary profession for the domestic image that "home" conjured up in their minds. But when the A.C.A. announced it would form a Committee of Eugenics, Ellen Swallow put her foot down. She demanded the chairmanship of the committee. Recruiting psychologists from the A.C.A., she threw all her prestige on the line.

My dear Miss Boggs:
The A.C.A. at Cincinnati set up a committee on Eugenics, appointed me chairman and suggested you as secretary. I am engaged in pushing my own term, Euthenics, which is better environment for the children now here, in distinction from Galton's Eugenics, better heredity or better births. This is clearly understood in England and I do not care to touch that side. I feel with Mr. H. G. Wells that we know too little as yet, and that environment must come first. We must live up to our [present] knowledge.

Now, which do you suppose the A.C.A. means, or does it know?

What is your interest? And if you take my side, will you serve as secretary with me? If you prefer Eugenics, then whom can you suggest as . . . chairman?

Take it or leave me out, she was saying. Psychologist Boggs preferred Ellen Swallow, environment, and euthenics. Now to swing the A.C.A. president, Laura Drake Gill, an old but cautious friend.

My dear Miss Boggs:
Not until today did I get the final word from Miss Gill. There was some hesitation about the name. . . . The Washington biologists did not think there was the objection to Eugenics which I make and the *Standard Dictionary* had not the word Euthenics in it. But it is decided that you and I are to have a committee and therefore they will take my word rather than lose me. I send you the outline. . . .

As the committee went about the work she assigned, the chairman concentrated her efforts outside the A.C.A., broadening the base of support for environmental education.

. . . Went to Minneapolis . . . a week in Albany . . . just back from Virginia . . . [now] . . . to Amherst. I am seizing on a few minutes before dinner. . . . Came up here [Morningside, New York] to do some water analysis and sanitary inspection . . . [before] a week's meetings. . . . to New York once a week this term . . . shall be in Washington for the A.C.A. A week in New York . . . a talk to the Ethical Society . . . gave two days to Philadelphia, another talk, [then] here [Washington] . . . back to Baltimore for 3 days and in New York for 3 more talks . . . home on the 16th. . . . We have been happy [in spite] of this Harvard merger hanging over . . . it will do us good to have . . . our faith tested. . . . Will be in Ithaca 13th to 19th . . . back for Saturday morning talks for Prof. Bailey. This is the first hour I have been able to choose what to do since I left. . . .

But it seemed worth it.

I believe it is only that the world is coming to believe that there is something in it that my talks have been more sympathetically received than ever before.

At last. She had caught their ear. Wherever they would listen, she would speak. And travel: New York, California, Georgia, Maine, Michigan. No town was too far away or too small.

> . . . To Merrimac, Mass., to speak to a small club . . . back in time to see Mansfield in Don Carlos. . . .

But if task took more and more time from amusement in her domestic life, it also took its toll of her.

> Tired . . . but this [cold] weather helps. . . . I am hoarse but hope camphor will make me alright for two lectures and a dinner to-morrow. Augusta left me to take care of her mother. It is these unexpected upsets that wear one. . . . Horrid weather . . . laryngitis . . . went to Hartford [at] 4 PM, spoke at 8 and went to bed at 10:30 [until] 1:30 AM, got up and took the 2:30 AM [train] and slept until 6:44 AM when we reached Boston. . . . went directly to the Institute. . . .

With such a schedule, it was only a matter of time. But she wouldn't stop. She saw progress.

> It is very interesting to note how many are coming out on the side of the great effects of environment as a potent factor. . . . I am pleased to see the interest the men on the newspapers take. Every paper sends up a reporter and I am pestered by them during the week. They are not always wise or correct, but . . . the editors are grasping the idea that [environmental conditions] are of the greatest importance . . . they mean to be useful. . . .

If the press was falling into step, others were less coordinated; the National Education Association was one. Swallow was on its executive council. But "it is too unsettled to do much original work," she reported. In truth, the NEA was in the throes of a power struggle. After a meeting at which she tried to advance her ideas, Ellen stopped to rest at Emma Roger's seaside estate in Newport.

> We lived through it, heat and politics. . . . Mrs. Young's election was not an argument for women's purifying politics . . . [but] I seem to have hit the nail on the head with my three speeches. . . .

Out of 298 people attending, 152 had come to hear her views.
Encouraged, she was back on the road.

> Two lectures in Newark, 21st . . . one in Bethel, 22nd . . . Cleve-
> land, 26th, Chautauqua . . . Ithaca . . . may go to California. . . . a
> dozen things waiting.

About this time, Swallow took on two new assistants. One,
"a young Canadian who is nice with my words." The other, the
tubercular daughter of an MIT professor, Lillian Jamieson. She
helped rough out a schedule.

4/10	10:00 AM	Mass Standards School
		1st of 3 lectures on Ed in Home
4/11	3:00 PM	Council of Jewish Women
		Economy in the Home
4/16		New Bedford Teacher's Assn.
4/24		2nd Lecture Mass Standards
4/28		Kingston, R.I., Opening new Dept.
		State Agricultural College
4/29		Jamaica Plain Fraternity of
		Churches "Cost of Living"
5/7		Boylston Street Church
		"Right Living"
5/10		A.C.A. Meeting

And then I am free of that. . . . This is dreadful, for I cannot have
enough ideas to go around. . . .

Then off to Seattle and San Francisco and back through Canada to Boston; a week later back to Canada again. Killing as it
was, it was bringing results. First, Clark University in Worcester
and then "more than one college" expressed their interest in a
euthenics curriculum. She had at least verbal encouragement
from other groups, too, such as the American Public Health
Association. Swallow stood tall in its growing interest with environmental issues she had raised years before. But the most promis-
ing sign for her environmental education came from America's
capital.

> Dr. Brown . . . will put all that is possible of the Government at
> our service. . . .

Dr. Elmer Brown was no less than United States Commissioner of Education, one of the most enlightened ever to hold that post. His 1898 report of the history of education would be good reading for students learning to teach today.

There were two more important steps to solidify her "1915 plan." First, she hoped to get support for euthenics from the American Association for the Advancement of Science, as she had for consumer and food sciences, earlier. Then, with the A₃S's distinguished backing, she was certain she could raise the money she would need—she had spent all of hers—from "the Carnegie," the foundation then becoming a force in American education. She never quite got that far.

Ellen Swallow had reached the zenith of her power and prestige. But her energy and time were rapidly running out. The spasm in her chest came more often and lasted longer. Her flesh was pale, her breathing labored. It was a steeper climb up the three flights of stairs to her laboratory at MIT. Travel, once the change that refreshed her, now tired her.

Alone at home one sweltering August night in 1910, she suffered her worst attack. Robert was out of town. The next day she went to work as usual, telling no one that she was ill. But on her office door she tacked a folded piece of paper with the name and number of a physician to be called "in case of illness." Then, an unexpected event seemed to give Ellen Swallow a lift through the long winter. Smith College announced it would bestow on her a doctor's degree, which MIT had denied her forty years before.

It was a dramatic scene on an October day that might well mark the official end to the professional suppression of women in the United States. Seven women were honored, five with Doctor of Humanities degrees and two with Doctor of Science degrees. Humanitarian Julia Ward Howe, with only days left to live, represented to Ellen an era past. The only other woman honored for her achievement in science that day symbolized the future, a woman born the year Swallow entered MIT, the next first lady of American science, the winner of the first Naples research prize and now an inspired believer in Swallow's work for "a controllable environment." Florence Sabin, who would soon prove that tuberculosis could be arrested by controlling environment, smiled across the stage to the older woman.

Of all those on stage that day, however, *LaFollette's Weekly*, a national magazine whose publisher would go to the United States Senate to become an American political legend, chose Ellen Swallow for its cover story a few weeks later. The biographical sketch inside was co-authored by Bella Case LaFollette and Caroline Hunt.

This belated recognition brought a new wave of public popularity to Ellen Swallow and a greater demand for her appearances. She couldn't pass up the chance to build more support for her environmental education. Back she went to the suicidal routine. It was a grueling winter—her last.

In January 1911, prodded by Smith's recognition, MIT's Women's Association held a luncheon to honor its sixty-eight-year-old first lady and presented her with a check for $1,000 to spend on "worthy research of her choosing." Swallow tried to decide. Should she use it for an education project or to further her new research into the feeding of anemic children? One was preventive, the other curative. Both were euthenic. She never had to decide, but the $1,000 kept Ellen Swallow from dying penniless; it was the only money she had to her name when she died two months later.

Shortly after the luncheon, Swallow was asked to prepare an address for the forthcoming Congress of Technology Arthur Little was organizing to celebrate MIT's fiftieth anniversary. With all her other activities, she began to review the past at home with Robert, sifting through Rumford's and Rogers's words to put their ideas into a modern frame.

St. Patrick's Day had become a wild event in staid Boston by 1911. That year, March 17 fell on a Friday. Late that afternoon, after class, Ellen Swallow traveled to Haverhill, Massachusetts, to lecture. As usual, she arrived early, stopping at her host's home for a reception. Leaving the house, the group started down the tree-lined street for the Universalist Church, "a stone's throw away," when Ellen Swallow's over-taxed heart convulsed. Reeling, she reached out instinctively for a tree to support her. It was spring, and the branches were beginning to bud. After resting a few minutes, she insisted on "carrying on her part of the program." The group went on to the church where she spoke, standing, for almost an hour.

At home that night, the dying woman took out tablet and pen to draft the address for MIT's fiftieth anniversary. Realizing the end was near, she gave new urgency to what she had to say. Much had been done. Much was happening. But so much more remained to be done.

Two days later, Sunday, March 19, she kept one more appointment. Addressing a large crowd in Boston's Ford Hall on the topic, "Is the Increased Cost of Living a Sign of Social Advance?" she showed it might be the opposite. For an hour after, she fielded questions—some antagonistic—from the floor. "Her mind was alert as ever," a friend reported, but the body was failing fast.

Monday and Tuesday Ellen Swallow went to her laboratory for the last times. Wednesday she stayed home to complete the anniversary paper. Up to now, strange as it seems, Robert Richards was unaware of his wife's condition. Like Yankee granite, she had always been there and he took it as a matter of course that she always would be. But this anchor to his life, once cut, would leave Robert Richards so awash that he would marry, within a year, hopeful, helpless Lillian Jamieson, Ellen's secretary.

Thursday night, March 23, Robert was awakened by the sound of a small bell ringing frantically from his wife's bedroom. A doctor was called. And now he knew. The weekend at 32 Eliot Street was uncommonly quiet. But even as the house was still, work was being done in that spartan bedroom on the second floor. Monday morning Ellen gave Robert a draft of the anniversary technology paper for President Maclaurin. He read it hastily and wrote:

Dear Mrs. Richards:
Prof. Richards brought in your paper for the forthcoming Congress and I read it with great interest. We are all greatly concerned to hear of the serious trouble through which you are now passing and hope that matters are progressing as satisfactorily as may be.

As so often happens at the end, Ellen Swallow rallied Tuesday. Wednesday she felt even better and sent out for a lounge to sit on and dictate from. If others were hopeful, though, she knew. Calling in her secretaries "one by one" she gave instructions for settling her affairs. Thursday morning she felt even stronger.

But it was just one last burst of the incredible force that ruled her life. During the day, she began to fail. At 9:25 PM, March 30, 1911, with Robert at her side in the airy, spic-and-span bedroom with its many plants and flowers, Ellen Swallow closed her eyes forever. But her work had made it possible for others to see. If only they would.

Sunday, April 2, was a warm, sunny spring day in Boston. Signs of life were everywhere. The leaves were rich and green on the trees, and along the Charles, early flowers had burst into bloom. On Copley Square, a block from the old Vendome Hotel, across the street from MIT, a growing parade of mourners began to fill historic, majestic Trinity Church. Robert and Ellen had crossed Boylston Street many times to sit in those pews. She had loved to hear his resonant bass voice work with the acoustics of the magnificent stone structure. Today, Robert Richards sat silent, alone with his family. Across the street, MIT's flags were at half mast.

Louisa Hewins, a friend and neighbor in Jamaica Plain, sat back a few rows and watched the honorary pallbearers, Maclaurin, Noyes, Crafts, Sedgwick, and two other officers of the corporation, escort Ellen Swallow's body to the front of the church. Louisa Hewins was a housewife whose daily routine had been brightened by the remarkable comings and goings at the house on the corner of Eliot Street; a woman whose life had been given new meaning by that of her neighbor. She wrote to one of the many visitors she had met at Ellen Swallow Richards's home.

> Dear Miss Mineah:
> . . . We are all stunned by this great change that has come into our lives. One so full of life and love and energy—but perhaps you would like to hear about the wonderful service in Trinity Church. [It] was filled with friends and so great was the feeling that you were impressed with it. Everyone present was in full sympathy with every other person—The beautiful singing by a choir of 50 men and boys I shall never forget. The hymns, "For All the Saints" and the "Alleluia," as the procession walked out of the Church. The casket was opened in the vestibule where the sun shone full upon it, the wind playing with her hair, her Doctor of

Science gown which she had on, a really beautiful expression [on] her face still lingers with me. A short service at the crematory which a few of us were invited to and then we are left with beautiful memories and a great appreciation of the high privilege we have enjoyed in knowing so valuable a life. . . .

My own appreciation of [her] friendship has been always very strong and I sometimes marvelled at her thought for me, as it was entirely one side of the larger interests in her life. I never could be of the slightest use to her in any of her work.

Mrs. Laura Richards has been staying with Prof. Richards for a week. She went home to Gardiner yesterday and Prof. Richards goes to Montana tomorrow for ten days. He is perfectly wonderful, so gentle and quiet, but like a man crushed. I hope he will be able to bear this but it seems as if everything had been taken from him. . . .

It will be a great pleasure to see you again sometime and [I] shall hope you will like occasionally to let me hear from you.
With kind regards and deep sympathy,
Very truly yours, Louisa Hewins

Boston newspapers carried several remembrances of Ellen Swallow in the next few days. In a symbolic way, the day her funeral was reported, so were the indictments of five companies for violating the new food and drug laws. Another story urged enforcement of new city ordinances to make the city's schools safe and clean.

William Sedgwick's eulogy to his "great teacher" was printed in full, and so was the unedited last paper written by Ellen Swallow in which she cautioned twentieth-century technologists not to mistake growth for maturity. Simultaneously, MIT announced the establishment of the Ellen Richards Memorial Fund to help sanitary scientists and engineers finance their education. Since it appears Ellen's $1,000 research gift reverted to this fund, in a strange way, even in death, she made the first contribution to this effort to improve the environment in the future.

The home economics and collegiate alumnae associations duly memorialized their founder, too, as did the Association to Advance Scientific Research by Women. The first international science prize for women was renamed to honor the woman who founded it in 1903. And in 1911, the year Ellen Swallow died, Marie Sklodowska Curie won her second Nobel Prize, this time in chemistry for the discovery of radium, and thus began the nuclear age. Like Swallow, Curie believed in bringing the sciences together to benefit man.

Years later, still one more memorial was established to Ellen Swallow, at Vassar College. When Madame Curie made her first visit to the United States, she consented to just two public appearances. Ironically, at the first, in New York's Carnegie Hall, Florence Sabin presented America's official welcome. Then, boarding a train for the journey up along the Hudson River to Poughkeepsie, Madame Curie, the only scientist at that time to win two Nobel Prizes, made her only formal American address as an "Ellen Richards Monograph."

So ended the life of Ellen Swallow. But her legacy lives on.

Epilogue

The "ever present granite" of New England rises in a sharp peak in the center of the town of Gardiner, Maine. On top, where the fog lifts late in the day, in the courtyard of a pre-Revolutionary War church, beneath a stone on which is carved

Pioneer—Educator—Scientist
An Earnest Seeker—A Tireless Worker
A Thoughtful Friend—A Helper of Mankind

rest the ashes of Ellen Henrietta Swallow Richards, 1842-1911.

Abiding by his wife's acrostic, Robert Richards waited a long time to join her on that hill a block away from his family home. Before he did, however, he found bitters in the FEAST of life. His second wife—weak, frivolous, and undisciplined—was a far less satisfactory partner. Robert had never had to learn the economics of Ellen's FEAST. Lillian Jamieson Richards spent him into near bankruptcy, a condition helped by the fact that the idealist refused royalties from his textbook in order to lower the price to students. Then, in 1914, he got caught in another pinch—one more attempt to merge Harvard and MIT.

This time, "Tech" would move across the Charles River to Cambridge to come under Harvard's shadow of influence. Unhappy with the plan, the irascible seventy-year-old Robert Richards was asked to resign. In one last act of loyalty, he tried to capitalize on the apparently certain merger to get an honorary degree from Harvard for his and Nellie's old friend, Arthur D. Little, now a renowned success with his commercial science

239

laboratory. Instead, MIT named Robert Richards Professor Emeritus, voted him a pension, and cut him loose. No one was ever on MIT's payroll longer. Each year for thirty years, Robert wrote his thanks for the stipend.

Mercifully, Lillian Richards soon passed away. And Robert returned to MIT occasionally, once when they named the school's mining laboratories in his honor, again in 1924 to attend the simple ceremonies unveiling a small bronze plaque in memory of Ellen. He occupied the rest of those thirty years as a mining consultant, at his brother's Camp Merriweather, as an MIT goodwill ambassador, or in the house once so full of life in Jamaica Plain. In 1944, nearly blind but alert to the last, Robert Richards, 100, joined his beloved Nellie on the top of the hill at Gardiner.

The Harvard-MIT merger went sour again. William Sedgwick went, too, taking the formidable sanitary science reputation Swallow helped build to Harvard where it became the renowned School of Public Health. She had warned MIT it would lose the lead. Now "the great sanitarian" she helped train helped her prophecy come true. MIT's role in the founding of ecology—never officially recognized, if realized—was lost in the shuffle. The environmental perspective embodied so uniquely in the eye and mind and work of Ellen Swallow was lost there, too.

If MIT passed lightly over Swallow's name and deeds, the home economics movement tried to claim them for its own. Paradoxically, just as her name was lost from the record of environmental science at MIT, home economics lost the environmental perspective she intended when she converted Oekology to organize the movement. Yet because of the truths on which they were based, Ellen Swallow's concepts were not so easily erased. Her name, perhaps, but not her work. She seemed to sense this inevitability when she wrote, a year before her death:

> In the vegetable kingdom it often happens that the seeds of [some] plant life sprout quickly, reach maturity quickly, and die soon. The hardy oak, however, grows slowly from a seed buried in the ground for perhaps two years. Similar laws seem to hold in the animal kingdom. Lordly man boasts of his long infancy as indicating a long life. . . .
>
> In the world of ideas, however, slow growth is not noticed, is

difficult to trace and the eager mind is often discouraged, thinking the seed [is] dead when it is only dormant, gathering strength for future development. It frequently means stability . . . this long waiting for the world to adopt the schemes presented to it.

She had reason for that point of view. The "schemes" she had presented in the course of her life she thought she saw coming to fruition in her last years. It gave her hope when, in 1904, Massachusetts established a state food laboratory under Albert Leach. Food science—nutrition, dietetics, and agricultural experimentation—were fully established. Even the mighty Carnegie Institution in Washington came to Boston to open a nutrition laboratory, leaning on Ellen Swallow for the more distasteful assignments, such as finding personnel for "scientific research . . . in the chemistry and bacteriology of feces. . . ."

In 1905, she had seen the American Society for Sanitary Engineering formed by those "missionaries" she had trained. In 1907, the year a national conference on weights and measures was called on behalf of the American consumer, the same year precedental laws were passed to improve labor conditions for women and children, the American School Hygiene Association was founded. The world was changing for the better, she thought. She held new hope for the future urban environment when, in 1909, the American Society for Municipal Engineers, the National Consumer League, and the American Society of Municipal Improvements were organized. She especially approved of the American Association for the Study and Prevention of Infant Mortality that met in New York City in 1910. Its goals were relative to her own for euthenics. Her books and schedule kept her from attending the sessions, but her designates and influence were very much present: Langworthy, Cushing, Brown and many others.

In her last days, Swallow could see the consumerism, food, and environmental sciences and professions she founded and synthesized taking form. Each was moving. Now, if they would just come together, as they did in her mind, in an education to improve environment for human development. She died believing they would, that her life had been "useful."

Three years after Swallow's death—about the time Robert was

put out to pasture by MIT—a zoologist from the University of Nebraska met a colleague from the University of Chicago at the traditional Christmas week meeting of the American Association for the Advancement of Science. Both schools had been touched by Swallow's programs, as indeed, had the A₃S. Citing Haeckel's life science proposal, the biologists felt ecology's time had come. In 1916, Robert Wollcott, C. V. Shreve, and a few others from the wing of life science, founded the Ecological Society of America.

In 1919, the society took over *Plant World* magazine, renaming it *Ecology*. Swallow would have been delighted by the remarks of President Barrington Moore the next year when he urged that human life be included in environmental studies, and by Stephen Forbes in 1922 when he proposed more interdisciplines within ecology. Even if she had lived to see it happen, however, she probably would have had to read about it. In spite of the increasing number of women biologists then coming out of Woods Holl and other laboratories she had influenced, in the early days of the Ecological Society the membership apparently was all male.

But at least, at last, ecology—that subversive science—was given an official structure. Many years would pass before its members would seek the subversive public participation she urged in 1892. Even then, it would be more of a financial invitation, far more narrow than what she had envisioned. But she anticipated that exclusivity, too, when she structured euthenics. Some outstanding ecologists, such as Sears and Cole, would preach the public potential of ecology. But whatever happened to euthenics?

The Association of Collegiate Alumnae (today the American Association of University Women) disbanded its committee on euthenics when its founder died. But true to her words that "slow growth . . . in the world of ideas . . . frequently means stability for future development . . ." euthenics did not die.

Others took up the issue of environment's influence on human development, some favorably, others in contention. Environment was still the sworn enemy of the hereditists. Only a very few saw their inseparability, mostly social scientists: psychologists, educators, and others who agreed with Swallow's dictum that "better people now" were the best chance for "better people tomorrow." In that dictum, Swallow had anticipated even the man who, in the 1950s, would break the genetic code, Sir Francis Crick, who said in 1968 at Northwestern University that education and environment will play a larger role than genes in modern human development. It wasn't so much that Ellen Swallow was before her time as it was that so many others of her time were far behind her. In many ways, that gap has not yet been closed.

In the 1920s when the School Hygiene Association and the Association for the Prevention of Infant Mortality were merged into the Child Health Association, Swallow's euthenics still circulated among hundreds of local and national groups concerned with improving community health and development of children. From that perspective, in 1924, her "promiscuous" science was given new life, fittingly, at Vassar College.

With the financial and political initiatives of trustee Minnie Cumnock Blodgett and the academic leadership of chemist Annie L. Macleod, and President H. N. McCracken, a Division of Euthenics was begun at Vassar. Social, physical, and perceptual environments came together in a remarkable comprehensive juncture for undergraduate, graduate, and summer study. Florence Cushing was there to see it. So was another Swallow protégée, Julia Lathrop. Now one of America's most distinguished persons, Julia Lathrop wrote an article for the dedication of the division in which she compared her former mentor with Pasteur, Fabre, and Steinmetz.

Vassar's experiment was a bold venture; too bold, as students deserted the individual disciplines for the more relevant cross-section. But the division left a legacy—the Summer Institute for Euthenics—that was the greatest ongoing experiment in child development, preschool education, and family and community studies ever undertaken by a major educational institution. It was an experiment that gave practice and following to Margaret Mead and Benjamin Spock, two of its faculty members, and attracted the support of no less a humanist than Eleanor Roosevelt.

The Institute grew through the 1930s, supported by a national media—none more positive than *The New York Times*—which saw in the venture hope to cope with an increasingly complex social environment. And once again there was a paradox. As support grew for the specifics of its work, the broader, less tangible environmental dimensions of the Institute began to fade. But not before Swallow's euthenics had won its place in the lexicon. Funk & Wagnall's *Standard Dictionary* listed it in a way that would have pleased her.

> Euthenics: . . . The science and art of improving the human race by securing the best external influences and environmental conditions for the physical, mental, and moral development of the individual, and for the maintenance of his health and vigor.

The only thing missing was the educational aspect of that science—art.

World War II dealt harsh blows to environmental humanism. In 1942, the Institute changed its name to the Vassar Summer Institute for Family and Community Studies. Perhaps it was the stigma suggested by Nazi Germany's "eugenics" to breed a "master race." Vassar's upper-middle-class students could be sensitive to such comparison.

Euthenics became for a while a school of thought within pediatrics, while the Vassar Institute, attaching itself more to the war-time family issues of rationing and patriotism, held on through 1945.

After the war, the baby boom indirectly gave the Institute new growth, at least in enrollment. Its work with child development and parental training was outstanding. So was euthenic pediatrics. But again, something had happened to Swallow's original idea. Once more the elusive environmental perspective was lost. Who had time to think about *that* illusive concept in the postwar rush to productivity and profit? New technologies had arrived. More were on their way. New miracles could compact time, space, and images of environment down to an instantaneous *now* almost anywhere.

Postwar population, prices, and affluence expanded with supply, demand, and technology. And Vassar, too, used the new skills of the period to market its wares. Like everything else thrown into the sophisticated supermarket of the electronic age, the Summer Institute, like the family, was "mom's apple pie" one day, corny the next, and outdated the day after. A few men and women tried to right its course. But they lost out to those who saw new programming, promotion, packaging, and sales as salvation.

The Institute's enrollment fell off. Like tail fins on the cars of the day, it had become more style than substance. It had always been limited, really; it was too selective in that men were not enough involved, and worse, it had largely upper-middle-class enrollment. The problems it meant to address were much deeper, much broader in family and community structures than a few upper-middle-class mothers and their children. So the Institute went the way of all snob appeals of the 1950s. The end was in sight the day it cooperated with promotions such as Vance Packard's *Reader's Digest* article, "I Sent My Wife to Vassar."

But if Swallow's vision of an interdisciplinary environmental education had become almost an alumnae promotion at her alma mater, euthenics was, like Thomas More's *Eutopia*, a hard idea to kill. Based on the belief that what man can conceive he can achieve, once planted, such ideas remain as future goals for intelligent life. This, then, is the ultimate facility of language: to give ideas circulation and meaning and to overcome space, time, and imperceptions.

About the same time Vassar dropped the word and concept of euthenics, Ellen Swallow's idea began to take root in another green environment. A chemist, Pauline Beery Mack, "encouraged to undertake research in food, clothing and shelter," steeped herself in the thoughts of her inspirator and opened the Ellen H. Richards Research Institute at Pennsylvania State University.

"The home economics people resented her because she was a chemist" and they got rid of the Institute soon after Mack left the campus, recalls one who watched the show. But there is a stubborn ecology to an idea. Once alive, it is not easily removed from the environment. Pennsylvania State University in the mid-1960s—before environment became a household word—opened perhaps the first Environment and Human Development Center in American higher education. The Center may lack the word euthenics in its title, but it does not lack the purpose Swallow intended for her second environmental science.

"Never mind the name by which it is known," she said in 1910. "It is the result we are after." Ironically, this chemist made that statement to the American Home Economics Association that grew so possessive of *her* name but dropped the environmental handle to her work.

Ellen Swallow was first, however, an environmental scientist, the most "compleat" of her time or since. Those who came after her could and did do what they wished with the broad body of her work. They split its whole into an almost infinite variety of bits, pieces, and fragments in their efforts to reduce things to smaller, concise, and manageable parts. But it was a great delusion. They were not more manageable in the long run. In fragmenting the environment as seen by Ellen Swallow, they only lost sight of its larger significance, its interconnections. Above all, the interplay of these environmental parts was lost sight of, especially the interplay between the environment and its most intelligent form of life, human beings, who became progressively more ignorant of the environment they were shaping. Since environment shapes everyone, it was the gravest imperception of all.

Ellen Swallow understood this, too. She must have had the universal frailty of human perception in mind when she said:

> There are among us many descendants of the old philosophers who . . . were agreed that *some object they could see* was the center of the Universe. The absence of facts, their ignorance and methods . . . did not daunt them, and the question furnished a subject of debate for twenty-five centuries. . . . (Author's italics.)
>
> *This did not affect the position of the center of the Universe, however.*

Neither did man's "lordly insistence" that he was above nature's laws alter the fact that he was creating the environmental judgment we face today.

People are now beginning to see the rising rates of heart, kidney, and lung disease she saw linked to the air, water, and food of a polluting physical environment.

People can now see, too, the increase in the pathologies of our social environment: crime, violence, drug abuse, alcoholism, and mental illnesses rising as people try to relate, respond, then regress or react to the reality of what surrounds them.

And finally, people are beginning to draw the connections, the interrelationships between the condition of our physical environ-

ment and the condition of our social environment and their com-
.bined influence on human health and development. Perhaps
people will soon be able to see what else the mind's eye of Ellen
Swallow saw—that the medium by which physical and social
environments interplay is a third environment: an environment
of information in which modern man lives and responds. Maybe
then man will be able to make real progress in improving environment and life.

"We have scarcely dreamed of the possibilities of . . . human
[beings]," she said.

1973 was the centennial year for environmental science. A
hundred years before, in 1873, German Biologist Ernst Haeckel
and American Chemist Ellen Swallow began, separately, the
science of life and environment in life's first environment: water.

It was fitting that a man named the science of "everyman's
house"; it was even more fitting that a woman arranged its
structure. Appropriately, a century later, ecology is the offspring
of the union of that man's and that woman's work. But the child,
though it bears a greater resemblance to the mother, has yet to
reach the maturity Ellen Swallow hoped for.

If she began with a grand design for environmental science, her
plan is hidden by the veil of her anonymity. More probably, it
was a plan that emerged as she graduated her study of environment, part by part. The result of her work is clear. More than
any other environmental scientist, then or now, hers was the most
comprehensive view.

Borrowing bit by bit from taxonomy and paleontology, from
physiology, botany, and zoology and more from bacteriology,
the chemist inched her way toward the *Life Sciences*.

Earth Sciences were brought in with her work in geology,
geography, mineralogy, metallurgy, and petrology; with her work
in the agricultural processes and their interaction with air and
water to produce food.

From the *Physical Sciences* she brought to Oekology the knowledge of heating, ventilation, humidifying, and other scientific
and engineering techniques.

With sociology, psychology, economics, and education, she
tried to bring the *Social Sciences* into ecology.

The chemist was always the mathematician. Astronomy, she

reserved as a hobby. But its meteorology was helpful in a better understanding of climate, winds, tides, rainfall, and vegetation. In Ellen Swallow's ecology, all the main branches of science over-lapped for cross-fertilization, "not in watertight compartments," she said. It was too much for the science purists of her time.

She was not satisfied merely with designing that "house"; she furnished it, cleaned it, equipped it and provided it with air, water, food, and knowledge. And then, like Nicostrata had in-vited the priests into the House of Letters she had made into the Roman alphabet, Ellen Swallow invited everyone into every-man's science house, only to get herself ejected for her trouble. Consequently, not even in its centennial year does ecology have quite the breadth and comprehension she intended for it.

For her work in bringing together the main bodies of science into ecology, Ellen Swallow might have helped clear the way for still other new sciences with her "interloping"; new sciences that have since tempered the age-old fight between heredity and environment as they find heredity and environment meeting in the biochemical processes of the body. But she will get no credit for that, either. Male science naturally resisted any effort to arrange a marriage. But they resented as unnatural a science union proposed by a woman, especially *this* woman who wanted to open the hallowed hall of the temple to nonscientists: engineers, architects, teachers, city planners, artisans, even farmers, chil-dren, and *housewives!*

If Hippocrates knew, 2,000 years ago, the vital relationships between air, water, food, soil, and human health, those who came after him reserved the study of those relationships as private domain. The problem with that limited privilege was that it was limiting in other ways, too. First, population was cut off from the knowledge of science. The priests of science would tell them what they needed to know. And second, the priests of science were only human themselves. They, too, were victims of the common limits of human perception. More and more, as they came through Hippocrates's guarded door, they gravitated to individual specialties of science, finite niches in the total en-vironment of knowledge.

They added a great deal to the depth of knowledge this way, but they also allowed great walls to grow up between the sciences

—blind spots to hide what people would do to the environment. When technology joined science, these blind spots became serious environmental liabilities. As science took knowledge apart, technology took the environment apart, redesigned it, and put it back together again for greater "utility." Then when science and technology linked up with government and industry for still greater productivity, profit, and progress, the walls and blindspots between knowledge became the sites for environmental dismantlement.

A new environment emerged, one in which human sensation was replaced at the interface by unfeeling man-made "things." Inorganic substitutions are fine, so long as nature agrees. But who was to know? Technology had grown from the hand and the eye of man. But the hammer and the wheel were remote technologies compared to the on-off switches and push-buttons of modern programmed environment.

Yet an intelligent organism is linked to its environment by something more than its stomach. The mind is a link, too. And among intelligent organisms you cannot break that connection or make substitutions in its circuitry without very careful consideration of the adjustments required or the consequences if the adjustments are not made. The stomach quickly sends its message when denied food. The mind, lacking knowledge, takes longer to get the message that something is wrong. Sometimes it is too late.

So the problem continued to build until it became crisis. Today, science and technology, government and industry stand together on one side of a huge credibility gap. A confused, distrustful population stands on the other side, exerting pressure, that, with the environment crisis Swallow warned about, is bringing the sciences together at last. But there is still missing from that meeting of the minds of science a major participant in the problem and its solution.

In her last paper, written in the pain and panic of her deathbed, Ellen Swallow addressed her accumulated understanding of the environment problem to the leaders of applied science and technology. Knowledge, she said, has too long been held captive as an instrument of private power, profit, and influence. In an age when environment is changing, we must give knowledge greater distribution, even reorganization, to restore the human link to environment, she told her peers.

She had hoped to appear in person in front of the fiftieth anniversary Congress of Technology to tell the participants that they must include human and environmental considerations in their work in the future. This was not just a way of "Elevating Applied Science to the Ranks of the Learned Professions"; it was the only proper dedication—human service—to qualify a body of knowledge and its practitioners to rank with "Theology, Law, and Medicine," she said. Theology, law, and medicine, she wanted to remind the twentieth-century's technologists, had overdone their private privilege as witnessed by their errors of the past, as witnessed by the early struggle of applied science to break away from their domination.

After fifty years, she pointed out, they had succeeded in establishing their own rapidly accumulating body of knowledge. After fifty years they had become, in fact, the dominant force in shaping man's modern environment. They must consider the human consequences and potential of that role. "Do not betray the rank and file," she wrote.

This then was the summary of Ellen Swallow's life—her final message to those she had worked with and those who would come after: renew, restore, and regenerate the interface between environment and population. She had tried oekology, ocology, and ecology and been rejected. So she had laid a structure for a second environmental science that would graft onto man's knowledge the means by which people could learn and live in harmony with environment. This social dimension was even more essential in 1911, she knew, than it had been in 1873 or 1892. Environment was changing faster and faster. It was necessary to re-educate the human perception that had learned that smoke rises, water drains, toilets flush, and the garbage man comes once a week to take garbage away. *It does not go away,* she knew; it can and will and is backing up.

Sixty years later, when it backed up into everyone's range of perception, the public believed it. But people have yet to include the social dimension she saw as a vital participant in environmental science. This perhaps, more than anything else, even her sex, was the major reason Ellen Swallow's name is missing from the environmental science record. Since people are the largest part of the environmental problem, they must become part of the basis of the solution.

Was Ellen Swallow an impractical, unbridled idealist?

In 1971, the man who sat on top of the pinnacle of the now most dominant branch of the sciences—and the most secretive body of knowledge in science history—wrote about "the good new days that a new science will bring." Glenn T. Seaborg, chairman of the United States Atomic Energy Commission, told a joint meeting of the American Geographical Society, the American Division of the World Academy of Art and Science hosted by the New York Academy of Science, that this new science will eliminate pollution and waste, poverty and crime, ignorance and disease. It will do so by joining the disciplines of science, not just with one another, but with technology, with the arts and humanities, and with all the modern information systems and facilities at our disposal.

The total of this massive reunion of knowledge will be greater than the sum of its parts, Seaborg said. From that difference there will evolve a new science with which to "rationalize" population to live in harmony with environment, physically and socially.

Ellen Swallow said the same thing almost seventy years before. She even named that new science. And she tried to establish it, just as she had tried to establish humanism in ecology. But if science rejected that philosophy at the turn of the century, it has not come far enough to include it even with less than thirty years to go to the twenty-first.

In 1971, an appraisal of the "State of the Environmental Sciences" by no less an establishment body than the National Science Board, almost completely overlooked education and the social sciences in making its evaluation. Officially, at least, the public chair Swallow tried to push into the house of environmental science still seemed empty.

In the early 1960s, however, a small group of science and professional people concerned with environmental conditions began to establish information monitors among the sciences. What they found—or did not find—warranted an effort in the mid-1960s to alert public and institutional awareness of the environment problem. In 1968, when environment had become a popular issue, the International Institute for Euthenics held a broad interdisciplinary conference, "Man, Information, and Environment," at the University of Illinois that confirmed Ellen Swallow's conclusions.

The new Institute for Euthenics set about the design and construction of a conceptual model of environment, a model on which to build an environmental education that interfaces *all* knowledge, subordinate to life-environment considerations. Unlike other existing environmental models, this one would benefit science, government, industry, and technology only indirectly. Its primary objective is, to use Seaborg's term, to provide environmental learning to help "rationalize" the social side of the problem.

Announcing this model of a public environmental science in 1973 is appropriate; it is one hundred years since Ellen Swallow started that work.

It is not strange that a woman founded environmental science. Rather, Ellen Swallow's role in ecology, limnology, and euthenics, like her work in food, consumer sciences, and education is really traditional for her sex.

There is a distinctly different environmental relationship between the male and female, a difference that exists in many, if not all, species of intelligent life. But among the highest order of intelligent animals, mammals—an order named for the female's unique life-environment function—it is especially pronounced in that family named for the male: Man.

The difference is rooted in the basic physiological design. The male is larger and stronger. He is, then, equipped for a more overt physical relationship with his environment. By this design and his social behavior, his role and function are influenced. Hence, so is his perception, the way he "sees" his environment. The male sees environment basically as a physical challenge, as something to penetrate, to overcome, and to exploit for his survival.

The female is fundamentally opposite, beginning with *her* physiology. Her social behavior, too, is influenced by design. And thus her perception of the environment reflects these differences and is reinforced by them. Physically smaller and muscularly weaker, the female "sees" environment as something to which she gives and from which she receives; something to cultivate, to nurture, and to improve for survival.

He is the environment's conqueror; she is its caretaker. Interplayed, these perceptions, roles, and designs have brought human development through no less than two great previous environmental crises, crises similar in seriousness and significance to the one humanity is now entering. And in each past crisis, the female had the initial role in the solution: nurturing a new life style—a new environmental relationship—for the species. Then, once the new relationship was established, the larger, stronger male exploited it. Both—nurturing and exploiting—have been necessary for the survival, evolution, and development of the human species.

The first environmental era in human development occurred when environmental changes wiped out vegetarian pre-man's food supply and required not only a new food supply—other animals—but a way of obtaining them in that environment. As man learned to hunt, he learned to cooperate and communicate. Human culture was born. The female, the first environment for man, was the source of that cooperative, communicative culture that made the hunt possible.

Adapting to and evolving from this new challenge, man became ever more adept at exploiting the environment. As he improved, he secured more food. As he secured more food, his population increased and he required still more food. The challenge of the environment and the exploitation by the hunt escalated. There is no permanent solution to the environment problem. Each solution only sets up a future, more demanding problem. Human intelligence evolves by the process.

Eventually, man went too far in his exploitation. The environment could not support his skill and his growing numbers. Other animal life became scarce. The hunt became more difficult and demanding. A division of labor was necessary, and the female stayed at the campsite to nurture future hunters and cultivate resources, while the male hunted farther from home. But it was painful and less productive for man. And once again, crisis was resolved by woman's "discovery" of agriculture at her campsite.

The discovery began a new environmental era in human de-

ELLEN SWALLOW

velopment. If the first had been physical, this one was social. Population settled in one place with a new food supply. Again, population expanded and needed still more food, yet more land to grow it. It was a new environmental relationship, always escalating, always more difficult. Rules, laws, and institutions; roles, property, and authority became more necessary. Woman nur-tured the new life style. Man exploited it. Both for survival, for more than 10,000 years.

Five hundred years ago, a new escalation of environmental exploitation was ignited by the new knowledge made possible by the printing press. That exploitation exploded, 200 years later, in the Industrial Revolution. Today the explosion is nuclear, a chain reaction of crises. The crises crisis.

The environment has about reached its limit to accommodate present exploitations. People are entering a new environmental era in which they face a new environmental crisis to which they must find a solution. This time the solution must be perceptual.

Ellen Swallow understood. Until she died, she worked to give form to what she felt was the only alternative to repressive or tyrannical management of a population living in disharmony with the environment.

Today's crisis would not surprise her. The first lady of science saw it coming in the nineteenth century. But the "caretaker" would be disappointed that man had not yet moved to prepare people, systems, and institutions. Ellen Swallow would be disappointed because she had an unshakable faith that human intelligence could solve this crisis, too.

If man does—without resorting to physical force, social repression, or perceptual constraint—he will almost certainly do so along the lines she proposed: a massive reorganization of our information and knowledge; a reformation of our education in order to produce a population harmonious with environment: *Environmentaculture*.

This crisis too, will require that *all* population—men *and* women—participate in the solution. But in forming environmentaculture, it will be especially interesting to watch the role of woman, who, in the past has initiated such adaptations. Today she not only outnumbers man and lives longer, she is both economically and politically enfranchised. And only the genetecists' test tubes can replace woman as man's first environment.

It is not strange that a woman founded environmental science and formulated a solution to a crisis she saw building, any more than it is strange that a later woman, Rachel Louise Carson, would be credited with reawakening public interest in the crisis long after Swallow was gone and forgotten. But the author of *Silent Spring* represents only one more legacy of the enormous influence of the pugnacious, brilliant woman from Dunstable.

Without Ellen, Swallow's work, Rachel Carson might never have had access to the knowledge she passed on to alert us. Two of the three schools from which Rachel Carson obtained that knowledge had felt the definite influence of the woman who founded environmental science: Johns Hopkins and Woods Hole Marine Biology Laboratory.

The roots of an idea are difficult to trace, Ellen Swallow said. Lifting the veil from the odyssey of her life and work, however, the roots of environmental science should be much more visible now.

Perhaps with that visibility, man can also see hope and direction in the future.

Sources

BOOKS BY ELLEN SWALLOW RICHARDS

The Art of Right Living. Boston: Whitcomb & Barrows, 1904

The Chemistry of Cooking and Cleaning: A Manual for Housekeepers. Boston: Estes & Lauriat, 1882

Conservation by Sanitation. New York: John Wiley & Sons, 1911

The Cost of Cleanness. New York: John Wiley & Sons, 1908

The Cost of Food. New York: John Wiley & Sons, 1901

The Cost of Living. New York: John Wiley & Sons, 1899

The Cost of Shelter. New York: John Wiley & Sons, 1905

The Dietary Computer. New York: John Wiley & Sons, 1902

Euthenics—The Science of Controllable Environment. Boston: Whitcomb & Barrows, 1910

First Lessons in Food and Diet. Boston: Whitcomb & Barrows, 1904

First Lessons in Minerals. Boston: Rockwell & Churchill, 1882

Food Materials and Their Adulterations. Boston: Estes & Lauriat, 1886

Guides for Science Teaching, sponsored by Boston Society of Natural History. Boston: D. C. Heath & Co., 1886

Notes on Industrial Water Analysis: A Survey Course for Engineers. New York: John Wiley & Sons, 1908

Sanitation in Daily Life. Boston: Whitcomb & Barrows, 1907

With Marion Talbot, *Food as a Factor in Student Life: A Contribution to the Study of the Student Diet.* Chicago: University of Chicago Press, 1894

With Marion Talbot, *Home Sanitation—A Manual for Housekeepers.* Boston: Association for Collegiate Alumnae, 1887

With Alpheus G. Woodman, *Air, Water and Food from a Sanitary Standpoint.* New York: John Wiley & Sons, 1904

ARTICLES, PAPERS, AND SPEECHES BY ELLEN SWALLOW RICHARDS

"An Account of the New England Kitchen and the Rumford Food Laboratory," address to the Massachusetts Medical Society, Boston, June 7-8, 1892

"The Adulteration of Groceries of Massachusetts," in the First Annual Report of the Massachusetts Department of Health, Lunacy and Charity, 1880

"Analysis of Samarskite from a New Locality," from Proceedings of the Boston Society of Natural History, 1872

"An Apparatus for Determining the Liability of Oils to Spontaneous Combustion," *Tech Quarterly,* Vol. IV, No. 4, December 1891

"Carbon Dioxide as a Measure of Efficiency in Ventilation," *Journal of American Chemical Society,* Vol. XV, No. 10, October 1893

"Desirable Tendencies in Professional and Technical Education for Women," Association of Collegiate Alumnae, 1904

"Dietaries for Wage Earners and Their Families," 17th Report, New Jersey State Board of Health, 1893

"Dietary Studies," United States Department of Agriculture Experiment Stations, Bulletin No. 129, 1903

"Domestic Economy," *The New England Farmer,* April 1883

"Domestic Economy in Public Education," in Educational Monographs, New York Teacher's College, 1899

"Domestic Science," *The Clubwoman,* Vol. 3, No. 6, March 1899

"Domestic Science," *The Outlook,* Vol. 55, No. 17, April 24, 1897

"Domestic Science as a Synthetic Study for Girls," in Proceedings of the National Education Association, 1898

"Estimation of Vanadium in an Iron Ore from Cold Spring, N. Y.," Thesis, 1873 (Vassar College Archives)

"Good Lunches for Rural Schools Without a Kitchen," Boston: Whitcomb & Barrows, 1906

"Hospital Diet," *American Kitchen Magazine,* Vol. 5, No. 1, 1896

"Housekeeping from the College Woman's Standpoint," *Vassar Miscellany,* December 1895

"Laboratory Notes on Sanitary Chemistry." (Unpublished; MIT Archives), 1896

"Laboratory Notes on Water Analysis." (Unpublished; MIT Archives), 1896

"A Lunch Room for Students," *New England Kitchen Magazine,* February 1895

"Municipal Responsibility for Healthy School Houses," Transactions of American Public Health Association, 1897

"Notes on the Chemical Composition of Some of the Mineral Species Accompanying the Lead Ore of Newburyport," Proceedings of the Boston Society of Natural History, Vol. XVII, 462-465, March 17, 1875

"Notes on Hospital Dietaries," *Journal of Insanity,* October 1895

"Notes on Some Reactions of Titanium," Colorado Meeting of the American Association of Mining Engineers, August 1882

"Notes on Some Sulpharsenites and Sulphantimonites from Colorado," Thesis, 1878, Massachusetts Institute of Technology

"Notes on the Water Supplies in the Black Hills of South Dakota and Vicinity," *Tech Quarterly,* December 1903

"On the Elevation of Applied Science to the Rank of Learned Profession," *Boston Sunday Herald,* April 2, 1911

"The Outlook in Home Economics," farewell address as president of American Home Economics Association in Proceedings, 1910

"The Place of Science in Women's Education," *American Kitchen Magazine,* Vol. 7, No. 6, 1897

"The Place of Vocational Science in the High School Curriculum," paper for the National Society for Scientific Study of Education, 4th Yearbook, 1905

"The Potable Waters of Mexico," Transactions of the American Institute of Mining Engineers, 1902

"The Relation of College Women to Progress in Domestic Science," paper for the Association of Collegiate Alumnae, October 24, 1890

"Sanitary Science in the Home," *Journal of the Franklin Institute,* 1888

"The Science of Nutrition," Wall-hanging pamphlet, 1897

"Scientific Cooking in the New England Kitchen," *Forum,* May 1893

"University Laboratories in Relation to the Investigation of Public Health Problems and to Commercial Work," Transactions of American Public Health Association, Vol. 25, 1900

"The Urgent Need for Sanitary Education in the Public Schools," American Public Health Association, 1898

"Wanted! A Test for Manpower," commencement address, Clarkson College, 1906

"Waste of Energy in Organization," *The Outlook,* December 1899

"The Water Supplies of Southeastern Alaska," *Tech Quarterly,* Vol. XVI, December 1903

With Edward Atkinson, "Nutritive Value of Common Food Materials," United States Department of Agriculture, 1894

With Edward Atkinson and Mary Abel, "The Right Application of Heat to the Conversion of Food Material," paper for the American Association for the Advancement of Science, August 1890

With L. A. Bragg, "The Distribution of Phosphorous and Nitrogen in the Products of Modern Milling," *Tech Quarterly,* Vol. III, No. 3, 1890

With Margaret Cheney, "A New and Ready Method for the Estimation of Nickel in Pyrrhotites and Mattes," *American Journal of Science and Arts,* Vol. XIV, September 1877

With T. M. Drown, "The Chemical Examination of Waters and Their Interpretation and Analyses," Boston 1889

With J. W. Elms, "The Colouring Matters of Natural Waters, Its Source, Composition, and Quantitative Measurement," *Journal of the American Chemical Society,* Vol. 18, No. 1, August 1895

With Arthur Hopkins, "The Normal Chlorine of the Water Supplies of Jamaica," Boston: Massachusetts Institute of Technology, March 1898

With Edwin O. Jordan, "Investigation Upon Nitrification and the Nitrifying Organism," 1890 (MIT Archives)

With Lily Kendall, "Permanent Standards of Water Analysis," *Tech Quarterly,* June 1904

With Elizabeth Mason, "The Effect of Heat on the Digestibility of Gluten," *Tech Quarterly,* Vol. VII, No. 1, April 1894

With Alice W. Palmer, "Notes on Antimony Tannate, No. II," *American Journal of Science and Arts,* Vol. XVI, November 1878

With George W. Rolfe, "Reduction of Nitrates by Bacteria and Consequent Loss of Nitrogen," *Tech Quarterly,* Vol. IX, No. 1, February 1896

BOOKS BY OTHERS

Atkinson, Edward, *The Industrial Progress of a Nation: Consumption Limited; Production Unlimited.* New York: G. P. Putnam's Sons, 1890

Frey, David G., *Limnology in North America.* Madison, Wis.: University of Wisconsin Press, 1963

Hunt, Caroline, *The Life of Ellen H. Richards.* Boston: Whitcomb & Barrows, 1912

James, Edward T., and Wilson, Janet (eds.), *Biographical Dictionary of Notable American Women, 1906-1950.* Cambridge, Mass.: Harvard University Press, 1971

McNeill, William H., *The Rise of the West—A History of the Human Community.* Chicago: University of Chicago Press, 1963

O'Neil, William, *The Woman Movement (Feminism in United States and Canada).* New York: Quadrangle Books, 1969

Prescott, Samuel, *When* MIT *Was "Boston Tech."* Cambridge, Mass.: Technology Press, 1954

Richards, Robert H., *His Mark.* Boston: Little, Brown and Co., 1936

Sarton, George A., *A History of Science: Ancient Science Through the Golden Age of Greece.* Cambridge, Mass.: Harvard University Press, 1952

Stern, Madeleine Bettina, *We the Women.* New York: Schultz Publishing Co., 1962

Talbot, Marion, and Rosenberry, Lois, *The First Fifty Years.* Washington, D.C.: American Association of University Women, 1931

Time-Life, *This Fabulous Century: Prelude 1870-1900.* New York: Time, Inc., 1970

————, *The Scientist* (Science Library). New York: Time, Inc., 1964

Williams, Henry Smith, *A History of Science.* New York: Harper & Brothers, 1904

Williamson, Harold Francis, *The Biography of an American Liberal.* Boston: Old Corner Book Store, 1934

Yost, Edna, *American Women of Science.* Philadelphia: Frederick A. Stokes Co., 1943

PAPERS, ARTICLES, AND REPORTS BY OTHERS

American Association for Study and Prevention of Infant Mortality, Proceedings of the First Annual Meeting, November 9-11, 1910. Baltimore: Johns Hopkins University

American Child Health Association, Index of Transactions, 1924

American Home Economics Association, Syllabus of Home Economics, 1913. Vassar College Archives

American School Hygiene Association, Proceedings of First, Second, and Third Congresses, November 1910

Association for the Advancement of Women, Constitution and Bylaws. Boston: W. L. Deland, 1877

Association for Maintaining the American Women's Table at the

Naples Zoological Station and for Promoting Scientific Research by Women, Reports, 1898-1903. Massachusetts Historical Society

Atkinson, Edward, Papers. Massachusetts Historical Society

———, "Suggestions Regarding the Cooking of Food," with Introduction by Ellen H. Richards. United States Government Printing Office, 1894

Baker, William Emerson, "The Consumers Protective Association—Bulletin and History," September 1, 1873

Boston Evening Post, "An Interview with Mrs. Ellen Richards," September 16, 1909

Brill, Julia, Correspondence re Ellen Richards Institute at Pennsylvania State University, July 9, 1972

Bryant, Alice G., "Mrs. Ellen H. Richards and Her Place in the World of Science," paper before the MIT Women's Association, December 2, 1936. Vassar College Archives

———, "Values for Which Mrs. Ellen H. Richards Stood," *Medical and Professional Women's Journal*, August 1933

Carter, H. E., "Challenge for the Seventies," Report of the National Science Board to the President of the United States on Environmental Science. National Science Foundation, 1971

Consumers League of Massachusetts, Constitution, Articles, History and Purpose, ca 1890

Dalton, Marshall B., "Edward Atkinson, 1827-1905, Patron of Engineering Science and Benefactor of Industry," memorial address, Newcomen Society of North America, 1950

Dearing, Albin, "Return to the Bad Old Days of 1870's? No Thanks." *Smithsonian Magazine*, 1972

Ecological Society of America, "Notes and Comments on Organization—1914-1919"

Farrell, Grace, "In Memory of Ellen H. Richards," *Journal of Home Economics*, Vol. 21, No. 6, June 1929

Forbes, Stephen A., "The Humanizing of Ecology," *Ecology Magazine*, Vol. III, No. 2, April 1922

Hunt, Caroline, "Ellen H. Richards: Scientist, Author, Teacher, Apostle of Right Living," *Home Economics Day*, December 3, 1912

Hunt, Caroline, and LaFollette, Belle C., "Woman of the Hour—Ellen H. Richards," *LaFollette's Weekly Magazine*, December 31, 1910

Journal of Home Economics, "Recollections of Ellen H. Richards," December 4, 1931

Marine Biological Laboratory, Fourth Annual Report, 1891

————, A Reply to the Statement of the Former Trustees. Boston: Alfred Mudge & Son, 1897

————, Tenth Report for the Years 1903-1906. Woods Hole, Mass., 1907

Massachusetts Department of Public Health, "Proud Heritage, The Story of the Lawrence Experimental Station," 1953

Montagu, Ashley, Alexander Graham Bell Lectures, Boston University, 1956

Moore, Barrington, "The Scope of Ecology," Presidential Address to Ecological Society of America, December 31, 1919, *Ecology Magazine*, Vol. I, 1920

New York Times, obituary of Robert Richards, March 28, 1945

Packard, Vance, "I Sent My Wife to Vassar," *Reader's Digest*, October 1951

Parloa, Marie, "The New England Kitchen," *Century Magazine*, December 1891

Seaborg, Glenn T., "Those Good New Days," *Saturday Review*, March 6, 1971

Sears, Paul B., "Toward a Design for the Future," Ecological Society of America. Bulletin ESA 52(3): 5-7, September 1971

Scudder, Samuel H., et al, "The Marine Biological Laboratory at Woods Holl, Massachusetts, *Science*, Vol. VI, No. 145, October 8, 1897

Society to Encourage Study at Home, Report, ca 1880

Warren, Katherine, et al, "Euthenics—What Is It?" *Vassar Quarterly*, November 1924

Women's Education Association, Annual Reports, 1870s, 1880s. Massachusetts Historical Society

Index

A

Abel, Mary Hinman, 118, 183, 186
  editor of *Journal,* 176
  New England Kitchen, 128,
    130, 132, 139-140
Acrostic for FEAST of Life, 64, 239
Addams, Jane, 171
  See also Hull House.
Air, study of, 40, 97, 224-226
  analysis, 149-150
  applied
    in factories, 124, 224-225
    in homes, 67-68, 224-225
    in MIT classrooms, 225-226
    in school rooms, 150, 224
    ventilation, humidification,
      and heating, 150
  publications and papers,
    150, 213-214
Advertising, concept of, 210
Agassiz, Louis, 108
Agassiz, Mrs. Louis, 62, 109
Agriculture, 138, 178, 241
  See also U.S. Department of
    Agriculture.
Aladdin Oven, 119-120, 126-127,
  132
Alaska, 190-191
Allen, Charles, 127
American Academy of Arts and
  Sciences, 28

American Association for the
  Advancement of Women, 43
American Association for the
  Advancement of Science,
    43, 54, 105-106, 127, 130,
    186, 223, 242
American Association of
  University Women. *See*
  Association of Collegiate
  Alumnae.
American Bacteriological Society,
  163, 182
American Centennial Exposition,
  Philadelphia, 100
American Geographical Society,
  251
American Home Economics
  Association, 177, 178, 183,
    186, 237, 246
  See also Lake Placid
  Conference.
American Household Economics
  Association, 171
American Institute of Mining and
  Mineralogical Engineers,
    98, 190
American Kitchen Magazine,
  165, 170-172, 176
  *See also New England Kitchen
  Magazine.*
American Public Health
  Association, 127, 148, 160-